Essentials of Psychological Assessment Series

Series Editors, Alan S. Kaufman and Nadeen L. Kaufman

Essentials

of Career Interest Assessment

Jeffrey P. Prince

Lisa J. Heiser

John Wiley & Sons, Inc.

NEW YORK · CHICHESTER · WEINHEIM · BRISBANE · SINGAPORE · TORONTO

ISBN 0-471-35365-5

Printed in the United States of America.

10 9 8 7 6 5 4 3 2 1

To our partners and parents for all their love, encouragement, and support:

Richard Keller, and Raymond and Lillian Prince
—Jeffrey Prince

Michael Sommer, and Gene and Vera Heiser
—Lisa Heiser

CONTENTS

SERIES PREFACE

I n the *Essentials of Psychological Assessment* series, our goal is to provide the reader with books that deliver key practical information in the most efficient and accessible style. The series features instruments in a variety of domains, such as cognition, personality, education, and neuropsychology. For the experienced clinician, books in the series offer a concise, yet thorough, way to master the continuously evolving supply of new and revised instruments, as well as a convenient method for keeping up to date on the tried-and-true measures. The novice will find here a prioritized assembly of all the information and techniques that must be at one's fingertips to begin the complicated process of individual psychological diagnosis.

Wherever feasible, visual shortcuts to highlight key points are utilized alongside systematic, step-by-step guidelines. Chapters are focused and succinct. Topics are targeted for an easy understanding of the essentials of administration, scoring, interpretation, and clinical application. Theory and research are continually woven into the fabric of each book, but always to enhance clinical inference, never to sidetrack or overwhelm. We have long been advocates of "intelligent" testing—the notion that a profile of test scores is meaningless unless it is brought to life by the clinical observations and astute detective work of knowledgeable examiners. Test profiles must be used to make a difference in the child's or adult's life, or why bother to test? We want this series to help our readers become the best intelligent testers they can be.

In *Essentials of Career Interest Assessment,* the authors provide detailed guidance in interpreting a number of today's most popular career interest tools. This volume focuses on three instruments in depth: the *Strong Interest Inventory,* the *Self-Directed Search,* and the *Campbell Interest and Skill Survey.* The authors highlight the foundations and applications of each instrument, and offer specific instructions for administering, scoring, and interpreting each tool. They also provide a detailed illustrative case example to draw attention to the similarities and differences among these instruments, and to demonstrate the value of using multiple measures. In addition, the authors review a number of interest assessment tools that are less traditional, including one from a computerized career guidance system (DISCOVER), one from an Internet-based career assessment site (Careerhub), and one experiential card sort (Talent Sort 2000). The authors provide the reader with the critical information needed to select an interest measure appropriate to the client's situation and to interpret it with expertise. They also provide annotated reference lists for each tool to direct the reader toward additional sources of information and training.

One

Interest inventories are among the most popular tools selected by career professionals today (Savickas, 1998). Over 200 reasonably valid and reliable interest measures are available (Walsh & Betz, 1995), providing a dizzying array of options for collecting information about individuals' preferences and motivations. New inventories enter the competition each year in a fast-changing market that promises lucrative rewards. Consequently, career counselors and human resource specialists are sometimes left overwhelmed with the responsibility for selecting an appropriate inventory and evaluating its soundness. Furthermore, many professionals find themselves in a dilemma: their formal training in assessment is years out of date, yet they have little time to wade through the range of newly available test manuals and textbooks.

This book was developed with the goal of providing an easy-to-read, practical, up-to-date, quick reference source that would guide the career professional through the essentials of using the most popular career interest tools. Its focus is twofold. First, it attempts to summarize and highlight important technical aspects of each inventory. Second, it offers step-by-step guidance in interpretation and use of the various inventories. Each chapter includes a number of "Rapid Reference" boxes that summarize important points. "Caution" and "Don't Forget" boxes also are included to emphasize critical issues for interpretation. This volume was not intended as a substitute for the manuals or user's guides for the selected instruments. In fact, the opposite is the intent. Annotated bibliographies are provided for each instrument to direct the reader toward specific resources that provide more detailed information and guidance.

Most of the instruments reviewed in this volume are products of a long history of research in interest measurement. In fact, the assessment of interests has been a critical focus of career counseling and guidance since the field of vocational psychology began. Frank Parsons (1909), considered the founder of vocational guidance, published the original model of career counseling, in which a fundamental step included gathering knowledge about an individual's interests. Ever since, counselors have relied on interest assessment to understand clients' motivations and to help them with career decisions and life planning.

The first formal interest assessment tool was the *Strong Vocational Interest Blank for Men (SVIB)*, developed by E. K. Strong and published in 1927 (Strong, 1927). Strong, a professor of Business Management at Stanford University, was interested in understanding the unique patterns of interests and disinterests that differentiated members of one occupational group from another. Over the course of the 20th century, research in interest measurement took a variety of directions. Extensive efforts focused on understanding the exact nature of interests and their links to abilities, genetics, and environmental factors (Walsh & Betz, 1995). Although these questions remain unresolved, it has become evident that interests are a complex and powerful source of information, and play a critical role in career behavior.

A recent survey of career assessment practices among counseling psychologists, across six different types of work environments, demonstrated the importance of interest testing to the current practice of career counseling. Researchers found that interest inventories were by far the tools these career practitioners used most frequently (Watkins, Campbell, & Nieberding, 1994). Specifically, they found that the *Strong Interest Inventory* (Harmon, Hansen, Borgen, & Hammer, 1994) and the *Self-Directed Search* (Holland, 1994) ranked first and second respectively across settings as diverse as private practice, universities, community mental health, and hospitals.

Selecting which instruments to include in this volume was a difficult task. Not only did we want to include the most widely used instruments, we also wanted to provide readers with a sampling of the different types of interest measures available to career professionals as well as the public. We decided to focus on three instruments in depth: the *Strong Interest Inventory (Strong)*, the *Self-Directed Search (SDS)*, and the *Campbell Interest and Skill Survey (CISS)* (Campbell, 1992). Both the *Strong* and the *SDS* were chosen because of their immense popularity and their solid research foundations. Each of these also represents a different type of interest measure. The *Strong* is a solid example of a formal inventory that measures interests using normative reference groups, and the

SDS is an excellent example of a self-administered and self-scored interest inventory that reports scores without reference to normative samples. The *CISS* was chosen because of its increasing popularity within organizational settings and because it is one of the few instruments that contrasts interests with skills confidence throughout its scales. We begin with the *Strong* in Chapter 2, and follow with the *CISS* in Chapter 3, since this instrument so closely resembles the *Strong* in both construction and format. We complete our featured reviews with the *SDS* in Chapter 4. Chapter 5 then provides an illustrative case example that highlights some similarities and differences among the three instruments when they are used in combination. When reviewing information on the theoretical foundations or interpretation, you can refer to Chapter 5 to view sample profiles of all three instruments.

In addition to the featured instruments, we selected the following career assessment tools to review briefly in Chapter 6: DISCOVER (ACT, Inc., 2000), *Careerhub* (Consulting Psychologists Press, 1999), and *Talent Sort 2000* (Farren, 1998). These tools are less traditional in format and they represent different modes of delivery. They also exemplify the diversity of career assessments on the market that integrate an interest assessment component. DISCOVER is an example of an established computerized career guidance system. *Careerhub* is an example of a state-of-the-art internet-based career assessment tool. *Talent Sort 2000* is an experiential card sort method for assessing interests.

There are many solidly constructed and useful instruments we would have liked to include in this volume but could not. We decided to focus on a limited number of tools in order to provide thoughtful and essential guidance on those, rather than a cursory review of a larger number of instruments. Our intention is to help the reader understand the essential information needed to administer, score, and interpret these well-regarded tools. We provide fundamental details about the instruments for each of the following dimensions: theoretical and research foundations, administration, scoring, interpretation, strengths, weaknesses, and counseling applications. In addition, we direct readers to critical reference sources through an annotated bibliography for each instrument.

Professional use of these measures requires a familiarity not only with basic statistical concepts, but also with legal, social, cultural, and ethical factors. Consequently, we assume the reader to have previous or concurrent training in psychological testing and to be well versed in the responsibilities and competencies necessary for proper test usage. Also, it is beyond the scope of this book to provide specific guidance in career counseling or to address the integration of interest assessment with other, related measures of personality, development, or ability. However, for readers needing further training, we have provided several references for this chapter to texts that address these concerns.

We hope that this volume will provide you with the essential information you need to understand and evaluate these valuable assessment tools. We also hope this book will lead you to use them with greater confidence and skill, to better meet the career development needs of your clients.

Two

STRONG INTEREST INVENTORY

INTRODUCTION

The *Strong Interest Inventory,* commonly referred to as "the *Strong,*" is a well-researched and dependable instrument that is the most widely used tool for identifying interests in the history of career assessment (Harmon, Hansen, Borgen, & Hammer, 1994). The *Strong* comes from a line of distinguished assessments that were among the first empirically-based tools used to assist individuals with making sound career choices. According to the test's publisher, Consulting Psychologists Press, over 30 million people have taken the *Strong*. The *Strong* is used in a variety of settings, including campus-based counseling and career centers, community-based and nonprofit career programs, career development centers in organizational and business settings, and outplacement and government-based employment centers. If there is one fundamental assessment tool to know and understand, the *Strong* is it. A sample profile for the *Strong* is displayed in Figure 5.1 in Chapter 5.

Today's *Strong* is the result of more than 70 years of research begun by E. K. Strong and continued by luminaries in vocational assessment research, including David P. Campbell and Jo-Ida C. Hansen. The most recent research team, and authors of the recently updated *Strong Interest Inventory: Applications and Technical Guide,* include Lenore W. Harmon, Jo-Ida C. Hansen, Fred H. Borgen, and Allen L. Hammer. The *Strong* has been continually updated and revised to reflect changes in our culture, careers, language, and dimensions of diversity. Due to the long and continuing research tradition on which the *Strong* is built, the *Strong* remains the most scientifically grounded tool in the assessment of interests used in career development today (Harmon et al., 1994).

The *Strong* measures an individual's work and personal interests and compares them to those of people employed in a wide range of occupations. Interests are organized, by John Holland's (1997) six vocational personality types, by a variety of specific interest content areas, by diverse and representative occupations, and by a set of personal style measures. The *Strong Interest Inventory* consists of 317 items. Respondents are asked to rate their level of interest in most sections according to a three-point scale of like, indifferent, and dislike. Responses are scored on standardized scales and presented on a six-page Standard Profile and in a variety of other narrative report formats.

The *Strong* consists of four different kinds of scales, which, when used together, provide a substantive and complementary picture of an individual's interest patterns. The SII scales include: 6 General Occupational Themes, 25 Basic Interest Scales, 211 Occupational Scales, and 4 Personal Style Scales.

The *Strong* is solely distributed by Consulting Psychologists Press (CPP). To purchase, administer, and interpret the *Strong,* one must have a degree from an accredited college or university and have satisfactorily completed one of the following courses at an accredited four-year college or university: Test Interpretation, Psychometrics and Measurement Theory, or Educational Statistics. Alternatively, one can attend a three-day qualifying workshop for the *Strong,* offered by organizations authorized by CPP, and be qualified by the publisher. For a brief overview of the *Strong Interest Inventory,* refer to Rapid Reference 2.1.

HISTORY

To understand the *Strong* in use today, it is helpful to have an appreciation of its origins. The *Strong* has undergone several important revisions and refinements since it was originally published as the *Strong Vocational Interest Blank* in 1927. For a brief history of the development of the *Strong,* refer to Rapid Reference 2.2.

The *Strong Vocational Interest Blank* (*SVIB*) was authored by Edward K. Strong, a dedicated psychologist and academic researcher at Stanford University, who first published the *SVIB* in 1927 through Stanford University Press. Strong authored a Women's Form in 1933 and revised the Men's and Women's forms in 1938 and 1946, respectively. As Strong was preparing to retire from Stanford in the late 1950s, he wanted to see research on the *Strong* continue. He developed associations with Minnesota psychologists Kenneth B. Clark and Ralph Berdie, who shared his dedication to interest measurement, which led

≡*Rapid Reference 2.1*

Strong Interest Inventory (SII) Overview

Strong Interest Inventory (Strong Interest Inventory of the Strong Vocational Interest Blanks, Form T317)

Author: E. K. Strong

Authors of Manual: Lenore W. Harmon, Jo-Ida C. Hansen, Fred H. Borgen, Allen L. Hammer.

Published by: Stanford University Press, Stanford, CA

Distributed by: Consulting Psychologists Press, Inc.
3803 East Bayshore Road
P.O. Box 10096
Palo Alto, CA 94303
Phone: 800-624-1765 or 650-969-8901
Fax: 650-969-8608
Web site: www.cpp-db.com

Copyright date: 1994.

The *Strong Interest Inventory* measures interests using three response formats, the most common being like/indifferent/dislike, in a wide range of areas such as occupations, school subjects, and leisure activities. The *Strong* compares an individual's preferences with Holland's typology, various specific interest domains, and the interest patterns of people employed in a variety of occupations who are satisfied with their work. The inventory is designed to assist individuals in identifying potential career fields as well as areas of leisure and other life interests in which the individual would likely find enjoyment and satisfaction.

Age Range: 14–adult

Administration Time: Paper and Pencil: 35–40 minutes; Online: 15–20 minutes

Qualifications: A baccalaureate degree and the satisfactory completion of a course in the interpretation of psychological tests and measurement from an accredited college or university, or a qualifying workshop recognized by CPP.

to the establishment upon his death in 1963 of the Center for Interest Measurement Research at the University of Minnesota.

In 1974, the first major revision of the *SVIB* was undertaken by David P. Campbell at the University of Minnesota and the instrument became known as the *Strong-Campbell Interest Inventory* (*SCII*). Campbell instituted two major innovations that made the *Strong* easier to use and more meaningful for both

Historical Highlights of the *Strong*

1927   E. K. Strong authors the first Men's Form and Manual, published by Stanford University Press.

1933   E. K. Strong authors the first Women's Form and Manual.

1938   First major revision of the Men's form and adoption of the modern profile.

1946   First major revision of the Women's form. First automated test-scoring machine is invented.

1959   First "modern" *Strong Vocational Interest Blanks Manual* published by Consulting Psychologists Press, Inc.

1963   The Center for Interest Measurement Research (CIMR) is created at the University of Minnesota, housing the Strong archives.

1966–69   Major revisions of the Men's Form and Women's Form and manuals.

1968   Basic Interest Scales are added to the *SVIB*.

1974   The first Merged Form (combined Men's form and Women's form), the *Strong-Campbell Interest Inventory*, using Holland's hexagon as an organizing structure, is completed at CIMR under the direction of David P. Campbell.

1981   The first revision of the Merged Form is completed at CIMR under the direction of Jo-Ida C. Hansen, resulting in additional gender-balanced occupational scales.

1984   The first interpretive manual, *The User's Guide for the SVIB-SCII*, is authored by Jo-Ida C. Hansen.

1985   The second revision of the Merged Form is completed under the direction of Jo-Ida C. Hansen, resulting in additional gender-balanced and non-college occupational scales.

1980   CPP begins publishing various interpretive reports.

1994   The largest revision of the *Strong*, the *Strong Interest Inventory*, undertaken by Harmon et al., results in a significant increase in the size of the general reference sample, new Basic Interest Scales, more Occupational Scales, a new set of scales called Personal Style Scales, improved reliabilities, and an enhanced profile.

1990s   Expanded resources and reports are published, including the *Strong and Skills Confidence Inventory Form*, the *Strong and MBTI Career Report*, *Interpretive Resource Manuals for College and Organizational Settings*, *Business Report*, *Entrepreneur Report*, and the *Making It in Today's Organizations* series. On-site software and web administrations are also offered.

2002–3   Target release date for newest revision of the *Strong*.

the practitioner and client. First, he incorporated an additional set of scales, the General Occupation Themes, utilizing John Holland's hexagonal model of occupational personality types to lend a theoretical framework to the instrument. Holland's RIASEC model was also used to guide the layout of the Basic Interest Scales and the Occupational Scales. Campbell's second major contribution was the effort to eliminate sex bias and discrimination by merging the Men's and Women's forms into a single booklet, eliminating references to gender in the items (e.g., changing *policeman* to *police officer*), developing several new scales that reflected non-traditional occupational choices for both sexes (e.g., adding scales for *female* veterinarians and physicists, and *male* nurses and elementary teachers), and scoring both sexes on all scales.

In 1981 and again in 1985, two major revisions of the *Strong-Campbell Interest Inventory* were undertaken under the direction of Jo-Ida C. Hansen at the Center for Interest Measurement Research at the University of Minnesota. With these revisions, Hansen undertook a major research effort to produce gender-balanced scales with equitable career options for both women and men. For example, for the 1981 version, 17 new female occupational scales were developed to match existing male scales (examples include *Biologist, Personnel Director, Public Administrator,* and *Realtor*) and 11 new male scales were developed to match existing female scales (examples include *Art Teacher, Flight Attendant, Occupational Therapist* and *Radiologic Technologist*). By the 1985 version, 101 pairs of scales had been developed on female and male samples for the same occupation, nearly tripling the 37 matched pairs available on the 1974 version of the instrument. In 1985, Hansen also added several more occupational scales for non-college occupations (examples include *Carpenter, Respiratory Therapist,* and *Chef*). Hansen also authored the very well-received *User's Guide for the SVIB-SCII* (1984), the first interpretive manual ever published on the *Strong*.

In 1994, during the next major revision of the instrument, in which 55,000 people in 50 occupations completed a research version of the *Strong* (Harmon, Hansen, Borgen & Hammer, 1994). In the 1994 revision, Harmon and her colleagues, updated the general reference samples with respondents in the 1990s and dramatically increased their sizes to 9,467 women and 9,484 men, compared to the samples of 300 men and 300 women used in previous versions. The language of the instrument was updated (e.g., the item *Typist* was replaced with *Word Processor* and the item *Pursuing bandits in a sheriff's posse* was deleted because it was too outmoded). The researchers added four new Basic Interest

Scales: the *Applied Arts, Culinary Arts, Data Management,* and *Computer Activities* scales. They also added fourteen more Occupational Scales, including, for example, *technical writer, corporate trainer,* and *paralegal,* to reflect contemporary occupations and future growth trends. Finally, the researchers added a new set of scales called the Personal Style Scales that measure preferences for work style, learning, leadership, and risk taking. The appearance of the profile was dramatically enhanced so users would not be overwhelmed by data. Visual cues such as color coding were used throughout the profile to more effectively guide the user through an interpretation. Throughout the 1990s, CPP developed new products and resources to support and enhance the use of this well-established and researched assessment instrument. Also, the publisher added internet and software administration and scoring capabilities. Rapid Reference 2.2 lists historical highlights in the development of the *Strong.*

THEORETICAL AND RESEARCH FOUNDATIONS

E. K. Strong constructed the original *SVIB* scales by comparing item responses of an occupational sample with those of a general reference sample. Items that showed large response differences between the occupational sample and general reference sample were incorporated into the occupational scale. The current Occupational Scales and two of the Personal Style Scales are constructed by these same methods today, assisted by the capabilities of computing technology.

The original *SVIB* included only the empirically constructed Occupational Scales. These scales demonstrated impressive validity and reliability. However, due to their empirical construction, the content and pattern of interests reflected in each occupational scale was not obvious to the client or the career professional. This limitation led to the development in the late 1960s of the Basic Interest Scales, which were constructed by identifying items that clustered together statistically. Today's Basic Interest Scales and two of the Personal Style Scales are constructed by identifying items that have strong item intercorrelations.

Although the Basic Interest Scales provided a set of homogenous and interpretable scales, they were too numerous to provide an overarching theoretical structure for the instrument. Factor analytic studies on interest and personality research in the 1950s and 1960s suggested that there was a much smaller number, perhaps five to seven, basic dimensions underlying the structure of interests. In 1959, Holland, following on earlier work of Guilford (Harmon et al., 1994) first published his proposal for six basic categories of occupational interests. These corresponded well to dimensions cited in the research with the *SVIB*. The General Occupational Themes were constructed by identifying items that corresponded to Holland's description of the six occupational-personality types. A variety of statistical procedures was used in the selection process, including item-scale correlations, item intercorrelations, and the endorsement of items among occupations of specific Holland types.

Item Content and Format

The 1994 revision of the *Strong* includes 317 items from a research pool of 379 items. The research version of the *Strong* was given to over 55,000 people and included the original 325 items from the 1985 version and 54 new items that were written to increase the number of occupations requiring less than four years of college, reflect occupations of growing importance as well as today's leisure pursuits, and to replace old items that worked well but appeared to be outdated. Final item selection depended on a range of item response characteristics. For example, items that were extremely popular or unpopular were excluded because they would not differentiate between groups (Harmon et al., 1994).

The General Occupational Themes

The Six General Occupational Themes (GOTs)—Realistic, Investigative, Artistic, Social, Enterprising, and Conventional—are homogeneous scales composed of 20–33 items. As described above, they are constructed on both a rational basis, that is, items are selected that best reflect Holland's typology, and on the basis of statistical evidence that indicate strong item-scale correlations, item intercorrelations, and popularity among occupations of related Holland types. Today's GOTs are constructed with enhanced reliabilities achieved by deleting items that had weak item-scale correlations and adding additional items with stronger item-scale correlations (Harmon et al., 1994). An effort was made in the 1994 revision to also minimize correlations among adjacent scales on the hexagon. For a full description of the themes, see Rapid Reference 2.3.

The *Applications and Technical Guide* (Harmon et al., 1994) provides data that

General Occupational Theme Descriptions

Realistic. Realistic people like activities, jobs, and coworkers who represent such interest areas as mechanical, construction, and repair activities; nature and the outdoors; and adventurous, physical activities. They enjoy working with tools, machines, and equipment. They are interested in action rather than thought and prefer concrete problems to ambiguous, abstract problems.

Investigative. Investigative people have a strong scientific, inquiring orientation. They enjoy gathering information, uncovering new facts or theories, and analyzing and interpreting data. They are most comfortable in academic or research environments and enjoy pursuing advanced degrees. They prefer to rely on themselves in their work rather than on others in a group project. They dislike selling and repetitive activities.

Artistic. Artistic people value aesthetic qualities and have a great need for self-expression. This type, more than any other, includes people who enjoy being spectators or observers (in this case, of the arts) rather than participants. Artistic types frequently express their artistic interests in leisure or recreational activities as well as in vocational activities or environments. With their typical verbal-linguistic bent, they are quite comfortable in academic or intellectual environments. The spectrum of the Artistic theme has a threefold content: visual arts, music/dramatics, and writing.

Social. Social people like to work with people; they enjoy working in groups, sharing responsibilities, and being the center of attention. Central characteristics are helping, nurturing, caring for others, and teaching and instructing, especially of young people. Social types like to solve problems through discussions of feelings and interactions with others. They may also enjoy working with people through leading, directing, and persuading.

Enterprising. Enterprising people are verbally facile in selling and leading. They seek positions of leadership, power, and status. They enjoy working with other people and leading them toward organizational goals and economic success. Enterprising people may like to take financial and interpersonal risks and to participate in competitive activities. They dislike scientific activities and long periods of intellectual effort.

Conventional. Conventional people especially like activities that require attention to organization, data systems, detail, and accuracy. They often enjoy mathematics and data management activities such as accounting and investment management. They work well in large organizations, but do not show a distinct preference for or against leadership positions.

demonstrate that the scales perform in predictable ways. While the sides of the hexagon are less regular than Holland's theory suggests, the intercorrelations between themes are generally highest between adjacent themes as arranged on the hexagon, and lowest between themes opposite one another on the hexagon (scales opposite one another have correlations that are all less than .1). The revised General Occupational Themes also show improved internal consistency reliability, with all reliabilities measuring above .9.

The GOT items are weighted such that a Like response on an item raises the individual's theme score (weight = + 1), a Dislike response lowers the score (weight = –1), and an Indifferent response has no effect on the score (weight = 0). Thus, if a person responds Like to the item *High school teacher* on the Social (S) Theme, this person's score on the S Theme increases. A Dislike response to the same item would result in a decrease on the Social Theme scale.

Evidence of construct validity is provided by correlations between Holland's *Vocational Preference Inventory* (VPI) and an earlier version of the *Strong* in which the correlations between the General Occupational Themes and *VPI* scales were high (median = .765). Evidence of concurrent and construct validity can be obtained by viewing tables in the *Applications and Technical Guide* (Harmon et al., 1994), which show the 15 highest- and 15 lowest-ranking occupations for each GOT falling out in predictable patterns; for example, the top three rank-ordered occupations on the Investigative GOT were Physicist, Science Teacher, and Chemist.

The general reference sample was used to create standard scores on the General Occupational Themes. Their raw score means and standard deviations on the six scales were used in the standardization formula that converts scores into distributions with standard score means of 50 and standard deviations of 10. The interpretive comments on the profile compare the individual with others of the same gender.

The Basic Interest Scales

Each of the 25 Basic Interest Scales are composed of items that statistically correlate with one another. While the General Occupational Themes are broader in their content, the Basic Interest Scales are more focused on measuring a specific interest area. They can be thought of as subdivisions of the General Occupational Themes, with each Theme having three to five Basic Interest Scales associated with it. Each Basic Interest Scale is composed of 5–21 items, with each scale name providing a summary of the item content of its scale. In the 1994 revision, one scale was deleted (Domestic Arts); four new scales were added (Applied Arts, Culinary Arts, Computer Activities, and Data Management); and one scale was moved to the Personal Style Scales and re-named (Adventure became Risk Taking/Adventure). The *Applications and Technical Guide* provides additional details about the 1994 revision.

Each Basic Interest Scale is arranged on the profile under the Theme to which it is closely related. The *Applications and Technical Guide* shows that the correlations tend to be highest (although not in every case) between the Basic Interest Scales and the General Occupational Themes within which they are grouped.

Basic Interest Scale items are predominantly weighted so that a Like response equals + 1, a Dislike response = –1, and an Indifferent response = 0. High scores on the Basic Interest Scales are achieved *primarily* by answering Like to the items on the scale, and low scores are achieved primarily by responding Dislike. Average scores are earned by responding with a mix of Like and Dislike responses to the items on the scale. However, it is possible in a few cases to get a point on a Basic Interest Scale by endorsing the Dislike response.

The Basic Interest Scales are normed against the general reference sample so that the mean of the combined gender sample is set to 50 and the standard deviation to 10. The interpretive comments on the profile compare the individual to others of the same gender.

There is substantial evidence for the construct and concurrent validity of the Basic Interest scales that can be obtained by observing the rank ordering of the 15 highest- and 15 lowest-ranking occupations on each of the Basic Interest Scales. For example, among the top five occupations on the Writing Basic Interest Scale were: English Teacher, Reporter, Public Relations Director, and Technical Writer. Thus, people in occupations related to the Basic Interest Scales scored higher than those in unrelated occupations.

The Basic Interest Scales can be used in a complementary way to provide enhanced meaning to the empirically derived Occupational Scales.

The Occupational Scales

There are 211 Occupational Scales representing 109 occupations. 102 scales are matched for men and women, and seven are represented by one gender only.

Five Occupational Scales have only female norms: Child Care Provider, Home Economics Teacher, Dental Hygienist, Dental Assistant, and Secretary. Two Occupational Scales have only male norms: Plumber and Agribusiness Manager. Individuals needed to meet the following criteria for inclusion in the Occupational Scales: (a) They had to be satisfied with their work (respondents who indicated any degree of dissatisfaction were excluded); (b) they had to have at least three years of experience in their job; (c) they had to be performing their job in a typical way (e.g., the individual trained as a lawyer who identified his primary occupation as a fiction writer would be eliminated); and (d) they had to be 25 years of age or older. Efforts were made to construct scales of about 40 to 50 items in length. Items that differentiated an occupational group's response rate from that of the general reference sample (GRS) by a difference of 16% or greater in either the Like or Dislike responses were the target for constructing the 1994 scales. Although the majority of scales meet this standard, some scales do not, and the actual range for the percentage difference is between 10% and 31%.

The items on the scale are quite varied, or heterogenous. Scores increase when individuals respond Like, Indifferent, or Dislike to the items that are weighted positively. Conversely, scores decrease when individuals respond Like, Indifferent, or Dislike to negatively weighted items. Item weights are determined by looking at the items that differentiate the occupational sample from the general reference sample and identifying whether the Like or Dislike response showed the larger difference. This difference is then weighted +1 or −1 depending on the direction of the difference. For example, in the female Physicist sample, 94% of female physicists say Like to the item *Doing research work,* compared with 32% of the female general reference sample. The difference is 62%. Because this difference is the larger difference (the Dislike response difference equaled −41), the Like response is positively weighted on the female Physicist scale. The opposite response, Dislike, is automatically weighted in the other direction, regardless of the difference. The Indifferent response is weighted if there is a 10 point difference; it is weighted +1 if the difference between the occupational sample and general reference sample is positive and −1 if the difference is negative. The scale is then normed on the occupational sample and raw scores are converted to standard scores with a mean of 50 and standard deviation of 10 for the occupational group.

The largest difference between the 1985 and 1994 versions of the scales are the length of the scales, with an average of 55 items for the 1985 Occupational

Scales and 45 items for the 1994 Occupational Scales. Despite their shorter length, however, the 1994 scales appear to be equally robust.

The Personal Style Scales

The four Personal Style Scales were constructed by two different methods. The Work Style and Learning Environment scales were constructed using an empirical approach, involving two contrasting groups, similar to that used in the construction of the Occupational Scales. The Work Style Scale was constructed by selecting 51 items that differentiated those individuals who consistently preferred people from those who consistently preferred one of the other three options (ideas, data, or things) on the items in Part VIII of the inventory, Preferences in the World of Work. The Learning Environment Scale was constructed by selecting 49 items that differentiated individuals in the 1994 general reference sample who had earned Master's or Ph.D. degrees from those whose highest degree was from a technical or trade school.

The other two scales, the Leadership Style Scale and Risk Taking/Adventure Scale, were developed using homogeneous scale construction techniques similar to those used for the Basic Interest Scales. The Risk Taking/Adventure Scale was originally constructed as one of the Basic Interest Scales by selecting items that correlated with one another and had similar content. The 1994 scale is similar to the original constructed in 1968, although a number of items have been updated to use more contemporary language. The Leadership Style Scale emerged clearly from factor analyses of the *Strong* items. Based upon the factor analysis, 23 items were selected that strongly correlated with one another. As with the General Occupational Themes and Basic Interest Scales, the Personal Style Scales were named on the general reference sample. Raw scores were converted to standard scores with a combined gender mean of 50 and a standard deviation of 10.

For a summary of the *Strong Interest Inventory* scales, including their item content and construction methods, see Rapid Reference 2.4.

Reliability

The 1994 revision of the *Strong* led to increased reliabilities for the instrument. For example, the test-retest reliabilities on the *Strong*'s General Occupational

≡Rapid Reference 2.4

Summary of the Scales on the *Strong Interest Inventory*

	# of Scales	Items/ Scale	Normed	Item Content	Scale Construction
General Occupational Themes	6	20–33	GRS*	Homogeneous	Rational Selection & Item-Scale Correlations
Basic Interest Scales	25	5–21	GRS	Homogeneous	Item Intercorrelations
Occupational Scales	211	23–70	OS**	Heterogeneous	Contrast Groups
Personal Style Scales:	4				
Work Style		51	GRS	Heterogeneous	Contrast Groups
Learning Environment		49	GRS	Heterogeneous	Contrast Groups
Leadership Style		23	GRS	Homogeneous	Item Intercorrelations
Risk Taking/Adventure		9	GRS	Homogeneous	Item Intercorrelations

*General Reference Sample

**Occupational Sample

DON'T FORGET 2.1

Options for Administering the *Strong*

The *Strong* can be administered in one of three ways: paper-and-pencil administration, software system administration, and Internet administration.

	Resources Needed	Procedures
Paper-and-Pencil Administration	Purchase pre-paid item booklet/answer sheets for mail-in scoring and plan to pay postage costs for scoring.	Review instructions of the appropriate item booklet/answer sheet with your client. Request client return the inventory to you for scoring.
Software System Administration	Purchase a license for the software system, pay annual license renewal fee, and purchase report administration (three below and Internet administration). Four administration options can be used with your software system. 1. On screen. Client takes inventory on screen at your site(s).	Depending on which option you are using, instruct your client in how to complete either the on-screen version or paper-and-pencil version (for scanning or manual key-in).

	Resources Needed	**Procedures**
Software System Administration (cont.)	2. Scan*. Client takes paper-and-pencil version and you scan data into computer (Note: You need an optical mark reader (OMR) scanner.) 3. Manual key in*. Client takes paper-and-pencil version and you key in responses manually.	For the paper-and-pencil version, instruct your client to return the inventory to you for scoring.
Internet Administration	Client takes inventory through a web administration. Results are sent to career professional electronically, or you download for scoring. Pay initial license fee for the first year (initial price includes web administration site and CPP software system), and pay annual renewal (which includes annual fee for software system).	Instruct the client to take the assessment at your customized home page, on which you can provide additional written instructions. Alternatively, you can direct your client to the CPP Web Administration home page.

*Software system combined item booklet/answer sheet can be scanned or keyed in to generate all *Strong* reports.

See the current CPP Catalogue or visit www.cpp-db.com for pricing and further information.

Themes for a sample of working adults over a three to six month period range from .84 to .92. The Realistic, Investigative, and Artistic scales demonstrate especially high reliability, with correlations above .90 for all three. The median three-year test-retest correlations for the Basic Interest Scales are excellent for adults (r = .82); however with high school students some changes should be expected over a three-year period (r = .56). The median test-retest reliability for the Occupational Scales for a sample of adults tested on the 1994 Occupational Scales over a three- to six-month period was .90 and ranged on the various scales from .80 to .95. The median test-retest correlation for a sample of college students tested over three months on the Occupational Scales was .85 and ranged from .71 to .96. Swanson and Hansen (1988) found the median correlation on the Occupational Scales over a 12 year period was .72 for a sample of women and .73 for men. Time will tell, but similar results are expected for the 1994 *Strong*.

Validity

After reviewing several studies of predictive validity, Harmon et al. (1994) concluded the hit rate is about 65% when predicting the occupations that individuals will enter based upon their earlier scores on the *Strong*. This rate is obtained by determining the percentage of the samples that entered occupations in which they had an Occupational Scales score of 40 or higher. Earlier researchers also have found that the chances are about 8:1 that individuals will not enter an occupation in which they have received an Occupational Scale score of 30 or lower (Hansen & Campbell, 1985). Researchers also have found the level of predictability to be higher for individuals who have well-defined interest patterns.

HOW TO ADMINISTER AND SCORE

Administering the *Strong*

The *Strong* can be administered one of three ways: as a paper-and-pencil instrument, interactively with a software system, or via the Internet. Don't Forget 2.1 summarizes the options for administering the *Strong*. Regardless of how the inventory is administered, there are certain instructions and cautions that should be provided to the client, either in a face-to-face introduction of the

DON'T FORGET 2.2

Keys to Competent Administration

- Tell clients the *Strong* generally takes an average of 35–40 minutes to complete using paper-and-pencil, and 15–20 minutes online.

- Remind clients they must complete the name or identification number and gender items in the demographics section for an accurate report to be generated.

- Indicate that the *Strong* is an inventory of interests, not a test. No one can fail the *Strong*.

- Remind clients that the *Strong Interest Inventory* is an assessment of interests designed to show the kinds of work they might enjoy by comparing their interests to those of people employed in a variety of occupations.

- Encourage clients to consider only their interests when completing the inventory. Reassure clients they should not worry about whether they would be good at a particular job.

- Remind clients that the *Strong* does not measure abilities or aptitudes; therefore, it cannot predict whether an individual has the skill to succeed in a given occupation or academic field.

- Tell clients the results of the inventory will suggest career fields or areas of academic interest for further investigation, but that the *Strong* is not designed to tell clients what they "should be" or "should do."

- Instruct clients to mark the response for the first answer that comes to mind. Results tend to be more indicative of respondents' true interests if they don't spend a lot of time evaluating which response to give.

- Point out the different sections of the *Strong* and indicate to the client the different types of response options they will be using.

- Indicate to clients that the *Strong* will provide information on 109 different occupations across all occupational types, and will include those requiring vocational/technical training as well as professional education, making it one of the most comprehensive inventories available.

assessment or via a personalized introductory page if you are using the option for interactive or web-based administration. Don't Forget 2.2 lists several suggestions for a competent administration of the *Strong*.

It is important to recognize the limits associated with administration. See Caution 2.1 that describes considerations such as reading level and language skills that need to be taken into account before administering the *Strong*.

CAUTION 2.1

Limits on Administering the *Strong*

Reading Level. The overall reading level for the *Strong* is between the eighth- and ninth-grade levels. However, not all of the vocabulary used in the assessment will be familiar to everyone, particularly some words associated with occupations and school subjects. In such cases, it is permissible and useful to describe or define the item. Doing so will yield more meaningful results than would be obtained if the respondent were to guess at the meaning of the item.

Age. Although the test authors indicate the inventory can be used with individuals from age 14 on, it is not usually administered to those who have not yet begun eighth grade (13- and 14-year-olds), since most people's interest patterns have not developed sufficiently before that age. If the *Strong* is administered to eighth-, ninth-, or tenth-graders, the scales that yield the most useful information will be the General Occupational Themes and Basic Interest Scales. Most high school counselors administer the *Strong* to eleventh- or twelfth-graders, as interests typically begin to stabilize by this age.

Language. For those whose first language is not English, the effectiveness of the *Strong* is limited to the extent that clients understand the meaning of the items. Check with the publisher for current translations of the inventory.

Scoring the Inventory

Counselors have several choices for the type of report they wish to generate for the completed inventory. The client will complete the same 317 items in the inventory regardless of the type of report that is produced. You will select the type of report and order it when purchasing the paper-and-pencil or electronic administrations.

If administered as a paper-and-pencil inventory, the *Strong* can be scored by the publisher at one of two CPP scoring centers. If administered on the web, clients take the assessment at the publisher's web administration site (or at one customized for the career professional) and results are delivered electronically to the career professional. Rapid Reference 2.5 provides additional details about scoring options.

Decisions about which administration and scoring methods to use are typically based upon factors such as cost, the turn-around time needed, and the level of organizational staff support for on-site scoring. Caution 2.2 suggests

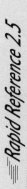

Rapid Reference 2.5

Options for Administering and Scoring the *Strong*

	Type of Administration	Procedures
Mail-In Scoring Provided by CPP Scoring Services	Used for paper-and-pencil administrations	After receiving the completed pre-paid combined item booklet/answer sheets from your clients, mail booklets to one of two CPP scoring centers: East Coast–Washington, D.C.; West Coast–Palo Alto, CA.
		When scheduling your interpretive session, allow sufficient time to get the completed item booklet/answer sheet back from your client and then allow about two weeks to get the results returned from the publisher's scoring service after you have mailed answer sheets for scoring (unless overnight delivery is requested).
Software System Scoring	Used for software system administrations (on-screen, scanned, and manually keyed in options)	Once the data have been entered either by your client on screen, or by you by scanning or keying in the item booklet/answer sheet, run the software system to complete the scoring.
		The CPP Software System runs on Microsoft Windows operating system. For optimum performance, 32 MB RAM, Pentium II processor-based computer, and HP LaserJet or other compatible Windows graphic printer is recommended.
		CPP Software allows for immediate access to scoring and reporting options. In addition, the system allows for batch reporting and a client management module which identifies the inventories a client has taken and the reports that were generated.
		Four-color paper is available for use with the *Strong Profile, Standard* and *High School* editions.
	Used for Internet administrations	Once your client has completed the inventory online, you will receive results electronically.

See the current CPP catalogue or visit cpp-db.com for pricing and other information.

CAUTION 2.2

Considerations for Selecting the Type of Administration

Administration	Considerations	Best Bet
Paper-and-Pencil Administration	**Pros:** Least expensive method of administration if ordering low volume of administrations.	Best used by cost-conscious operations where a fast turn-around time is not necessary.
	Cons: Generally about three weeks are needed to get the assessment back from the client, to the publisher, and the results returned to you before a follow-up session can be scheduled.	*Example: Nonprofit community based career centers serving an adult population.*
Software System Administration	**Pros:** On-site scoring capability allows for immediate access to results. Provides convenience for clients. With scanning option, provides enhanced speed, accuracy, and flexibility in scoring.	Best used by high-volume operations that have sufficient staffing and appropriate scanning equipment. *Example: High-volume, large-scale university counseling or career centers serving students.*

Administration	Considerations	Best Bet
Software System Administration (cont.)	**Cons:** Additional staff time is required to print reports. *For On-screen option*, clients need to have time to remain at your site to take the inventory. *For Scan option*, OMR scanner represents a significant expense. *For Manual key-in option*, additional staff time is required to key in results.	
Internet Administration	**Pros:** Clients can take the inventory via the Internet from any remote location, at any time. On-site scoring capability allows for immediate access to results. Provides enhanced speed, accuracy, and flexibility in both administration and scoring. **Cons:** Most expensive method of administration. Requires that you and clients have a PC or Macintosh, Internet connectivity, and appropriate browser.	Best used by operations that have clients in diverse or remote locations and where there is a client expectation, need, or desire for convenient access or quick turn-around times. *Example: Outplacement firms or career development centers serving sophisticated clients from diverse locales in time-limited sessions.*

relative advantages and disadvantages associated with each type of administration, to assist you in determining which approach may be best for your setting.

Report Formats

A variety of report formats exist that are tailored for use in different situations and vary in both the amount of information provided and, as a result, the cost. The standard report format is the Profile, Standard Edition. It is a four-color, six-page format with a "Snapshot" of results and includes the 6 General Occupational Themes, 25 Basic Interest Scales, 211 Occupational Scales (109 occupations), 4 Personal Style Scales, and Administrative Indexes. This format works particularly well in group programs and in individual sessions that are time-limited. Experienced practitioners find the standard Profile adequate for most purposes.

Another popular format is the narrative report called the *Strong Interpretive Report*. It provides both a copy of the Profile and an expanded narrative report of the *Strong* results. The expanded report includes a personalized General Occupational Theme hexagon, the highlights of which are further explained in terms of occupations, leisure interests, and personality descriptors; the Basic Interest Scales printed in rank order with short descriptions of the typical activities associated with the scales; and the top 10 Occupational Scales with descriptions of work tasks, related occupations, and associated Dictionary of Occupational Titles (DOT) codes. This report works well for clients who wish to have more detailed information available to them. New professionals often prefer the *Strong Interpretive Report* because of the wealth of interpretive information available. It is important to note, however, that the narrative report can be problematic for novice practitioners because it relies on numerical scores, rather than patterns of scores, to determine the top two to three Occupational Themes and top 10 Occupational Scales. Since other scales with high scores, and in some cases, equally important scores, will not be included in these interpretive highlights, some practitioners will overlook other important data in the inventory by relying on the *Interpretive Report* alone. Remember the *Interpretive Report* can provide a wealth of very valuable information, but it is used most appropriately in conjunction with the Profile, which provides additional important details of benefit to many clients.

A variety of narrative reports have been developed to complement the Profile. See Rapid Reference 2.6 for a summary of Strong Report Formats. In ad-

Summary of *Strong* Report Formats

Report Format	Description
Profile, Standard Edition	Presents a summary of individualized career interests.
Profile, High School Edition	Provides high school students and parents with career exploration and planning information.
Profile, College Edition	Provides college students and college counselors with information pertaining to choosing majors and careers.
Interpretive Report	Identifies and explores personalized career development options. Summarizes who the person is.
Professional Report	Identifies interests in professional occupations requiring a college degree. Summarizes what the person would like to do.
Business Report	Organizes interests into functional areas within an organization to supplement Holland categories (e.g., marketing, sales, customer service, etc.).
Strong and MBTI Career Report	Combines *Strong* results with personality preferences for comprehensive career exploration.
Strong and MBTI Entrepreneur Report	Identifies how interests and personality preferences fit with tasks required to run a business.
Strong Interest Inventory and Skills Confidence Inventory	Measures interests and perceived skills for focused career planning.
Strong, Skills Confidence, and MBTI Entrepreneur Report	Identifies confidence-interest patterns and how interests and personality preferences fit with tasks required to run a business.

More information can be obtained from your CPP regional representative or at CPP's web site: cpp-db.com.

Adapted from the CPP 2000 catalogue.

dition, you could select among several Profiles: High School Edition; College Edition; or Skills Confidence Inventory Profile. Several "second-level" interpretive reports also are available to supplement an initial interpretation of a Profile.

HOW TO INTERPRET THE *STRONG*

Because the *Strong* can be used for so many different reasons and in such varied settings, you will need to focus your interpretative strategy to address your specific goals and your client's individual needs. The following guidelines are intended to provide a general framework or template from which you can customize an interpretation suitable to your unique circumstances.

This model for interpreting the *Strong* will be divided into two sections, (1) preparing for the interpretation and (2) sequencing the interpretation. Quick reference boxes are provided throughout, summarizing the highlights of each.[1] If you are not familiar with the *Strong* refer to the sample profile in Chapter 5 (Figure 5.1) as you review the following guidelines.

Preparing for the Interpretation

Take time to review the *Strong* Profile prior to your interpretation to begin building hypotheses and planning your interventions. The following steps (also listed in Rapid Reference 2.7) outline a thorough preparation strategy. Once you are familiar with interpreting the *Strong,* these steps can be completed quickly.

Step 1: Assess the Validity of the Profile
Before planning your interpretation, assess whether the Profile appears to be valid for interpretation. Page 6 of the Profile contains two general measures that can alert you to possible validity problems. Both measures can be found toward the lower right corner of the page. The first is the number of total responses

---

[1] This model generally follows the interpretation methods detailed in the following two sources that provide in-depth treatment for interpreting the *Strong:* Harmon, Hansen, Borgen, & Hammer, 1994 and Prince, 1995.

(maximum 317). If this number is less than 300, the Profile may be invalid, and a warning is printed on the Profile. If this occurs, review the Booklet/Answer Sheet to identify which items were left blank. Typically, a low number is due either to the respondent inadvertently skipping a page or group of items, or to improperly darkened ovals. Plan to discuss with the client the reasons for the omission; the Booklet/Answer Sheet can be rescored after the client has properly completed the missing information.

The second measure is the number of infrequent responses. This measure is indexed to the number of

> ≡ *Rapid Reference 2.7*
>
> ### How to Prepare for the Interpretation
>
> **Step 1:** Assess the validity of the profile
>
> **Steps 2 and 3:** Review client's response style
>
> **Step 4, 5, 6, and 7:** Review each section of profile—note highlights, patterns, and inconsistencies
>
> **Step 8:** Determine a preliminary theme code
>
> **Step 9:** Summarize highlights that address client's presenting concerns
>
> **Step 10:** Choose an interpretive sequence to follow

items that the client answered differently from typical respondents of the same gender. This index includes 11 items for females and 14 items for males. Generally, less than 1% of women endorse more than four infrequent responses, and less than 1% of men endorse more than six infrequent responses. Scores are calculated using an inverse scoring technique so that one point is subtracted from a constant for each infrequent response that is endorsed. The resulting highest total score for women is five and the highest total score for men is seven. The lowest possible score for women is –7, and the lowest possible score for men is –8. However, the counselor only needs to remember that a negative number indicates that the client responded to items in a highly unusual way. A negative score also may result from random responding, or some other error in completion of the Booklet/Answer Sheet. However, a negative score does not necessarily indicate invalidity. A negative score may occur for individuals with interests highly atypical for their gender. When a negative score occurs, first check the Profile to see if the score can be explained by patterns of interests on Basic Interest Scales and General Occupational Themes that reflect non-traditional interests for that person's gender.

Step 2: Review the Summary of Item Responses

These scores (see page 6 of Profile) provide a general view of the client's response distribution: the percentages of items endorsed as Like, Indifferent, and Dislike for each section of the inventory. Note the SUBTOTAL line for any extreme percentages (over 80% or under 20%). Extreme response percentages will affect the overall elevation of the Profile's scores, particularly the General Occupational Themes and the Basic Interest Scales, since these scales achieve elevation primarily when Like responses are endorsed.

Prepare to discuss with the client any extreme response patterns, and be prepared to explain how they might influence the scores on the various sections of the client's Profile. For example, on the one hand, someone with a high percentage of dislikes may be stating a generally negative attitude toward assessment, or toward a broad range of activities in general. On the other hand, the same pattern may indicate a mature individual who, over time and experience, has narrowed her or his interests into a clearly defined domain.

Step 3: Review the Snapshot—A Summary of Results

The Snapshot page of the Profile (page 1) provides a good starting place. It summarizes the client's scores on the General Occupational Themes, listing them from highest to lowest interest as measured against the general reference sample of the respondent's same sex. The Snapshot also lists the top five Basic Interest Scales and top 10 Occupational Scales. Review this page with an eye toward identifying those interest Themes that repeat across the different sections of the inventory, and note any surprises or inconsistencies. For example, is there a consistent pattern, across the different sections, of high scales with Social interests? Alternatively, is there an inconsistency, such as a number of high Social Basic Interest Scales, but a lack of Occupational Scales with a Social theme code? If all the client's scores in any section of the Snapshot fall below average, a special cautionary note is printed on that section of the Snapshot. (See Don't Forget 2.3 to prepare yourself for interpreting such Profiles.)

Step 4: Review the Personal Style Scales

Note the scores on these scales, and how they might fit or conflict with your knowledge of your client's work environment or work style. (See Page 6 of Profile.) Prepare to discuss in positive terms those scores that fall toward the left pole, since these scores may be misinterpreted by your client in a negative light. For example, a score toward the left pole on the Leadership scale should not be misinterpreted as a lack of leadership interest. It may represent a greater interest in being a consensus-oriented leader, an individual contributor, or a manager of projects rather than people. Also, familiarize yourself with work activities and environments that correspond to each of the scales' poles, so that you are prepared to engage in a discussion about how these scores may fit with various tasks.

Step 5: Review the General Occupational Themes

Begin by evaluating which two or three of the six General Occupational Themes summarize your client's strongest interests. Notice the specific scores for each of the themes and their relative elevations. With Profiles that have no scores of "High Interest" or "Very High Interest," you will need to prepare for questions or negative reactions from your client (see Don't Forget 2.3).

Step 6: Review the Basic Interest Scales

Notice which scales are highest and which are lowest among these 25 scales (see page 2 of Profile). Also, be prepared to describe the content that each scale reflects. Familiarize yourself with the brief descriptions that are listed in each of these scales in Rapid Reference 2.8.

Step 7: Review the Occupational Scales

Notice which occupational groups appear to have interests similar to your client (scores 40 and above), and which occupational groups appear to have interests dissimilar to your client (scores below 30) (see pages 3, 4, and 5 of Profile). Keep in mind these interpretations for the related standard scores: 19 and below—very dissimilar; 20–29—dissimilar; 30–39—mid-range; 40–49—similar; 50 and above—very similar. Identify commonalities among the highest Occupational Scales. Are there Theme codes or other characteristics that they share? This preparation will help you explore similar occupations with your client, beyond those listed on the Profile.

Prepare to discuss any mismatches and matches with the occupational settings in which your client currently works, or which your client is considering moving toward. Also, prepare yourself for questions that your client may ask about these scales. They are complex scales, both in terms of their construction and presentation on the Profile. Are you able to describe in general terms the composition of the sample of these occupational groups? Are you clear about the meaning of the standard scores that appear on the Profile? Do you

Basic Interest Scales—Definitions

Theme Code	Basic Interest	Typical Activities
R	Agriculture	Working outdoors
R	Nature	Appreciating nature
R	Military Activities	Working in structured settings
R	Athletics	Playing or watching sports
R	Mechanical Activities	Working with tools and equipment
I	Science	Conducting scientific research
I	Mathematics	Working with numbers or statistics
I	Medical Science	Working in medicine or biology
A	Music/Dramatics	Performing or enjoying music/drama
A	Art	Appreciating or creating art
A	Applied Arts	Producing or enjoying visual art
A	Writing	Reading or writing
A	Culinary Arts	Cooking or entertaining
S	Teaching	Instructing young people
S	Social Service	Helping people
S	Medical Service	Helping people in a medical setting
S	Religious Activities	Participating in spiritual activities
E	Public Speaking	Persuading or influencing people
E	Law/Politics	Discussing law and public policies
E	Merchandising	Selling retail or wholesale products
E	Sales	Selling to potential customers
E	Organizational Management	Managing or supervising others
C	Data Management	Analyzing data for decision making
C	Computer Activities	Working with computers
C	Office Services	Performing clerical and office tasks

Text is taken from the Snapshot of the *Strong Interest Inventory*™ Profile, 1994, Stanford, CA: Stanford University Press. Copyright 1994 by Stanford University Press. Reprinted with permission.

understand the reasoning for having separate male and female scales? Can you explain why individuals commonly score higher on opposite-sex scales? If you are not familiar with interpreting the *Strong,* review the Rapid Reference 2.11, which provides a number of answers to questions that clients typically ask about these scales.

Step 8: Determine a Preliminary Theme Code

The Theme Code listed on the Snapshot page is derived simply from the scores of the General Occupational Themes. This Theme Code may or may not accurately represent the full interest patterns of your client once the scores on the Basic Interest Scales and Occupational Scales are taken into account. Take a moment to review the full profile to determine which Theme Code most accurately summarizes the full array of scores. First, notice whether the most similar Occupational Scales cluster within one or two of the Themes, and whether the least similar scores cluster in other Themes. Next, determine whether the same patterns are evident across the Basic Interest Scales and General Occupational Themes. Then choose the two- or three-letter Theme Code that best summarizes the highest interest patterns.

Note any inconsistencies between the Themes suggested by the Occupational Scales and those suggested by the General Occupational Themes and Basic Interest Scales. For example, if a pattern of high scores occurs among the Investigative Basic Interest Scales, but not among the Investigative Occupational Scales, the Investigative Theme may represent avocational, rather than occupational interests. The individual is stating an interest in specific Investigative topics, but not in the broader interest patterns shared among workers in Investigative careers.

Finally, given the preliminary Theme Code you have selected, how might you plan to adjust your interview style and interpretation strategy to match it? For example, you might anticipate that a client with an Investigative Theme Code will ask you many questions about the meaning of scales, whereas one with a Realistic Theme Code may expect practical suggestions.

Step 9: Summarize the Important Highlights

Rarely do we have the time to review the inventory with the client in all its detail, and rarely are clients interested in every scale's meaning or nuance. As a final step in preparing for the interpretation, therefore, try to summarize two or three highlights that you think would be important to stress during your interpretation.

For example, you may want to highlight the significance of the Theme Code. You might also note ways in which the Theme Code appears to be consistent with scores on particular Personal Style Scales. For example, does the client have a high Enterprising General Occupational Theme, and also a Leadership Style score indicating a preference for directing others? Also, look for any inconsistencies or unusual patterns among the scales that may shed light on the client's presenting concerns. Are there particular scales that confirm the client's career plans, or others that raise questions? Keep in mind, however, that all of your hypotheses will need confirmation from the client during the interpretation.

Step 10: Select an Interpretive Sequence

Having reviewed the full Profile, tentatively decide which sections or scales provide the information that you consider most useful or relevant to your client's concerns. (During your interpretation, you may need to adjust or change this plan depending on the client's reactions.) Then develop a tentative plan for how you will apportion your interview time, since not all sections of the inventory will be equally relevant to your counseling goals. Also, consider the order in which you will interpret the inventory. Do you plan to follow a traditional order, as described in the Interpretive Sequence below, or does it make more sense to begin with a particular set of scales that address a particular concern of your client?

The Interpretation Sequence

Following is a seven-step model for interpreting the *Strong*. Although designed for individual interpretations, these steps can be used for small group interpretations as well. Completing all the steps can easily fill a typical 50-minute interview; however, it may work best with some clients to break up the interpretation into sections, covering the seven steps over the course of several sessions. Rapid Reference 2.9 provides a summary of the seven steps.

Step 1: Introduce the Results

Investigate client's reactions to completing the Strong Ask the client what it was like to complete the *Strong*. What thoughts, reactions, or questions occurred? This provides an opportunity to dispel misconceptions about the inventory and to build rapport. Remind the client that you will be explaining the meaning of the scores. However, emphasize that a number of factors can influence the results, and you will rely on the client to confirm their degree of accuracy.

Clarify goals of the interpretation   Review with the client again the goals for the interpretation. Discuss any misconceptions or unrealistic expectations the client may hold, and come to an agreement about the purpose of your interpretation. (review Caution Box 2.3). Highlight, in particular, the fact that the *Strong* does not measure the client's abilities. Also, remind the client that the *Strong* is a useful tool for getting to know your client's interests and preferences better, but it will not tell the client which career to choose.

Describe the Profile's organization, and how you will proceed   Explain that the *Strong* has four different sections, and that each assesses the client's interests in a different way. Describe each section briefly and indicate the order in which you will review them. For example, you might say:

> *Rapid Reference 2.9*
>
> **Seven Steps to Interpreting the *Strong***
>
> **Step 1:** Introduce the results
> **Step 2:** Explain Holland's theory and the General Occupational Themes
> **Step 3:** Discuss the Basic Interest Scales
> **Step 4:** Interpret the Occupational Scales
> **Step 5:** Review the Personal Style Scales
> **Step 6:** Summarize results
> **Step 7:** Encourage exploration beyond the profile

"Your Strong *Profile includes over 200 scales. These scales are organized into four sections; each section addresses a different question about your interests. We will review each of the four sections in turn. First, we will review the section called the General Occupational Themes. These summarize your interests according to a personality theory, and indicate which of six different personality types might most closely describe you. Next, we will review the section called the Basic Interest Scales. This section organizes your interests into topic areas and highlights what you said you like, and what you said you do not like. Next, we will review the Occupational Scales. These indicate which types of people, across a wide range of occupations, share interests in common with you. Finally, we will discuss the fourth section, the Personal Style Scales. These measure four ways in which your personal preferences or styles might influence your choice of a work environment."*

You can use the Snapshot page to help you introduce and summarize each section of the inventory. This is particularly helpful if you have little time to re-

CAUTION 2.3

Interpretive Do's and Don'ts

- **Do** clarify clients' expectations for the interpretation.
- **Do** explore clients' previous experiences with interest testing, both positive and negative.
- **Do** explain that interests are only ONE piece of information needed for good career decision-making.
- **Do** remind clients that the *Strong* assesses a full range of life interests, not just career-related interests.
- **Don't** give the *Strong* Profile to a client without a personalized interpretation.
- **Don't** confuse interests with skills or abilities: the *Strong* measures interests, not skill or ability.
- **Don't** lead clients to believe that the *Strong* indicates which occupation they "should" pursue.
- **Don't** use the word "test"; the *Strong* is an "inventory," and you cannot pass or fail it.

view each page of the profile in detail. Otherwise, you might move the Snapshot page to the last page of the Profile, and use it as a tool for summarizing the results at the end of the interpretation.

Structure the interpretation to be a dialogue rather than a lecture. For example, explain that you will describe the meaning of the scales and scores, and draw attention to the highlights. However, emphasize that you will need the client to explain to you, at each step, how the scores fit or do not fit. Encourage the client to ask questions throughout the interpretation session. Point out, on the reverse side of the Profile, the thorough description of the Profile's scales, numbers, and graphs. Encourage the client to read this fully following the interview.

Step 2: Explain Holland's Theory and the General Occupational Themes
Provide an overview of Holland's themes   Explain that Holland's theory is used to organize the client's interests into six broad patterns, or themes. Use the brief descriptions printed on the Profile following each General Occupational Theme as helpful terms to understand each Theme (see Rapid Reference 2.10).

For more in-depth descriptions of Holland's themes, see Chapter 4, the *Self-Directed Search*. Mention that the definitions of the six Themes may not be obvious from the terms used to label them. For example, a typical association with the word "conventional" is "commonplace," whereas the meaning of Holland's term "Conventional" is quite different and specific.

Remind the client that no one fits any one type perfectly; most people have interests in all six types to varying degrees. Typically, however, two or three types in combination describe the general interest patterns of individuals.

Emphasize the broad nature of the Themes. For example, remind clients that, in addition to work related interests, the Themes can help identify leisure interests, values, motivators, and potential skill areas. Describe how the Themes are similar and dissimilar to one another: those adjacent to one another on the Profile have more in common with each other than those that are farther apart. Use the hexagon provided on the reverse side of the Profile, on the color version, or in the accompanying document, understanding your results on the *Strong*, for the software version, to demonstrate (see Figure 2.1: Holland's Hexagon). For example, point out how the similar Themes of Realistic and Conventional are actually adjacent to one another, and the dissimilar Themes of Realistic and Social lie at opposite ends of the Hexagon.

Another way to describe the similarities and dissimilarities among the themes is to draw attention to how the Themes differ from one another according to two general dimensions: people versus things (Realistic versus Social) and data versus ideas (Conventional and Enterprising versus Artistic and Investigative). Figure 2.2 (Prediger, 1982) illustrates this point.

≡ *Rapid Reference 2.10*

Summary of General Occupational Theme Descriptions

Theme	Description
Realistic	Building, repairing, working outdoors
Investigative	Researching, analyzing, inquiring
Artistic	Creating or enjoying art, drama, music, writing
Social	Helping, instruction, care-giving
Enterprising	Selling, managing, persuading
Conventional	Accounting, organizing, processing data

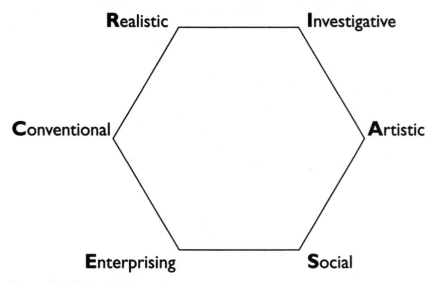

Figure 2.1 Holland's Hexagon

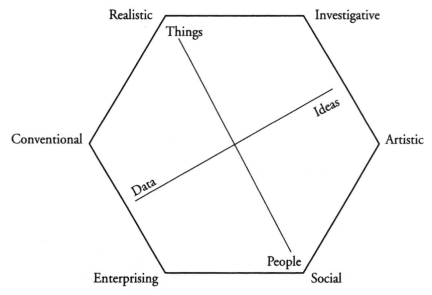

Figure 2.2 Underlying Dimensions of the Six Themes According to Prediger

Define the Scores   Outline the three different ways in which the client's General Occupational Theme scores are presented: interpretive comments, standard scores, and standard scores plotted to graphs.

The printed *interpretive comment* printed immediately under each General Occupational Theme refers to the client's score in comparison to a reference sample of the same gender. The people used for these comparisons are a large sample of employed individuals (over 9,000 of each gender). There are five possible comments, ranging from Very Little Interest to Very High Interest. Each label indicates the following percentile bands:

Very High Interest	91st% and above
High Interest	76th%–90th%
Average Interest	26th%–75th%
Little Interest	11th%–25th%
Very Little Interest	10th% and below

Note that the Average Interest band is the widest and includes a 50% range. Consequently, when you have a client with few or no scores falling into the High or Very High Interest categories, you may need to point out the importance of the highest scores that fall in the upper end of the Average Interest range.

The numbers appearing to the right of the scale are *standard scores,* not percentiles. Standard scores result from a conversion of a client's raw scores; they provide a meaningful way to compare a client's scores across scales. These scores have a mean of 50 and standard deviation of 10. A client who has a score of 60 on the Enterprising General Occupational Theme Scale and a score of 50 on the Social Scale, for example, is indicating a significantly higher interest in the Enterprising theme. Because there is always some degree of error in any measurement, it is important not to infer meaningful distinctions between standard scores that differ by only a few points. Scores that differ by only three or four points should be considered essentially equivalent. Unlike the interpretive comments, these scores are derived from comparing the client's responses with those of the general reference sample, *both* men and women. A score of 40 represents relatively little interest, and a score of 60 represents relatively high interest compared to the general reference sample.

Point out that the *standard scores plotted to graphs* are not percentiles; the number is plotted by a dot on the graph for ease of interpretation. Be careful to avoid giving a lecture on statistics when interpreting these scores. (Note: If you are using the color Profile, rather than the black-and-white software version, you can draw attention to the explanation of the graphs provided in the upper right hand corner of this page of the Profile (see page 2 of Profile).

Mention that the dot is plotted to the graph corresponding to the client's own gender; show clients how to read the score with respect to the graph of the opposite gender as well. The lighter graph represents the female sample, and the darker graph represents the male sample. Also, demonstrate how the bar graphs provide a way to convert the standard score to a percentile score, since most clients understand the meaning of percentiles. (See Figure 2.3 for an explanation of how to interpret the bar graphs in this manner.) In other words, the client's score at the 90% level reflects very high interest in that topic, since it reflects interest greater than that shown by 90% of the men or women in the general reference sample.

Discuss each of the themes   Provide the client with a more in-depth explanation of the six General Occupational Themes. You can begin with the Realistic Theme and end with the Conventional Theme, or discuss the themes in the order they appear on the Snapshot, from highest to lowest scores. If you are using the color Profile, use the chart on the reverse of the Profile Figure 2.4 as a visual aid as you discuss each Theme. For software users, the same chart appears on page 2 of the separately printed text, "Understanding Your Results on the *Strong*."

These themes address the question: "What are you like?" Discuss the client's reactions to each of the six General Occupational Theme Scores to confirm their degree of accuracy. Usually, no one person fits the full prototypical description of any of the Themes, so ask clients to identify which specific adjectives or descriptors of each Theme fit them, and which do not. If you have time, this discussion can extend into an exploration of the client's positive and negative past experiences with activities in each of the six areas.

After reviewing all of the General Occupational Themes, summarize this section by highlighting those two or three themes that the client agrees are most descriptive of them. You can do this, for example, by writing on the Profile, or circling those Themes' scores and titles.

Step 3: Discuss the Basic Interest Scales

Provide an overview of the scales   Explain that the Basic Interest Scales measure more narrow interests than do the General Occupational Themes. These

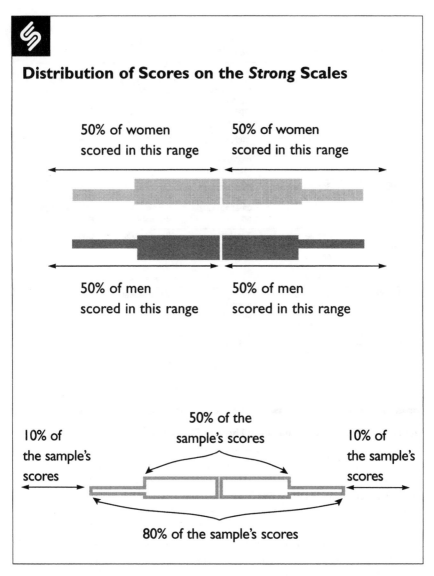

Figure 2.3 Distribution of Scores on the *Strong* Scales

THEME	INTERESTS	WORK ACTIVITIES	POTENTIAL SKILLS	VALUES
Realistic (R)	Machines, tools, outdoors	Operating equipment, using tools, building, repairing	Mechanical ingenuity and dexterity, physical coordination	Tradition, practicality, common sense
Investigative (I)	Science, theories, ideas, data	Performing lab work, solving abstract problems, researching	Math, writing, analysis	Independence, curiosity, learning
Artistic (A)	Self-expression, art appreciation	Composing music, writing, creating visual art	Creativity, musical talent, artistic expression	Beauty, originality, independence, imagination
Social (S)	People, team work, human welfare, community service	Teaching, explaining, helping	People skills, verbal ability, listening, showing understanding	Cooperation, generosity, service to others
Enterprising (E)	Business, politics, leadership, influence	Selling, managing, persuading	Verbal ability, ability to motivate and direct others	Risk taking, status, competition
Conventional (C)	Organization, data, finance	Setting up procedures, organizing, operating computers	Math, data analysis, record keeping, attention to detail	Accuracy, stability, efficiency

Figure 2.4 General Occupational Themes Descriptions

scales address the question: "What specific topic areas do you like?" The 25 Basic Interest Scales help to organize and prioritize those topics and activities that the client likes and dislikes. The scores on the Basic Interest Scales are interpreted in a manner similar to the scores on the General Occupational Themes (e.g., the labels, standard scores, and graphs are presented similarly and have similar meanings). Note that the 25 Basic Interest Scales are different from the General Occupational Themes. They are arranged on the Profile beneath the six Themes, but they are not part, or subsets of, the same scale. In fact, it is quite possible to score high on a particular General Occupational Theme, yet have only "Average" interest in all the Basic Interest Scales that are grouped under it, since different items are used to construct the two different types of scales. Also, the topics covered by the Basic Interest Scales grouped under a particular Theme do not exhaustively sample the domain of that Theme. For example, it is possible for a client to show "High Interest" on the Artistic General Occupational Theme, but show "Little Interest" on all of the Artistic Basic Interest Scales. This pattern would suggest a general interest pattern or personality style that fits Holland's description of the Artistic Theme (such as an interest in self-expression, creativity, independence, and originality), but no specific interest in the particular topics of music/drama, art, applied art, writing, or culinary arts.

Explain that the Basic Interest Scales reflect interests that can be fulfilled not only through work tasks or work environments, but also throughout one's general lifestyle—though hobbies, friends, family, volunteer activities, and home environment, for example. Often an unhappy individual who is not ready to make major life or career changes can find increased satisfaction in life simply by increasing attention to a particular Basic Interest Scale area that has been ignored.

Review each scale individually   Review each of the Basic Interest Scales individually, and discuss the client's reactions to the scores. Ask the client for examples of how the scores might reflect specific interests or disinterests. Describe in more detail the content of any scale not understandable to the client. (See Rapid Reference 2.8 for a quick descriptive phrase for each.)

As you discuss the scales, spend extra time discussing the client's highest scores. Ask the client to identify how these interests are finding expression through work or non-work related activities. Also, discuss which of these higher interests the client would like to incorporate into a job or career. Take time to discuss any high interest areas that are not finding any expression in the client's lifestyle, and help the client strategize how to begin exploring that interest area.

Discuss, also, the client's reactions to the lowest scores, and ask for examples of how these scores match the client's self-ratings for these interests. Low scores typically reflect a dislike of that Basic Interest area. However, be careful with this conclusion, since some clients obtain low scores not because they dislike the area, but because they have never been exposed to that particular Basic Interest area. Interest might develop with additional life experience.

Summarize the client's results on the Basic Interest Scales by emphasizing those scales that the client agrees represent her or his highest interest areas. Remember that the interpretive comments compare the individual's responses to a same-sex reference sample, and the standard scores compare the individual's responses to a combined-sex reference sample. Consequently, due to gender differences, it is not unusual for someone to have the same standard score on two Basic Interest Scales yet have different interpretive comments for each.

Step 4: Interpret the Occupational Scales

Provide an overview of the Occupational Scales   Before reviewing the Occupational Scales with the client, give a brief overview of their construction and purpose. Explain that they differ from the General Occupational Themes and the Basic Interest Scales in the following two ways:

1. These scales do not address the content of the client's interests directly; instead, they address the question: "What types of people have interest patterns similar to the client?" The General Occupational Themes and the Basic Interest Scales are constructed as homogeneous content scales—the items that comprise each of the scales reflect content obviously related to the scale's label. A client's score generally is raised only when the client endorses Like responses to such items. (For example, endorsing Like to the item "Discussing Politics" raises one's score on the "Law/Politics" scale.)

   The Occupational Scales, by contrast, are constructed by empirical methods, using both the client's Like and Dislike responses. The items that comprise each scale are those that strongly differentiate a particular occupational group from a general reference sample. Consequently, the items in the Occupational Scales may have little or no obvious relationship to the scale's label. (For example, a Dislike response to the item "Fashion Model" raises one's score on the female Physicist scale.) A client could conceivably achieve a score in the Similar range on the female Physicist scale, for example, not because the client shares interests with female physicists, but because the client dislikes many of the same items that female physicists dislike.

2. The Occupational Scales do not compare the client's interests to those of the general reference sample. Clients' interest patterns are compared to carefully selected samples of men and women in 109 different

occupations. Each of these samples are described in detail in Appendix A of the *Applications and Technical Guide* (Harmon et al., 1994). These samples contain, on average, more than 200 individuals, drawn from nationwide directories and associations. They include only individuals who:

- perform their work in a manner typical for the occupation
- are satisfied with their work
- have been doing this work for at least three years
- are at least 25 years old

Explain how the Occupational Scales can be useful   The Occupational Scales are the best predictors on the *Strong* of what typical day-to-day work activities the client is likely to enjoy. They can be helpful in a number of ways, including the following:

- to confirm the fit of a client's intended career choice
- to suggest new occupational fields for the client's consideration
- to identify types of people the client may enjoy spending time with as coworkers, clients, or friends

You may need to remind the client of the following two points:

1. These scales do not indicate what occupation the client "should" pursue. The Occupational Scales represent only 109 occupational areas. There are thousands of related occupations not measured by the *Strong,* and the client will need to view each occupational scale as a representative example of a much larger family of occupational titles worth further investigation.
2. These scales do not measure the client's skill or lack of skill for any of the occupations.

Describe how the Scales are organized and presented   Begin interpreting the Occupational Scales by pointing out that the occupations are organized according to the six themes. You can choose to begin with the occupations grouped under the Realistic Theme and proceed in RIASEC order, or you can start with the occupations under the theme listed first on the Snapshot. Choose an Occupational Scale in this group, such as Carpenter (third in the list under Realistic), as an example for interpreting the scores. Point out the Theme Codes listed in the columns labeled female and male to the far left side. Explain that these letters refer to the first letter of the General Occupational Themes on which individuals in this occupational sample scored highest. For example, female carpenters, as a group, scored highest on the Realistic Theme, second on the Investigative Theme, and third on the Artistic Theme ("RIA"). In other words, female carpenters' interest patterns consist of three dominant themes, Realistic being the strongest. Note that the male carpenters' interest pattern is slightly different ("REA") from the female carpenters' pattern.

The Carpenter Scale is an example of an occupational sample that is described by three different and significant themes. However, note that some of the occupations have more narrowly defined interests, and can be described with just one letter (e.g., Auto Mechanic, R).

Next, point out that men and women within the same occupation sometimes have very different interests. Point to the first occupation listed, Athletic Trainer, as an example. The female Athletic Trainer sample has primarily Realistic interests, whereas the male Athletic Trainer sample has primarily Social interests. Consequently, the male code, SIR, appears in parentheses to indicate that the male scale can be found under the Social Theme instead. Only a few scales (two female and five male) have no code listed, such as female Plumber. An asterisk appears, instead of a Theme Code, indicating that an occupational scale for that gender does not exist; the test developers have not collected enough individuals who fit the criteria for a solid occupational scale. The key at the top right of the page provides a brief explanation for these codes and scores (see Page 4 of Profile).

Next, explain the numbers appearing under the columns titled: "Your Scores." These scores are standardized for each occupational sample so that a score of 50 represents the mean score of individuals included in that occupational sample. The meaning of the numbers (which can range from a negative number to over 80) may be confusing to the client. You may need to emphasize that these scores are the client's own scores, not scores belonging to people in the occupation. Explain that the score for the client's same gender is the score that is plotted with a dot, using the scale that appears to the right of the scores. *Similar Interest scores*   Scores 40 and higher are labeled "Similar Interests." These scores indicate that the client and typical individuals from that occupation sample share common interest patterns—both likes and dislikes. A score in the Similar range or higher indicates that the client may enjoy the work associated with that occupation, since individuals with interest patterns similar to the client enjoy working in that field. Therefore, that career field may be worth the client's further exploration. However, the scale does not measure, necessarily, the degree to which the client is interested (or skilled) in performing the actual tasks of that particular occupation. In fact, an individual may score in the Similar range on a number of occupations that she or he would not want to pursue. For example, the occupation may require skills or education that the client is not interested in developing, or the work tasks may not fit the client's values or lifestyle needs. Nevertheless, the client may enjoy working with individuals from these occupations as clients, or may enjoy spending leisure time with them, given the interests and disinterests they share.

Dissimilar Interest scores   Scores below 30 are labeled "Dissimilar Interests." These scores indicate little overlap between the client's interests and the interests of that occupational reference sample. In other words, the client and typical individuals from that occupational sample do not share similar interest patterns. A score in this range usually indicates that the individual is not interested in the occupation. However, be cautious that the client does not interpret dissimilar scores as a strong directive to avoid an occupation, or as an indication of lack of skill for an occupation. Instead, dissimilar scores indicate that the client will find her/himself having little in common with the *typical* worker in that occupation. If the client wants to consider that occupation, however, the implications of entering that field should be discussed. For example, you might point out the need to find support outside one's work environment, as well as the advantage of your client's ability to contribute a different perspective from that of the typical worker.

The Occupational Scales are the most complex scales on the *Strong* to interpret. Consequently, you may find it helpful to review the frequently asked questions listed in Rapid Reference 2.11.

Step 5: Discuss the Personal Style Scales

Provide an overview of the Personal Style Scales. (See Rapid Reference 2.12 for a brief summary of these scales.) First explain that these four scales measure very general styles or preferences for interacting with people and approaching new tasks or activities. Indicate the key in the upper right corner of page 6 of the Profile that describes how to interpret scores for these four scales.

Explain that the scores, graphs, and reference groups for the Personal Style

≡ Rapid Reference 2.11

Frequently Asked Questions about the Occupational Scales

1. Why does the Strong list only these particular occupations?
There are thousands of occupations in the world of work. The *Strong* attempts to sample popular occupational fields that represent a broad range of interests, activities, and educational requirements. Each scale is selected as a representative of a much larger family of related occupational titles not specifically listed on the inventory, but worth consideration as well.

2. What is the range of possible scores, and what is the significance of a negative number?
The scores listed for each male and female Occupational Scale are standard scores, not percentages or percentiles. A standard score has a mean of 50, which on these scales indicates an interest pattern similar to the average person in the scale's occupational criterion group. Although the meaning of any standard score is the same across all the occupational scales, the range actually varies from scale to scale from a low in the –40's to a high of 90. Consequently, the number itself is not as useful to interpretation as is where the plotted score falls along the continuum from dissimilar to similar. A negative score, therefore, simply indicates an individual's interest pattern is very dissimilar to that of the particular occupational sample.

3. Why are there separate male and female scales instead of just one combined scale?
Although men and women in most occupational groups have interests similar to one another, research indicates that men and women within some occupations have significantly different interest patterns from each other. Also, there continue to exist strong culturally-based gender differences in interest patterns. Consequently, the occupational scales, like all other scales on the *Strong*, provide both male and female scores so that the individuals can choose to compare their interests to either or both reference groups.

4. Why can I score high on a Basic Interest Scale (e.g., Culinary Arts), yet dissimilar on its corresponding Occupational Scale (e.g., Chef)?
These sets of scales are constructed differently. The Basic Interest Scale measures your specific interest in cooking and entertaining, whereas the Occupational Scale measures how much your broad interests and disinterests overlap with those of employed chefs. You may like cooking, but not the other interest patterns that characterize chefs.

5. My top five occupations seem very different from one another. How do I make sense of this?
Look at the Theme Codes listed before each occupational title to determine the general interest patterns the occupations share with one another. The

Theme Codes reflect core motivators, values, and activities shared among the occupations. Use these Themes, as well as your top five occupational titles, to identify similar or related occupations not listed on the *Strong*. Begin by reading job descriptions in a career library or on the Internet.

6. What does it mean when I score higher on a particular Occupational Scale for the opposite sex than on the Occupational Scale of the same sex?

Simply put, you share interests and disinterests with opposite-sex individuals in that occupation. If you were to pursue that occupation, and work primarily in environments with individuals of the opposite sex, you would probably find you share common interests with your coworkers. Also, research whether men and women in that occupation may tend to pursue different specializations in that field; evaluate how well the different specializations within that occupation fit your interests.

7. What does it mean when I have several scores that are higher on Occupational Scales for the opposite sex than Occupational Scales for my same sex?

This is a common occurrence when scales are constructed with separate scales for men and women. For example, females are more likely to score higher on traditionally female occupations when scored on the male scales than on the female scales. The opposite is true for men. An example can help your clients understand this. Take the elementary school teacher scale. Females will generally score higher on the male Elementary School Teacher Scale than on the female scale. The reason? An item that differentiates male elementary school teachers from men in general, for example saying "Like" to "Teaching children," would be built into the male Elementary School Teacher Scale. However, this same item would not differentiate female elementary school teachers from women in general, since most women enjoy teaching children. So, when the typical female respondent says "Like" to the item "Teaching Children" she is getting a point on the male Elementary School Teacher Scale, but not on the female Elementary School Teacher Scale, leading to a higher score on the male scale. This is just a by-product of the scale construction with separate male and female scales. It is less important to be concerned about the overall level of the score, than it is to note if your client scores in the similar range for both same sex and the opposite sex scales if it is an occupation he or she is interested in.

Scales are generally similar to those described earlier for the General Occupational Themes and Basic Interest Scales. However, there is one important difference: the Personal Style Scales are constructed with two poles, one at each end of a continuum, whereas each of the General Occupational Theme Scales and Basic Interest Scales measure only one preference from "less interest" to "more interest." A client's score on each of the Personal Style Scales falls some-

≡ Rapid Reference 2.12

The Four Personal Style Scales

	Poles	
Work Style	Left	Prefers to Work Alone
		versus
	Right	Prefers Working with People
Learning Style	Left	Prefers Practical Learning Environment
		versus
	Right	Prefers Academic Learning Environment
Leadership Style	Left	Prefers to Lead by Example
		versus
	Right	Prefers Taking Charge and Motivating Others
Risk Taking/ Adventure	Left	Prefers to Play It Safe
		versus
	Right	Prefers Adventure and Risk Taking

Scores of 55 and above typify the right; scores of 45 and below typify the left pole; scores in the mid-range, 46–54, occur for people who have a mix of preferences, or no strong preference.

where along the continuum, showing the degree of preference for one pole versus the other. As with other scales on the *Strong,* these scales do not measure the abilities or skills associated with the dimensions. Review each of the four scales in turn, provide a brief description of the bipolar dimensions, and discuss some ways in which the scores might describe the client's current or ideal work and lifestyle preferences. The following sections provide descriptions of these four scales and guidance for interpreting each.

Work Style   This scale can help identify and confirm the client's preferred ways of dealing with work tasks or academic activities. Scores toward the left pole (<47 for women; <41 for men) indicate a preference for working alone with ideas, data, or things. Scores toward the right pole (>60 for women; >53 for men) indicate a preference for people contact, working with people in groups or one-to-one, or in a helping role. Scores between these points indicate a preference for some amount of each. It is usually best to point to the bar graphs for a general reference to the score's meaning, rather than to discuss the meaning of actual scores with clients. Typically, individuals with strong Realistic and Investigative interest patterns tend to score toward the left pole; those with strong Social and Enterprising interests tend to score toward the right pole. However, it can be helpful to explore further the experiences of a client who scores opposite of this pattern. For example, an individual with a Realistic interest pattern may score strongly toward the "working with people" pole. This individual may be able to make unique contributions to the workplace compared to typical coworkers with Realistic interest patterns. On the other hand, this difference may be a source of confusion to the client, or may lead the client to feel different from or misunderstood by Realistic coworkers.

Learning Environment This scale measures the client's preferred style of learning. Scores toward the left pole (<43 for women; <44 for men) indicate a preference for learning by doing, and a practical or instrumental approach to education or training. Scores toward the right pole (>57 for women; >56 for men) indicate a preference for learning through traditional academic courses or classroom lectures. Such scores typically indicate an interest in learning for its own sake, rather than as a means to an end. Scores in the middle range (43–57 for women; 44–56 for men) indicate an interest in learning though a range of methods. Again, refrain from interpreting actual score numbers to clients, and focus instead on where the dot falls on the bar graph.

This scale does not measure academic ability or intelligence in any way, nor does it predict academic success. It is an indication of the style of learning the individual is most comfortable with, not an indication of whether the client enjoys learning or not. Individuals who score toward the left pole typically enjoy learning practical skills, and prefer pursuing time-limited or goal-oriented education. Individuals who score toward the right pole typically enjoy learning theoretical material and may enjoy taking a course or pursuing an advanced degree even if they are unsure of its practical use. Explore with the client which learning style fits best. Also, help the client identify the style she or he would be most comfortable using to approach future career development activities or educational plans. Scores of 55 and above are typical of individuals who have achieved the PhD degree. Scores of 45 and below are typical of those in occupations that require practical training.

Leadership Style This scale indicates the style of leadership that an individual prefers to assume. Scores toward the left pole (<44 for both men and women) indicate a preference for leading by example. Individuals with such scores typically are not interested in actively directing others. Instead, they prefer to do a job well themselves and thereby set an example for others to follow. For example, they may prefer to lead though project management rather than organizational management.

Scores toward the right pole (>58 for women; >57 for men) indicate a preference for leading others in a directive manner, through motivating or actively organizing others. Scores in the middle range (44–58 for women; 44–57 for men) indicate an interest in some characteristics of both leadership styles. Individuals with Investigative, Realistic, and Conventional interest patterns typically score toward the left pole. Individuals with strong Enterprising interests typically score toward the right pole. When a client's scores vary from the typical pattern, it can be useful to discuss the implications of the score further; this can lead to an enriched understanding of the individual's complex interests and experiences. Although this scale is not a measure of leadership potential, it can be a useful tool for discussing the client's previous work experiences and future career goals that involve leadership tasks.

Risk Taking/Adventure   This scale measures the client's general comfort with taking risks across a variety of circumstances. Scores toward the left pole (<40 for women; <47 for men) indicate a preference to "play it safe." Individuals with scores in this direction usually prefer to take time to examine situations carefully and to thoroughly prepare before taking on something new or unknown. Scores toward the right pole (>54 for women; >60 for men) indicate a preference for adventure and taking chances. Individuals with scores in this direction usually enjoy exploring new and adventurous activities in a number of areas of their lives. Scores in the middle range (40–54 for women; 47–60 for men) suggest some interest in risk taking, such as taking measured risks or taking risks under specific circumstances. It can be useful to discuss the client's score with respect to her or his approach to choosing a career or job. For example, is the client playing it too safe, and avoiding taking risks necessary for career advancement or job hunting? Alternatively, does the client typically make impulsive but poorly planned career-related decisions just for the thrill of it? Exploring the client's comfort with risk taking can assist in planning the pace of her or his career exploration activities.

Step 6: Summarize Results

Use the Snapshot page of the Profile to review the client's interest patterns and highlights. This section of the Profile provides a summary of the highest scores for the General Occupational Themes, Basic Interest Scales, and Occupational

Scales. In addition, it provides a summary Theme code based on the client's scores from the General Occupational Themes. Begin by reviewing the General Occupational Themes and the summary Theme code. The Themes are listed in order from highest to lowest scores. Discuss the client's reactions and answer any remaining questions. If the summary Theme code is different from the one you and your client derived earlier from the full profile, remind the client that this one is based solely on scores from the General Occupational Themes.

Because of such potential disagreements, understanding the derivation of the summary Theme code deserves particular attention. It is based upon the three highest Themes (of Average Interest or higher level) in descending order. An individual with only one or two themes in the Average Interest or higher categories will have, correspondingly, a one or two letter theme code instead of three. Profiles with no Themes in the Average Interest or higher categories do not list a summary Theme code. (For these profiles, refer to Don't Forget 2.3.) Consider the summary Theme code only a tentative summary code, since it is based only on the General Occupational Themes, not on the full range of scales from the Profile.

Review the Basic Interest Scales section of the Snapshot. It lists in rank order the client's five highest Basic Interest Scales, along with the General Occupational Theme that each is most closely related to. Some clients may have more than five important interests, and adding these to the list by writing them on the page will provide a more accurate summary. Other clients will have very narrow interests, and of the five, several may be of little interest. In this instance, draw attention to those few that are the highest by circling them. Next, assist the client in determining which Theme Code or Codes best summarize these top interests.

Move on to the Occupational Scales section, which summarizes, in rank order, the ten occupations to which the client's interest patterns are most similar. The Theme code corresponding to each occupation is also provided. As with the summary of the Basic Interest Scales, add to or delete from this list if these 10 do not adequately reflect those occupational scales of importance to the client. Again, determine a Theme Code (one, two, or three letters) that best summarizes the themes in this list.

Compare this code to the summary Code listed on the Profile above. Does it confirm the pattern, or conflict with it? Note that the instructions encourage the client to explore occupations with codes that contain any combination of the three letters, so the exact ordering of the codes does not need to match.

DON'T FORGET 2.3

Tips for Interpreting Profiles with Few Elevations

A "Flat" Profile, or one with very few scores at or above the "Average Interest" level on the General Occupational Theme Scales or Basic Interest Scales, will occur when the client endorses a high percentage of items in the Indifferent or Dislike direction. Elevations occur primarily when a client responds Like to items on these scales. Similarly, the Occupational Scales will have very few scores at or above the "midrange" level when the client endorses a high percentage of items as Indifferent, since elevations on these scales result primarily from Like and Dislike responses.

Common reasons for Flat *Profiles:*
- Lack of work or life experience
- General indecisiveness
- Narrowly defined or unique interests
- Depressed mood or disinterest in working
- Took inventory grudgingly

How to Interpret
Determine reasons for response patterns, and consider the following suggestions:
- Focus interpretation on scores that are highest for client, ignoring labels and reference groups
- Emphasize any defined interests and extrapolate to domains not listed on Profile
- Use Basic Interest Scales to interview client about past and present interests and experiences
- Administer the *Strong* again with instructions to endorse more likes and dislikes
- Suggest client take the *Strong* at a later date after gaining further experience

However, if the two codes differ widely, then the client needs information about which to use as a guide for further career exploration. For most adults, aged 25 or older, the code you determined from the Occupational Scales is the better predictor for the actual day-to-day work activities the individual might enjoy. However, for younger individuals, or those with little work experience, the Occupational Scales may not be as valid a predictor; these individuals may profit more from exploring their general interest patterns further, as represented by the summary Theme code printed on the Profile.

The Snapshot does not summarize the individual's scores from the Personal Style Scales. However, to complete your summary, write on the Snapshot page any scale for which the client showed a clear preference for a particular pole. Highlight those preferences that confirm the client's Theme code (e.g., a work style preference toward the "working with people" pole, along with a high interest in the Social theme), and explore how apparently inconsistent interests may fit together for the client (e.g., how an individual might express through a combination of work and life roles a leadership style preference toward the "taking charge of others" pole, but little interest in the Enterprising theme).

Finally, summarize the Snapshot by drawing attention to two or three points that appear to be most important. The *Strong* Profile includes such a large number of scales, and such a variety of information about the client's interest patterns, that you may need to help the client focus upon those few pieces of information that will be most useful. Here your best judgment and the client's goals will need to guide your choice. For some individuals, for example, you may want to highlight the summary Theme code to direct occupational information gathering. For others, you may want to draw attention to important Basic Interest Scales that represent areas not finding expression in the client's current job or lifestyle. Alternatively, ask the client to summarize two or three points that appear most important to remember from this array of information. This strategy can also help you address lingering misconceptions, such as a belief that the Occupational Scale with the highest score is the field to pursue.

Step 7: Encourage Exploration beyond the Profile

Conclude the interpretation by reminding the client to read the detailed, descriptive information provided on the reverse side of the Profile (or contained in the separately printed "Understanding Your Results of the *Strong*," if you are using a software-generated Profile). Although the client's next steps will vary depending upon her or his specific career planning needs and goals, provide some further resource for researching occupational or educational areas suggested by the *Strong*. Library research using the *Dictionary of Holland Occupational Codes* (1996), or Internet-based research using the *O*NET* (1998), for example, can be used to explore occupations related to those listed on the *Strong*, and to gather career information about specific career fields, such as day-to-day activities, work environments, salary ranges, or employment prospects for particular career fields. The publishers of the *Strong* also offer an excellent workbook, *Where Do I Go Next,* that helps clients use their *Strong* results to focus their career search. If at all possible, arrange a follow-up appointment or workshop to check on clients' progress, and help them deal with unforeseen obstacles they may have encountered.

The interpretive guidelines presented in this chapter focus primarily on "typical" Profiles. It is not rare, however, to encounter Profiles that have very few or very many scale elevations. Such "atypical" Profiles are some of the most challenging ones to interpret. Don't Forgets 2.3 and 2.4 summarize some helpful hints for dealing with these situations. You should also refer to the *Ap-*

DON'T FORGET 2.4

Tips for Interpreting Profiles with Numerous Elevations

An "Elevated" Profile, or one with numerous high scores throughout the Profile, results from a high percentage of Like responses. The General Occupational Themes and Basic Interest Scales will be more strongly influenced by this response pattern than will the Occupational Scales, where elevations also result from Dislike responses.

Common Reasons for "Elevated" Profiles
- Client truly has multiple, wide-ranging interests
- Attempt to "look good" (e.g., completed *Strong* as part of job or school application)
- Uncomfortable endorsing Dislike (e.g., due to cultural norms, or to avoid displeasing others)
- Afraid of ruling out career options prematurely

How to Interpret
Discuss the reasons for such a response pattern, and consider the following options:
- Use the Snapshot to prioritize a few highest ranking scales for each section of the Profile
- Focus the interpretation on general interest patterns, such as the three Theme codes that occur across all sets of scales
- Discuss ways to integrate diverse interests throughout work and life roles
- Suggest focusing on different interests at different times in life
- Administer the *Strong* again with instructions to purposely endorse fewer Likes

plications and Technical Guide as well as to the *Resource Guides* for more in-depth assistance with such Profiles.

STRENGTHS AND WEAKNESSES

The *Strong*'s many strengths have been described in the preceding sections. Rapid Reference 2.13 highlights some key strengths of the inventory. In addition, important limitations of the *Strong* are summarized in Rapid Reference 2.14.

APPLICATIONS

The *Strong* has a long history of applied use in both organizational and educational settings. The following review highlights the broad range of settings in which career professionals have effectively used the *Strong*.

≋*Rapid Reference 2.13*

Key Strengths of the *Strong*

- The *Strong* is based on a strong tradition of research and is one of the most thoroughly grounded instruments available for the purpose of career assessment.
- The researchers analyzed data on over 67,000 people in developing the 1994 revision of the *Strong*.
- Large sample sizes were used to construct the Occupational Scales. Median sample size for criterion samples was 250.
- The *Strong* has excellent reliability for the various scales.
- The *Applications and Technical Guide* has extremely useful appendices that can be used to learn about occupations identified on the instrument and to extrapolate from the Occupational Scales to related occupations.
- The *Applications and Technical Guide* is an outstanding manual. It combines both detailed technical information and comprehensive guidelines for interpretation.
- The color-coded profile is easy to understand and interpret.
- The use of Holland's typology for the assessment provides a well-researched and familiar framework in which to understand interest patterns.
- Numerous options for customized reports are available to meet various needs.

≡ *Rapid Reference 2.14*

Key Limitations of the *Strong*

- Respondents are limited to only three options (e.g., Like, Indifferent, and Dislike). These do not capture the degree or strength of a respondent's interests or disinterests.

- The Basic Interest Scales are limited in length, ranging from only 5 to 21 items. Small changes in responses can lead to significant changes in standard scores.

- Sampling for the Occupational Scales relied on returns from mail-in responses. Consequently, a sample's representation of the range of subspecialties within a particular occupational field can be limited.

- The Occupational Scales were constructed using Tilton's limited statistical procedure for "percent overlap." More comprehensive response comparisons available through modern computational methods have not been integrated into the scale construction.

- Discrepancies between scores on different types of scales can be cumbersome to explain to clients due to the different scale construction methods used.

- Profiles with either few or numerous scale elevations are challenging to interpret.

- The Standard Profile essentially measures interests, with no other information on skills or abilities that would give the respondents data on how likely they would be to successfully perform the work in which they show high interests.

- Scores on opposite-sex scales can be time consuming to explain.

Applications in Organizations

The *Strong* can be of great use to adults in organizational settings and has a variety of applications. Many organizations have established internal career development programs to maximize productivity in their organizations and as a benefit to employees (Gutteridge et al., 1993). The *Strong* can be used to assist employees with various career tasks over the lifespan. For employees who seek assistance in planning their next career move, the inventory is never used in absolute terms to predict satisfaction. Yet, the data obtained can either confirm or call into question potential steps the employee is considering, which then, require further investigation. Following are some of the ways, based upon our experience in working with adults in organizational settings, in which the *Strong* can be used effectively with employees in business, industrial, government, health care, and other corporate or organizational settings. Illustrations, when provided, reflect specific clients or a composite of clients presenting the same issue. (See Rapid Reference 2.15 for a brief summary of these applications.)

Career Exploration

As Super (1984) has suggested in the reformulation of his stage theory, career exploration tasks traditionally associated with adolescence in fact take place throughout the life span. The *Strong* is a useful tool that can support adults engaging in career exploration activities in organizations as they seek to move from a "job" to a "career," to find job opportunities that are congruent with more of their interests, or to determine whether to take on additional or different roles within their chosen career field.

Moving from job to career   Many employees who utilize internal career programs are motivated to find work that they would enjoy, that would utilize more of their talents, and in which they might find a greater sense of fulfillment. These individuals are often dissatisfied with their current positions and most have never had the benefit of career counseling. Many are in entry-level jobs, such as clerical or administrative positions, that have primarily provided them a means to earn a living, but aside from salary, benefits, and other extrinsic rewards provide little else in the way of intrinsic job satisfaction.

The *Strong* is an excellent tool to assist these clients in clarifying their interests and discovering new career opportunities that might lead to an increased sense of satisfaction. The *Strong* often confirms possibilities that an individual has been considering, but has been afraid to act upon. For example, an administrative secretary who has one year of college education and hopes to become a human resources professional would be reassured that she might well enjoy a human resources career if she sees that she has high scores on the Social and Enterprising General Occupational Themes and the Human Resources Director Occupational Scale.

Career Refinement

Many clients who use internal career development programs are in their 20s and 30s and in the Establishment phase of their career (Super, 1984). Frequent job changes occur in the early stages of establishing careers, as new professionals seek opportunities that are increasingly congruent with their interest

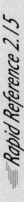

Rapid Reference 2.15

Applications of the *Strong* in Organizations

The *Strong* can be used to assist employees with career development tasks over the life span.

When the employee need is:	**Use of the *Strong* assists employees in:**
Career Exploration	Exploring their career interests as they relate to new job opportunities, lateral moves, or changes in role or job tasks.
	Discovering career opportunities that provide more intrinsic satisfaction.
Moving from Job to Career	*Clarifying which job activities are preferred and how these relate to potential career moves, such as lateral moves.*
Career Refinement	*Evaluating potential shifts in job responsibilities or role changes; e.g., taking on a team leader role.*
Role Expansion/Change	
Career Advancement	Determining whether they would likely be satisfied with a higher level of responsibility, such as people or project management.
Career Enrichment	Identifying new activities within the job, department, or organization that will provide greater satisfaction with work and increased skills.
Career Change	Assessing whether a contemplated major career change is well supported.
Work Environment Concerns	Clarifying whether the source of job dissatisfaction is related to job content or the work environment.
Training and Development	Identifying longer-term career goals and the requisite training and experience needed to achieve the goals.
Outplacement and Inplacement	Re-evaluating their current career and other potential career possibilities under consideration.
Life Planning	Satisfying their interests in the larger context of their lives, such as community service, education, part-time work, and leisure pursuits.
Retirement Planning	Identifying complementary or supplementary interests for pursuit in second careers, entrepreneurial or part-time work, or volunteer or leisure activities.
Team Building	Appreciating differences in team members' interests and personal styles and applying this understanding to enhance the effectiveness of the team.

patterns. The *Strong* is a useful tool to help the new professional identify what his or her next career step will be. The *Strong* provides language, either in the descriptions of the Occupational Scales in the Interpretive Report or in Appendix A of the *Strong Interest Inventory Applications and Technical Guide,* that identifies work tasks associated with the top 10 (or more) jobs identified from the interpretation. You can conduct a useful exercise with these descriptions. Ask your client which of those tasks he or she would enjoy doing, which are currently part of his or her position, which are not present, and whether there are positions within the organization that would offer responsibilities more congruent with his or her interests. (Exercise adapted from Judith Grutter's 1998 series *Making It in Today's Organizations,* a useful set of tools for career counselors in organizational settings.)

Role expansion or change   Some employees are at crossroads in their careers. For example, successful technical experts are often approached to take on leadership roles in their chosen profession. A research scientist who has been asked to join the management team has to decide whether it will be a good decision to reduce the amount of time spent doing research. The *Strong* can be extremely helpful to this individual who is having trouble predicting his or her likely satisfaction in this new role. For the scientist who scores low on the Enterprising GOT and Organizational Management BIS, and in the low to mid range on the Research and Development Manager OS, the *Strong* can call into question whether he or she will likely enjoy the tasks associated with this opportunity.

Career Advancement

Many individuals who seek internal career assistance are eager to pursue advancement opportunities. The *Strong* can be helpful to these individuals in supporting or clarifying their longer-term goals within the organization and in identifying the education and skill-building activities that will be needed to pursue them. Dalton and Thompson (1993) describe a four-stage model of career development in organizations in which employees in professional careers move through identifiable stages from apprentice to individual contributor, then to mentor, and finally, in a few cases, to sponsor. Although the roles and structures of work have changed and continue to change dramatically, these stages can still provide a template for using the *Strong* to understand where a client stands in regard to shifting job role expectations.

For example, the *Strong* can be extremely helpful to successful employees who are no longer satisfied with their work and are feeling restless about next steps. The *Strong* can help to clarify whether the person is still interested in his or her field. An individual in marketing or accounting, for example, who has high scores on the Enterprising General Occupational Theme, Organizational Management Basic Interest Scale, and several of the Manager Occupational Scales may be ready to move on from the role of independent contributor to that of a people or project manager.

Career Enrichment

Many organizations, however, have reorganized into flattened hierarchies and may not have the advancement opportunities that were previously available. The *Strong* can suggest job enrichment activities that will enable most employees to take on more rewarding responsibilities and will also enhance employees' skill sets, which in turn can lead to greater recognition and compensation. The same applies to individuals who are not yet prepared to leave their current job for any number of reasons. For example, an administrative assistant whose ideal career would be a "writer" but who is limited in her educational background, would be reinforced in her career dream if she takes the *Strong* and sees her high scores on the Artistic General Occupational Theme and the Writing Basic Interest Scale. She could also be coached to gain invaluable experience by volunteering to write for her departmental newsletter or organizational news and information service, which would lead to increased job satisfaction and an expanded portfolio, that may prove beneficial if she were to apply for actual writing jobs later.

Career Change

Some clients who pursue internal career counseling are seeking support in coming to a decision about making a career change. Many of these clients are mid-career professionals who have had success in their fields, but for whom there are few remaining challenges. They may have been in their current job for many years and have become motivated to find another challenge and greater satisfaction in their work lives, often in greater alignment with a sense of life purpose and an increasing need for generativity. The *Strong* can be very helpful in working with these clients to confirm or, alternatively, to raise questions about possibilities they are considering.

For example, the very successful development officer for a major organization who has been feeling increasingly empty about her current career, and is considering a career as a therapist, would be well supported in exploring this and related options further if she scores high on the Social GOT and Very Similar on the Social Worker and High School Counselor Occupational Scales.

Work Environment

Employees who are unhappy in their jobs often need assistance in clarifying whether it is because of issues associated with that work environment, such as poor relationships with a supervisor or peers, or the actual content of the job itself, such as the work tasks. The *Strong* can be very helpful in clarifying what employees' interests are and the associated job tasks they would find enjoyable. Again, using either the descriptions of the Occupational Scales in the *Interpretive Report* or Appendix A of the *Strong Interest Inventory Applications and Technical Guide,* the career professional can use the *Strong* to confirm that an employee's career field itself is congruent with the employee's interests. If so, the career professional would then focus the discussion on the work environment, identifying the particular stressors in the environment that are leading to dissatisfaction with the career. The career professional might further support the employee by helping him or her consider whether there are ways the environment can be adapted to make it more satisfying, such as through a team-building intervention, or whether the best avenue may be to find a similar position in another department or division of the organization.

Training and Development

Many organizations offer tuition reimbursement or educational benefits to their employees for college and university courses and a full range of internally-offered training courses and workshops, from technical courses to courses on soft skills such as interpersonal, communication, management, and leadership skills.

The counselor can utilize the *Strong* to help employees identify short- and long-term career objectives and then support the employee further by helping him or her review internal and external training and development opportunities that would support these career objectives. For example, the administrative manager who is interested in a career in training would be supported in his career decision-making if his *Strong* results revealed high scores on the Artistic, Social, and Enterprising General Occupational Themes and the Corporate Trainer Occupational Scale. The career professional could further assist him in planning educational and developmental opportunities in support of his goals, including completing a Training and Development Master's program and taking on well-targeted volunteer training opportunities.

Outplacement and Inplacement

At times, through no fault of their own, employees will lose positions due to budget cuts, restructuring, or downsizing. This can be a time of great crisis for individuals who are forced to make a career transition they have not chosen. While the counselor's first priority is often to meet the employee's "survival" needs, the *Strong* can also be of great benefit to employees facing this crisis when presented at the appropriate time. The career professional needs to give the employee some time to cope with the emotions of shock, betrayal, anger, and fear that are commonly aroused with this type of crisis. When timed well, typically about three to four weeks after a Reduction in Force notification, the *Strong* can offer affected employees an opportunity to assess whether they want to pursue the same career path, or whether this crisis may indeed present an opportunity to shift career tracks in a major or minor way.

Life Planning

For some employees, there are few opportunities for career enrichment or advancement in either their jobs or their organization. For such employees, their jobs may be critical to their lives for the economic and health benefits they provide for themselves and their families, not for higher order needs such as "esteem" or "self-actualization."

In such instances, savvy career professionals have been able to use the *Strong* to assist employees in looking at ways to satisfy their interests in the larger context of their lives. This involves expanding the definition of career to include one's paid job, educational pursuits, community activities, and leisure interests. In a large U.S. government agency, for example, employees have been encouraged by their career services provider to create a development plan for themselves each year that incorporates developmental activities that could satisfy interests, as identified on the *Strong,* in each of these four dimensions of their lives.

Retirement Planning

As employees prepare to leave an organization, some are eager for assistance in considering what to do next in their lives. Retirees can be divided into three general types. The first type pursue primarily leisure activities and interests they could not enjoy when working. The second type pursue meaningful entrepreneurial, part-time work or volunteer activities. These endeavors might be associated with their previous career field or may reflect work interests they were unable to pursue during the time of their employment. The third type of retirees pursue neither vocational nor avocational interests, and often feel disengaged from and unappreciated by the world around them.

The *Strong* can be an extremely useful tool with all three types, since the instrument suggests both vocational and avocational activities. The General Occupational Themes and Basic Interest Scales can be particularly helpful in planning for a meaningful retirement. They encompass beloved leisure pursuits as well as career interests that are either *complementary* or similar to interests in the person's activities during employment. In addition, these scales can be used to identify *supplementary* interests that differ from the interests pursued during employment (Hansen, 1990).

Team Building

The *Strong* can also effectively be used to assist in team building. For example, by conducting group interpretations for intact teams, group members can come to appreciate the ways in which they differ in their interests and personal styles. For example, an interesting exercise developed by David Campbell (1996) for working with groups is to have the individuals line up in a "human histogram." You might use the Risk Taking/Adventure Personal Style scales, for example. This type of exercise can build awareness of differences in how team members feel about taking risks, new ideas, and change. The career professional can help groups better understand one another and use that understanding for improved communication and problem-solving.

The career professional can also assist the team leader in utilizing the insights gained from the *Strong* in assigning tasks that are congruent with team members' interests. For example, based upon the interpretation of the *Strong,* one manager in charge of a conference facility dramatically improved two team members' job satisfaction when she reassigned the front desk duties (reception, trouble-shooting) to the staff member who scored high on the Social General Occupational Theme and low on the Conventional General Occupational Theme, and reassigned the logistics and facility planning tasks to the team member who scored high on the Conventional General Occupational Theme and low on the Social General Occupational Theme.

Applications to Educational Settings

The *Strong* has a long history of use in both high school and college settings. One of the most powerful applications of the *Strong* for these populations is its comparison of students' interests to those of working adults. In addition, it has been shown to reliably predict students' future academic and occupational choices. The *Applications and Technical Guide* includes two chapters that summarize research demonstrating its usefulness with these populations. One chapter describes when and how to use the *Strong* with high school students. The other describes how to use the *Strong* to help college students identify extracurricular activities, choose a major, or choose a career. Applications of the *Strong* for counseling graduate students are also described. In addition, two resource guides provide thorough instruction for interpreting the *Strong* in educational settings (Rumpel, S. K., & Lecertua, K., 1996; Prince, J. P., 1995). The following brief summary provides a few examples of the variety of ways in which the *Strong* can be used with students of various ages. Rapid Reference 2.16 also provides a summary of these applications.

General Career Planning

Frequently, the *Strong* is used to help students with the self-assessment stage of career planning (i.e., as a general tool for identifying, assessing, or prioritizing students' interests). However, the *Strong* can be a useful tool at each stage of the career planning process. Prince (1995) suggests emphasizing different scales of the *Strong* to focus an interpretation toward the relevant career planning stage. For example, he suggests ways of using the Basic Interest Scales to help students explore college majors, student activities, and internships. Similarly, he outlines ways to help students set career development goals and confront barriers through careful interpretation of the Personal Style Scales and Holland Theme Codes.

Lesson Plans for the Academic Classroom

Incorporating the *Strong* into lesson plans in high school or college classrooms as a tool for educating students about careers or as a means of promoting career maturity is a goal for many high school career guidance programs and college career centers. The *Strong* can be introduced easily as an educational tool for students in a range of classes on topics such as career development or academic success. Providing group interpretations of the *Strong* in classroom set-

≡*Rapid Reference 2.16*

Applications for the *Strong* to Educational Settings

Individual career planning—frequently used in self-assessment stage of career planning, but also for guiding information gathering, goal setting, and barrier identification.

Lesson plans for the academic classroom—educational tool for group career development activities.

Academic decision making—to assist with choosing courses, colleges, majors, or graduate programs.

Academic success and retention—to involve students in campus life through identifying campus organizations and extracurricular activities that fit interest patterns.

Interventions with specific populations—as a vehicle for addressing career concerns and challenges of particular student populations.

tings has several advantages. Large numbers of students can be reached at one time in group settings that are already structured and scheduled. Also, the stigma of counseling is removed, since students do not have to identify themselves as clients or seek out a counselor to obtain an interpretation.

Decision Making

The *Strong* is an ideal tool for assisting students with a range of academic and career decisions, such as choosing courses, choosing a college, selecting a graduate program, or finding a first job. Individual interpretations can be focused toward expanding options for those students with limited experience or toward narrowing options for those students with multiple and conflicting interest patterns. The *Strong* can be a tool for increasing students' self-confidence through reinforcement of existing career plans, or a tool for stimulating exploration of new domains.

Academic Success and Retention

Many educational institutions offer the *Strong* to all students at matriculation or during orientation programs. Group or individual interpretations are then offered to help students identify organizations and activities that fit their interest patterns. Early identification and integration into campus activities can have dramatic effects on students' adjustment to a new educational institution.

For example, involving students in extracurricular activities they find interesting can lead to higher retention rates by reducing isolation and increasing exploration of the full range of one's interests.

Interventions with Specific Populations

Diverse populations of students in most educational settings often share specific career development challenges. Prince (1995) outlines ways to tailor group interpretations of the *Strong* to meet the specific needs of student athletes; students with disabilities; racial and ethnic minority students; and lesbian, gay, and bisexual students. Group interpretations can be offered within pre-established student group settings and designed specifically to address the group's needs. In this context, the *Strong* becomes a valuable tool for campus outreach activities and a vehicle for discussing common career and academic challenges, such as confronting stereotypes, preparing for job interviews, or balancing individual, family, and cultural values related to career choice.

 TEST YOURSELF

1. **All the Basic Interest Scales and Personal Style Scales were developed by identifying items that clustered together statistically with strong item intercorrelations.** True or False?

2. **In determining item weights for the Occupational Scales, if the Like response shows the greater difference and is positively weighted, the Dislike response is automatically weighted negatively.** True or False?

3. **The 1994 revision of the *SII* has matching men's and women's Occupational Scales for all occupations.** True or False?

4. **Individuals in the occupational samples had to meet several criteria, including being satisfied with their work, performing their job in a typical way, and being at least 25 years old.** True or False?

5. **When checking the Infrequent Response Index, a positive number indicates that the profile is probably valid.** True or False?

6. **The General Reference Sample used in the latest revision of the *Strong* is comprised of 600 people.** True or False?

7. **An individual can earn a high score on most Occupational Scales only by responding Like to specific items on the scale.** True or False?

8. **Flat profiles with no scores above average on the General Occupational Themes and Basic Interest Scales should not be interpreted.** True or False?

(continued)

9. **The ethical counselor will restrict interpretive comments about the General Occupational Themes, Basic Interest Scales, Occupational Scales, and Personal Style Scales to career issues only.** True or False?

10. **Interpretive comments on the General Occupational Themes and Basic Interest Scales compare the individual with members of his or her own gender.** True or False?

11. **Which of the following would you review first to determine whether the Profile is valid?**

   (a) Elevations on the Occupational Scales

   (b) The standard score for the Work Style Scale

   (c) The Administrative Indexes

   (d) The Basic Interest Scales

12. **If a client responds with an extremely high percentage of Likes, which scales would show higher scores?**

   (a) All the General Occupational Themes

   (b) All the Occupational Scales

   (c) All the Personal Style Scales

   (d) None of the above

13. **Which scales first appeared on the earliest edition of the *Strong*?**

   (a) Basic Interest Scales

   (b) Occupational Scales

   (c) General Occupational Themes

   (d) Personal Style Scales

14. **Which scales have the largest number of items?**

   (a) General Occupational Themes

   (b) Occupational Scales

   (c) Basic Interest Scales

   (d) All Scales on the *Strong* are the same length

15. **What is the mean standard score of the general reference sample on the Social General Occupational Theme?**

   (a) 50

   (b) 40

   (c) 60

   (d) None of the above

Answers: 1. False; 2. True; 3. False; 4. True; 5. True; 6. False; 7. False; 8. False; 9. False; 10. True; 11. c; 12. a; 13. b; 14. b; 15. a

Three

CAMPBELL INTEREST AND SKILL SURVEY

The *Campbell Interest and Skill Survey (CISS)* is the product of over 35 years of interest measurement research conducted by David Campbell. Its purpose is to help individuals with career planning and decision making. Specifically, it attempts to map self-reported interests and self-reported skills to the occupational world. A sample profile for the *CISS* is displayed in Figure 5.2 in Chapter Five. It is one of six surveys in the *Campbell Development Survey (CDS)* battery. Rapid Reference 3.1provides an overview of The Campbell Development Survey battery.

The *CISS* consists of 200 interest items and 120 skill items. Respondents are asked to rate their level of interest according to a six-point scale (e.g., from Strongly Like to Strongly Dislike). Similarly, respondents are asked to rate their level of skill along a six-point scale. For example, the skill items include response options ranging from "Expert: Widely recognized as excellent in this area" to "None: Have no skill in this area." Responses are scored on standardized scales and presented on an 11-page graphic profile. Interest scales measure the level of an individual's attraction for each area, and skill scales measure the level of an individual's estimate of self-confidence in performing well in that area.

The *CISS* scales include 7 Orientation Scales, 29 Basic Scales, 60 Occupational Scales, and 2 Special Scales. There are also three scales designed to detect problems in administration or processing. Both interest and skill scores are presented for each scale to allow comparisons between an individual's strength of interest and strength of self-confidence for each area. The Profile is organized around the seven Orientation Scales. Patterns of interest and skill scores provide the individual with suggestions for possibilities of satisfaction and success in the world of work. Four patterns are presented: Pursue (High Interest-High Skill), Develop (High Interest-Lower Skill), Explore (Lower Inter-

≡ Rapid Reference 3.1

Campbell Development Survey (CDS) Battery

- The Campbell Development Survey (CDS) battery was designed for use in a range of settings including, educational institutions, human resource departments, training and development programs, individual career counseling or coaching, and community interventions.
- All of these surveys have identical item formats, scale construction methods, norming techniques, and profile layouts.
- It is easy for a user who is familiar with one of the surveys to quickly become proficient with the others.
- The battery includes the following six instruments:
  - —Campbell Leadership Index (Campbell, 1990)
  - —Campbell Organizational Survey (Campbell, 1991)
  - —Campbell Interest and Skill Survey (Campbell, Hyne & Nilsen, 1992)
  - —Campbell-Hallam Team Development Survey (Hallam & Campbell, 1994)
  - —Campbell-Hallam Team Leader Profile (Hallam & Campbell, 1999)
  - —Campbell Community Survey (This is in the final stages of development)

est-High Skill), and Avoid (Low Interest-Low Skill). Rapid Reference 3.2 presents an overview of the *CISS*.

THEORETICAL AND RESEARCH FOUNDATIONS

A cursory review of the *CISS* profile reveals an obvious similarity to the *Strong Interest Inventory* profile. In fact, the origins of the *CISS* are closely linked with those of the *Strong Interest Inventory*, since David Campbell was a primary developer of both instruments. From 1958 until 1988, he was involved in researching and revising the *Strong-Campbell Interest Inventory*. However, in 1988, having moved on to a new professional setting, the Center for Creative Leadership, he parted company with the publisher of the *Strong-Campbell Interest Inventory*, which was then renamed the *Strong Interest Inventory*. In his new environment, he began to apply his extensive knowledge of vocational assessment to developing a new career assessment tool that would be more "user-friendly" for both the practitioner and the person being assessed. In describing his devel-

≡Rapid Reference 3.2

Campbell Interest & Skill Survey (CISS)

Authors: David P. Campbell, Susan A. Hyne, and Dianne L. Nilsen

Publisher: National Computer Systems Assessments
P.O. Box 1416
Minneapolis, MN 55440
612-939-5000

Copyright Date: 1992

Description: The CISS helps individuals understand how their interests and self-reported skills relate to occupational and career environments. It includes 200 interest items and 120 skill items presented on a six-point scale. It can be used in a variety of settings, including educational institutions, human resource departments, training and development programs, and individual career counseling.

Profile Summary: Available though mail-in service, computer software, and direct Internet access (www.usnews.com/usnews/edu/careers/ccciss.htm). Includes 7 Orientation Scales, 29 Basic Scales, 60 Occupational Scales, 2 Special scales (Academic Focus Scale and Extraversion Scale), and 3 Procedural checks. A CISS Quadrant Worksheet is also provided with each profile to help respondents identify important patterns within their scores.

Age Range: 15 years to adult

Minimum Reading Level: approximately sixth-grade level

Administration Time: 35–45 minutes

Qualifications: The CISS profile is self-interpretive and respondents can understand their results with little outside help. However, to use the CISS for educational or career planning, the authors recommend interpretation by a Master's-level counselor who has completed coursework in psychological testing and personal counseling.

opment of the *CISS,* Campbell stated (Campbell, Hyne, & Nilsen, 1992), "the traditional academic issues of reliability and validity took a back seat to the more immediate concerns of efficiency, perceived usefulness, and especially social sensitivity" (p. ii). His goal was to develop an inventory that would be useful to "real people in the real world" and that would be free of bias in its vocabulary, grammar, norms, analyses, and profile presentation.

An additional distinct influence upon the development of the *CISS* was

Campbell's long-term experience (from 1969 to 1996) on the Board of Directors of National Computer Systems (NCS), the publisher of the *CISS*. This entrepreneurial background in marketing, production, and processing of tests on a large scale influenced his approach to both constructing and distributing the *CISS*. Campbell was joined in the production of the *CISS* by Susan Hyne, who contributed to its design and interpretation, and Dianne Nilsen, who assisted with its technical development.

The theoretical and research foundations of the *CISS* include a variety of psychometric and research methods. The authors used state-of-the-art construction techniques and took advantage of knowledge accumulated from over 30 years of experience with interest measurement research. The construction of the items and the different types of scales relied on an array of methodologies. Consequently, the research foundations for each segment of the *CISS* will be summarized separately.

Item Content and Format

Hundreds of items were originally written to comprise the *CISS* item pool. Items selected for final inclusion in the *CISS* were chosen on the basis of item response characteristics, such as response distributions over a wide range of occupations and strength of correlations with items in similar and different item clusters. In addition, item content and grammar were screened to avoid content that was biased or that might be offensive to people of different genders, races, or ethnicities. One of the unique aspects of the *CISS* interest items on occupations is that each occupation is defined. This undoubtedly yields more meaningful results than would be obtained if respondents without a wide experience base or limited language skills were to guess at the meaning of the items.

A six-point, free response format was chosen for the *CISS* instead of a two- or three-point choice format. Rapid Reference 3.3 reviews the response options for the *CISS* Interest and skill items. The provision of a six-point continuum allowed respondents the option of expressing their intensity of attraction to each item in finer gradations. The decision for this format was based on Campbell's experience with respondents to the *Strong-Campbell Interest Inventory* who had complained about being restricted to a narrow three-point

≡ *Rapid Reference 3.3*

Response Options for the *CISS* Interest and Skill Items

For interest items, the response options for most items are:

L = STRONGLY LIKE

L = Like

l = slightly like

d = slightly dislike

D = Dislike

D = STRONGLY DISLIKE

For skill items, the response options are:

E = EXPERT: Widely recognized as excellent in this area

G = Good: Have well developed skills here

sa = slightly above average: Average, or a touch above

sb = slightly below average: Average, or a touch below

P = Poor: Not very skilled here

N = NONE: Have no skills in this area

item response format. The goal of the even-numbered, six-point scale was to force a respondent to state at least a mild preference toward one direction or the other for each activity. This format also eliminated the option of a neutral response such as "indifferent" or "don't know." Item statistics provided in the manual appear to support the decision. They indicate relatively flat item response distributions over the entire six-point range for both interest and skill items (p. 35, Campbell, Hyne, & Nilsen, 1992). The authors suggest that a quick and easily remembered rule of thumb for the percentages of responses over both the six interest and skill response options is approximately: 10, 20, 25, 15, 15, 15.

Self-Assessed Skills

The *CISS*'s incorporation of self-assessed skills, along with self-assessed interests, was an innovation for interest measurement. The addition of skill items acknowledged the importance of an individual's self-confidence to career decision making. It also provided counselors with a means for assessing the degree of similarity or discrepancy between a client's interest and skill in a particular domain. The skill items on the *CISS* reflect an effort to measure an individual's belief about being able to perform a range of activities. In other words, these items were designed to be measures of an individual's self-confidence, not direct measures of their skills. However, research data reported in the manual indicate that an individual's self-assessed skills and behavioral ratings of those same skills are highly correlated, supporting the contention that measures of self-assessed skills often approximate those of actual skills. For example, an individual would typically estimate her level of skill in spelling at the same level that would result from a written test of her spelling ability.

The Orientation Scales

The *CISS* profile is organized around seven factors, referred to as Orientations. They are Influencing (I), Organizing (O), Helping (H), Creating (C), Analyzing (N), Producing (P), and Adventuring (A). Campbell offers the following humorous phrase to remember his seven-letter typology, IOHCNPA: I Often Hear Counselors Naturally Prefer Anchovies. This typology generally corresponds to Holland's six types (Holland, 1997), with Holland's Realistic type split into two, creating the seventh orientation (Adventuring). The labels of the Orientations differ from Holland's labels in two important ways. They are action-oriented words, or gerunds, instead of adjectives, and the meaning of each word is more obviously related to workplace activities. Rapid Reference 3.4 provides a comparison between the two structures.

The definitions of several of the Orientations differ slightly from those of their corresponding Holland types. The Influencing Orientation is defined to measure more leadership factors, whereas Holland's Enterprising type is focused more strongly toward sales. Similarly, the Organizing Orientation includes a stronger management and financial services factor, whereas the Conventional type has a stronger emphasis on office and clerical work. The major difference between the two typologies is that the Realistic type is divided into two components on the *CISS*: the Producing Orientation, which includes mechanical, construction, and farming activities, and the Adventuring Orientation, which includes military, police, and athletic activities.

≣ *Rapid Reference 3.4*
....

Comparison between *CISS* Orientations and Holland Types

CISS Orientations		Holland Types
Influencing (I)	_____	Enterprising (E)
Organizing (O)	_____	Conventional (C)
Helping (H)	_____	Social (S)
Creating (C)	_____	Artistic (A)
Analyzing (N)*	_____	Investigative (I)
Producing (P)	_____	Realistic (R)
Adventuring (A)	_____	Realistic (R)

* Note that the letter *N* is used for Analyzing rather than *A* to avoid confusion with Adventuring.

The seven Orientation Scales were constructed in an attempt to identify a small, manageable number of dimensions that would encompass the range of domains measured by the Basic Scales. Earlier research was used for guidance, specifically the array of studies by Holland, Campbell, Thurstone, and Strong that had identified five to seven broad interest dimensions. Campbell et al. (1992) analyzed the interest and skill scales separately. Based upon their findings and for ease of interpretability and consistency, a seven-component structure was chosen so that interest and skill scales could be presented in matching sets. The loadings for the Basic Scales on the seven components showed good support for the IOHCNPA structure.

Items for the Orientation Scales were selected based on statistical data and face validity. Specifically, items were chosen that met two criteria: their content represented the construct of each Orientation, and they had high item-scale correlations. Each Orientation contains a few items from each Basic Scale that is clustered within that Orientation. Similarly, all items in each Orientation Scale are included in the corresponding Basic Scales. The *Manual* (Campbell et al., 1992) provides a complete list of the items that comprise both the interest and skill scales for each Orientation. The item-scale correlations are also provided; they are generally high with a median of .59 for interests and .58 for skills.

The *Manual* (Campbell et al., 1992) provides data indicating that intercorrelations among the Orientations are low, supporting the claim that the Orientations are generally measuring different dimensions. These correlational data also support the validity of the arrangement for the seven factors in the IOHCNPA order. The median correlation between the interest and skill Orientations is .70, supporting the claim that interests and skills have strong covariance.

As an additional test of validity, the 60 occupational samples were rank ordered for each of the Orientations. Results indicated that the five highest-ranking occupational samples for each Orientation clearly conform to common sense expectations, indicating that the Orientations measure what they intend to. For example, the five highest-scoring samples on the Influencing Interest Scale included: Media Executive, Marketing Director, Hotel Manager, Public Relations Director, and Manufacturing Representative (Campbell et al., 1992).

Reliability data for the Orientation Scales also are strong. The *Manual* (Campbell et al., 1992) reports a median alpha coefficient for both interest and skill scales of .87. Similarly, test-retest correlations over a 90-day period demonstrate a high level of stability. They are reported to average .87 and .81 for interests and skills respectively.

Basic Scales

The 29 Basic Scales each include one interest and one parallel skill scale. They measure an individual's level of attraction to and confidence in a range of occupational activities. They were designed essentially as homogeneous subscales of the Orientation Scales, and were constructed by identifying and clustering items with high intercorrelations. Three criteria were followed for assigning items to each scale based on the following questions: (a) Did the items in each cluster correlate with each other? (b) Were their correlations with items in other clusters low? and (c) Did the items appear to belong together, given their content? The *Manual* (Campbell et al., 1992) identifies all items in each of the scales along with a complete listing of item-scale correlations. Correlations are high, averaging in the .50s and .60s, with many above .70.

Evidence supporting the validity of the scales relies primarily on rank orderings of the 60 occupational samples on each Basic Interest and Skill Scale. Generally, the occupational samples scored in predictable ways, indicating that the Basic Scales measure what they purport to measure. For example, on the Leadership Basic Interest and Skill Scales, the highest-ranking occupations were School Superintendent, Military Officer, and Human Resources Director. The lowest ranking occupations on these scales were Commercial Artist, Musician, and Veterinarian.

Reliability data for the Basic Scales indicate that the scales are internally consistent and stable, at least over short periods of time. Internal consistency data indicate a median alpha coefficient of .86 for the interest scales, and .79 for the skill scales. Similarly, test-retest correlations over a three-month period were high, averaging .83 for the Basic Interest Scales and .79 for the Basic Skill Scales (Campbell et al., 1992).

Occupational Scales

The Occupational Scales, unlike the Orientation Scales and Basic Scales, were developed using empirical scale construction methods. Samples of employed workers who reported enjoying their work were collected from a wide range of occupations. All data were collected by mail, typically through the use of occupational mailing lists. The response rate is not reported in the manual. The modal level of education for these samples was a bachelor's degree; the median sample size was 75. Individuals' responses were compared with responses of a larger, broader general reference sample comprised of all respondents from 65 occupational areas (1,790 women and 3,435 men). Those items that best discriminated between an occupational sample and the general reference sample (typically by a 0.55 standard deviation or higher) were selected as items for that particular occupational scale. This procedure is similar to that used in constructing the Occupational Scales for the *Strong Interest Inventory*. The Occupational Scales differ from the Basic Scales in a number of ways. Rapid Reference 3.5 summarizes these differences. The Occupational Interest Scales include items that reflect both likes and dislikes typical for an occupation. However, the Occupational Skill Scales are similar to the Basic Scales in that they contain no negatively weighted items. The rationale is that it appears conceptually unwise for a client to make a positive decision based on negative data, such as, "You have the same lack of skills as an accountant; therefore you should consider accounting."

To construct the Occupational Scales, mean differences for items were calculated from the six-point response format. This procedure differs from that used with the *Strong,* where calculations were based on a three-point response format. The authors of the *CISS* argue that this difference allows the *CISS* to use occupational scales that are shorter than those found on the *Strong.*

Another significant difference between the *CISS* and the *Strong* is the use of combined, rather than separate, gender scales on the *CISS.* This decision was made to ease interpretation and to minimize attention to gender differences. Statistical procedures were used to balance gender differences for those occupations with unequal numbers of men and women. (See Rapid Reference 3.6 for a listing of important differences between the *CISS* and the *Strong*).

≡ *Rapid Reference 3.5*

How the Occupational Scales Differ from Basic Scales

The Occupational Scales are:

- empirically, not intuitively derived; items were not selected on the basis of their content.
- longer and contain at least twice as many items.
- heterogeneous in content; the items on any particular scale cover a range of topics rather than just one.
- constructed with both positively and negatively weighted items.

Similar to other scales on the *CISS,* a raw-score to standard-score conversion formula is used to standardize all scores on the Occupational Scales. The general reference sample has a standard score mean of 50 and a standard deviation of 10. The mean for each occupational sample varies from scale to scale depending on the degree to which the sample's members differ from the general reference sample. These data are displayed on the profile with bar graphs that represent the scores for the middle 50% of each occupational sample. The mean scores for the occupational samples are approximately 65 to 70, or one and one–half to two standard deviations above the mean of the general reference sample.

Final minor adjustments were made to the Occupational Scales to enhance the technical quality and power of the scales. For example, statistically weak items were eliminated following preliminary analyses.

Validity

One source of support for the construct validity of the Occupational Scales is evident from the ordering of the scales on the profile. Scales are clustered according to the Orientations with which they have the highest correlation. For

≡Rapid Reference 3.6

Important Differences between the *CISS* and the *Strong*

CISS	Strong
Combined gender scales	Separate gender scales
Items offer six-point response options	Items offer three-point response options
Can be purchased directly by consumer	Needs trained interpreter to purchase
Compares interests with self-reported skills	Does not measure self-reported skills
Organizes interests by seven Orientations	Organizes interests by six Themes
Order of Orientations: Influencing closer to Adventuring than to Helping	Order of Themes: Enterprising closer to Social than to Realistic
Provides four tags to describe interest/skill Patterns (*Pursue, Develop, Explore, Avoid*)	Does not provide descriptive tags
Occupational Scale Score of 50 represents mean score of **general reference sample**	Occupational Scale Score of 50 represents mean score of **occupational sample**

example, the Attorney Scale correlates most highly with the Influencing Orientation and the Secretary Scale with the Organizing Orientation.

Additional data support the claim that the Occupational Scales reflect unique interests and skills of specific occupational groups (Campbell et al., 1992). The median separation between workers in a particular occupation and the general population is close to two standard deviations. In addition, those occupations that are obviously similar to one another generally show the highest correlations with each other. For example, the three highest scoring occupations on the Accountant Scale are Statistician, Bookkeeper, and Financial Planner.

Reliability

Test-retest data for the Occupational Scales over three months are generally high, indicating stability at least over short periods of time. Correlations are reported to be .87 for the Interest Scales, and a slightly lower .79 for the shorter skill scales (Campbell et al., 1992).

Special Scales

The two Special Scales, Academic Focus and Extraversion, offer important information about how clients prefer to apply their interests in academic and work settings. Rapid Reference 3.7 provides a quick summary of these two scales.

≡ Rapid Reference 3.7

Special Scales

Academic Focus Scales	Measure interest, motivation, and self-confidence in formal academic pursuits.
Extraversion Scales	Measure interest and confidence in working with others and through others.

Academic Focus Scales

The Academic Focus Scales were designed to measure a respondent's interest and confidence in doing well in formal academic pursuits. These scales were constructed by comparing the responses of people from a diverse sample of occupations that varied by level of education. Those items rated highly by people with high levels of formal education were chosen for inclusion in the scale and given a positive weighting. Items rated low by these people also were chosen for inclusion and assigned negative weights. The interest and skill scales include positively weighted items that reflect content areas such as science, literature, and the arts. Negatively weighted interest items reflect content areas that emphasize business and sales. No negatively weighted skill items were included. A full listing of the items for both the interest and skill scales are reported in the *Manual* (Campbell et al., 1992). Norms were designed so that individuals with a bachelor-level degree score about 50. The scales were constructed to show virtually no mean differences between genders.

The strongest validity data for the Academic Focus Scales indicate higher scores on both the interest and skill scales for groups with increased education. For example, groups whose highest education was "Some High School" show the lowest scores, and groups who attained "Doctoral-level Degrees" show the highest scores. The mean difference between high school dropouts and individuals with doctoral degrees was found to be roughly one and one-half standard deviation on both scales. Test-retest reliabilities over a three-month period are similar to those for other scales on the *CISS*: .87 for interests and .77 for skills (Campbell et al., 1992).

Extraversion Scales

The Extraversion Scales were designed to measure the respondent's interest and confidence in working with people as opposed to working alone. The scale was constructed empirically by comparing observer ratings with *CISS* items. The criterion sample consisted of 207 individuals who had completed both the *CISS* and the *Campbell Leadership Index* (*CLI*). The *CLI* is an instrument with 100 personality–oriented adjectives. It is completed by three to five observers who know an individual's working style well. The Extraversion interest and skill scales were created by selecting and positively weighting *CISS* items that correlated with "Extraverted" and "Likable" descriptions. Similarly, additional items that correlated with "Introverted," "Private," and "Solitary" observer ratings were selected and negatively weighted for the interest scale. The skill scale did not include any negatively weighted items. Norms for these scales were established using the general reference sample. Statistically weighted samples of men and women were created so that both genders would obtain a mean score of 50 and have a standard deviation of 10.

Validity of the Extraversion Scales was examined by correlating these scales with the Orientation Scales, Basic Scales, and Occupational Scales. As expected, the highest correlations for both interest and skill scales were generally with the Influencing and Helping Orientation Scales. The highest correlations with the Basic Scales occurred with the Leadership, Public Speaking, Adult Development, and Counseling Scales. The Occupational Scales with the highest correlations included Guidance Counselor, School Superintendent, and Corporate Trainer. These data support the proposition that the Extraversion Scales reflect interest and confidence in working with people in either entrepreneurial or helpful ways. Test-retest reliabilities over three months for the Extraversion scales are similar to those of other scales, .85 and .82 for interest and skill scales respectively (Campbell et al., 1992).

HOW TO ADMINISTER AND SCORE THE *CISS*

The *CISS* can be administered in several ways: The booklet can be purchased directly from National Computer Systems (NCS) by individuals who have a bachelor's degree and have completed either coursework in psychological assessment or an NCS approved workshop. Software is also available from NCS for on-site scoring and data storage. USNews, in conjunction with NCS Assessments, currently offers the *CISS* at its *USNews and World Reports Online* web site (*www.usnews.com/usnews/edu/careers/ccciss.htm*). For a modest fee, consumers can download the *CISS* booklet, print it, complete it by hand, and return it by mail directly to NCS for scoring. Within a maximum of two to three weeks, respondents receive in the mail a 12-page report along with an action planning guide. Don't Forget 3.1 offers tips for properly administering the *CISS*.

DON'T FORGET 3.1

Tips for Counselors Administering *CISS*

- Explain why you are asking the individual to complete the *CISS* (e.g., "This survey can help guide our discussion of your career planning.").
- Briefly describe the *CISS* (e.g., "This survey will ask you to rate your interests and skills in a variety of areas.").
- Estimate time to complete (e.g., "It will take about 35–45 minutes to complete.").
- Describe the next steps (e.g., "Your answers will be analyzed and compared to those of people in a wide range of occupations.").
- Point out that it is not a "test" (e.g., "You cannot fail or pass; you will not be timed; and there are no 'right' or 'wrong' answers.").
- Suggest that respondents answer questions quickly but seriously, without spending too much time thinking about any particular item.
- Point out the two different sections, interests and skills, and indicate the types of questions each includes.
- Be sure someone is available to answer questions a respondent may have about the instructions.
- For group administrations, read aloud the instructions for both the interest and skill sections, and allow time to answer questions.
- For clients completing the *CISS* by mail, include a cover letter explaining why they are being asked to complete it, along with instructions for completing it.
- Prior to submitting booklets for scoring, scan booklets to insure they are fully completed and that demographic information is entered correctly.
- Have your hypotheses confirmed by clients during interpretation.
- Remember that no one fits any Orientation perfectly, and everyone resembles all Orientations to some degree.

HOW TO INTERPRET THE CISS

As with the section on the Interpretation of the *Strong*, the model for interpreting the *CISS* will be divided into two sections: (1) preparing for the interpretation and (2) sequencing the interpretation. The focus here will be on providing individual interpretations.[1] For a detailed treatment of how to provide a group interpretation of the *CISS*, see the *Manual for the Campbell Interest and Skill Survey* (Campbell et al., 1992) and Campbell's article, "The Use of Interest Surveys With Groups: A Useful Team-Building Technique" (Campbell, 1996). If you are not familiar with the *CISS*, refer to the sample profile provided in Chapter 5 (Figure 5.2) as you review the following guidelines.

Preparing for the Interpretation

Take time to review the *CISS* profile prior to your interpretation to identify highlights of the profile and to begin building hypotheses about your client. If you have met with your client in a previous intake or counseling session, note the ways in which the data on the profile provide preliminary confirmation or disconfirming evidence of the interests and goals your client previously discussed. Rapid Reference 3.8 summarizes the steps in preparing for an interpretation of the *CISS*.

Step 1: Assess the Validity of the Profile

Assess whether the profile appears to be valid by reviewing the procedural checks on page 11 of the profile. There are six procedural checks performed by the computer, designed to indicate possible problems in the client's completion of the answer sheet or in the processing of the answer sheet. Three of the procedural checks are for interest items and three are for skill items.

Response Percentage Check   The Response Percentage Check (one each for interests and skills) indicates the percentage of times that the client selected each of the six possible response options. For the Interest Items, response percentages are provided for the three subsections: Occupations, School Subjects, and Varied Activities. An Overall Percentage also is provided for the entire section on Interests. For the Skill Items, response percentages are reported for the

---

[1] This model generally follows the suggestions provided in the *Manual for the Campbell Interest and Skill Survey* (Campbell, Hyne, & Nilsen, 1992).

=Rapid Reference 3.8

How to Prepare for the Interpretation

Step 1: Assess the Validity of the Profile

Step 2: Review Overall Patterns on the Profile

Step 3: Review the Orientations

Step 4: Review the Basic Scales

Step 5: Review the Occupational Scales

Step 6: Review the Special Scales

Step 7: Determine a Preliminary Orientations Code

Step 8: Summarize the Important Highlights

Step 9: Select an Interpretive Sequence

See the sample *CISS* profile, Figure 5.2, in Chapter 5 to apply the following suggestions.

Varied Activities in the skills section. The response percentages are calculated in the case of the Interest Items for the response options: STRONGLY LIKE, Like, slightly like, slightly dislike, Dislike, and STRONGLY DISLIKE. The response percentages are calculated for the Skill Items for the response options: EXPERT, Good, above average, below average, Poor, NONE. If any of the six response percentages in either the interest or skill section is over 80%, or if any four of the six response percentages in either section is three percent or less, the pattern is reported as Doubtful. If this is the case, a warning phrase is printed on the front of the profile indicating that one or more of the procedural checks is doubtful. Otherwise, the Response Percentage Check is reported as valid. Extremely high or low response percentages should be explored with a client. For example, an extremely high STRONGLY DISLIKE response percentage might be indicative of a client's reaction to his or her current situation or to the testing process itself. It also can indicate a narrow and highly focused interest pattern, not uncommon among artists and scientists.

Inconsistency Check   Next, review the two Inconsistency Checks, one each for the Interest and Skill items. The Inconsistency Checks include 10 pairs of closely related items for each of the Interest and Skill sections. For example, in the Interest Section, one pair includes the items *Develop new varieties for plants and*

DON'T FORGET 3.2

Procedural Checks for Omitted Items

Number of Items Omitted

Interest	Skill	Result
0–12	0–8	Valid
13–20	9–12	Doubtful
21+	13+	Invalid (The survey will not be scored)

Note: The survey also will be considered Invalid if a combination of 30 or more interest and skill items are omitted.

flowers and *Raise exotic plants, such as orchids.* A pair will be counted as inconsistent if two very different responses are selected for the pair, for example, Strongly Like is selected for one item and Strongly Dislike is selected for the other. If six or more inconsistent pairs are selected, the Inconsistency Check will be labeled as Doubtful, and a warning will be printed on the front of the profile. If the number of inconsistent pairs is five or fewer, the Inconsistency Check will be considered Valid. A Doubtful label is unusual. If it occurs, the client may have reading problems, or may not be taking the assessment seriously.

Omitted Items Check Finally, review the two Omitted Items Checks, one each for the Interest and Skill sections. Each check identifies the number of un-answered items. The most common reason for omitted items is that the client did not complete a section of the booklet. Don't Forget 3.2 summarizes the number of omitted items used to determine whether the assessment is Valid, Doubtful, or Invalid.

Step 2: Review Overall Patterns on the Profile—Note highlights, inconsistencies

Review the Response Percentages Review the response percentages to identify patterns in the way your client has responded. As mentioned previously, the average percentages for interest and skill responses across the six response op-tions, for example in the case of interests, STRONGLY LIKE, Like, slightly like, slightly dislike, Dislike, STRONGLY DISLIKE, is 10, 20, 25, 15, 15,15.

If your client has a higher than average percentage of interest "Strongly like,

Like, and Slightly Like" responses and skill endorsements, the client's profile will have many Pursue tags. If there is a high percentage of interest "Likes"and a low percentage of skill endorsements, the profile will have several Develop tags. If the client is confident he or she has many skills, but has a low percentage of "Likes", the client's profile will have many Explore tags. If both interest and skill endorsement percentages are low, the client's profile will have many Avoid tags.

Reviewing the Skill item response percentages can give you a sense of the client's overall confidence. Add the EXPERT and Good response percentages. Since the average combined response is about 30%, 50% would suggest a client with a very positive view of his or her abilities. If the combined percentage is over 58%, it suggests the client has a great deal of confidence. On the other hand, if the combined response percentage is less than 25%, or the client has 0% in the Expert response category, your client may have an unduly harsh or critical self view.

High scores, which result from high interest "Like" and skill endorsement percentages, can be accurate and reflect a multi-talented individual with multiple attractions. They may also reflect a client's desire to keep options open, the client's response bias for higher ratings, a belief that low interest or skill ratings are "bad", limited life or work experience that leads to an inability to differentiate interests and skills, an optimistic or positive focus or attitude, or an unrealistically inflated self-assessment.

Conversely, low scores, which result from low interest "Like" and skill endorsement percentages, may reflect limited life and work experience and lack of opportunity to develop or know interests or to develop and be able to estimate skills, the client's general response bias for low ratings, low self-esteem, a pessimistic outlook, a desire to appear modest, a unique pattern of interests/skills not covered by the *CISS*, a possible lack of a career orientation, very high standards, or depression.

What does your client's response pattern say about the client and how does it fit with other information you have? In one case, for example, a practitioner worked with a woman who was highly successful in her career, but still had low self-esteem. The counselor was able to show how the client's lack of confidence (low percentage of positive skill endorsements) was not in synch with her career success. This led to an important discussion about how her self-image had not caught up with her success.

Review the Orientations, Basic Scales, Occupational Scales, and Special Scales Next, review the sections on Orientations, Basic Scales, Occupational Scales, and Special Scales to identify patterns that repeat across the survey and note any surprises or discrepancies. For example, is there a consistent pattern, across the different sections, of high scores on the "Influencing" interest and skill scales? Alternatively, is there an inconsistency, such as a number of high scores on "Influencing" Basic Scales but a lack of high scores on Occupational Scales with an "Influencing" Orientation Code?

The *CISS*'s great strength lies in the provision of both interest and skill scales. At the same time, the number of scales and the combination of interest and skill scales can make interpretation confusing for the client and counselor. The suggestions below, in Steps 3–7, and the following section on Interpretation are intended to help you sort out the important nuances of the profile.

Notice the overall pattern of interests and skills. Are scores on Interest and Skill scales generally similar, denoting compatible interests and skills? Are there generally more high scores on Skill scales than Interest scales, suggesting a client with high confidence in a broader range of his or her abilities, and more focused areas of interest? Are there generally more high scores on Interest scales than Skill scales, suggesting a client with a broader range of interests, and confidence in a smaller range of his or her abilities?

Step 3: Review the Orientations

Turn to page 2 of the profile and identify the Orientations with the highest interest and skill scale scores. First, review all the Orientations labeled "Pursue" (both interest and skill scores are 55 or above). If there is more than one Orientation labeled "Pursue," consider the nuances between them by first identifying any Orientations with both interest and skill scales in the *Very High* range; second, any Orientations with interests in the *Very High* range and skills in the *High* range; third, any Orientations with skills in the *Very High* range and interests in the *High* range; and fourth, any Orientations with both interests and skills in the *High* range. Identify a preliminary two- or three-letter orientation code. Does this Orientation code support or disconfirm the interests and confidence in skills that your client has previously discussed?

Step 4: Review the Basic Scales

Next, glance over the Basic Interest and Skill Scales. Remember that a high score on a Basic Interest Scale reflects attraction to or enjoyment of the specific activities in that area. A high score on a skill scale reflects confidence in being able to perform the activities in that area and is also likely related to experience the client has had with these activities. As with the Orientations, it can help to identify the Basic Scales with the highest interest and skill scale scores. Among those labeled Pursue, you might again identify first any Basic Scales with both interest and skill scales in the *Very High* range; second, any Basic Scales with interests in the *Very High* range and skills in the *High* range; third, any Basic Scales with skills in the *Very High* range and interests in the *High* range; and fourth, any Basic Scales with both interests and skills in the *High* range. Are those Basic Scales with the Pursue tag (especially those with the highest interest and skill scales in combination) reflected in your client's current work life, hobbies, or plans? Conversely, are those Basic Scales with the Avoid tag areas that your client is indeed able to avoid? Are those Basic Scales labeled with the Develop tag areas that your client wants to develop skills in, has an underlying aptitude for, or wishes to maintain as a hobby? In the case of those Basic Scales labeled Explore, is there a way to transfer skills to areas of activity that your client is more interested in or that would relate more to your client's values? Be prepared to describe the content that each scale reflects. Familiarize yourself with the brief descriptions of each of these scales as summarized in the Rapid Reference 3.9.

Step 5: Review the Occupational Scales

Note which occupations are labeled Pursue, indicating that your client has interests and confidence in skills similar to people in that occupation. Do the Occupational Scales with the Pursue tag support the hypotheses that you have about the career goals of your client? What additional directions, in terms of your client's current work life, avocational pursuits, or future plans, might be suggested by the occupational scales labeled Pursue? Are there occupations labeled with the Develop tag? If so, what development plans might those scales suggest? Would your client prefer to express those interests in hobbies or leisure pursuits? Are there ways that your client might transfer skills that he or she already has into new career directions for those careers labeled with the tag Explore? Or is your client ready to move on from the tasks associated with these careers? Are there any occupations labeled with the Avoid tag? If so, do those make sense in light of the intake conversation you had with your client? Is your client able to avoid those occupations or the work tasks associated with

≡ Rapid Reference 3.9

Basic Interest and Skill Scale Descriptions

Basic Scales	Activities Covered
• Leadership	Acquire resources, inspire others to high performance
• Law/Politics	Debate issues, be politically active, negotiate
• Public Speaking	Give interviews to the media, deliver speeches, conduct training
• Sales	Make sales calls, persuade others to purchase goods or services
• Advertising/Marketing	Develop marketing strategies, design advertising campaigns
• Supervision	Manage others, plan budgets, schedule work
• Financial Services	Coordinate financial planning, investments, study economics
• Office Practices	Perform secretarial duties; handle schedules, supplies, and files
• Adult Development	Teach new skills to adults, work with students
• Counseling	Counsel, help, advise, support people
• Child Development	Teach classes, play with children, tell stories
• Religious Activities	Conduct religious programs and services
• Medical Practice	Provide health care services, first aid
• Art/Design	Draw, create works of art, design room layouts
• Performing Arts	Play music, act, sing, dance, direct plays
• Writing	Research topics, write and edit materials
• International Activities	Travel, work overseas, speak foreign languages
• Fashion	Design fashions, buy and sell clothes, jewelry
• Culinary Arts	Prepare gourmet meals, manage a restaurant
• Mathematics	Write computer programs, analyze data, teach mathematics
• Science	Perform lab research, work with scientific concepts and equipment
• Mechanical Crafts	Work with cars, machines, and electrical systems
• Woodworking	Do carpentry, build furniture and decks

Basic Scales	Activities Covered
• Farming/Forestry	Raise crops, manage timber, care for livestock
• Plants/Gardens	Design, plant, and care for gardens
• Animal Care	Care for pets, raise and train animals
• Athletics/Physical Fitness	Exercise, coach, compete, stay fit
• Military/Law Enforcement	Use military strategies in challenging or dangerous situations
• Risk/Adventure	Engage in high-risk, exciting, physically strenuous activities

them? Do those careers labeled Avoid confirm your client's expressed career aversions?

Step 6: Review The Special Scales

Academic Focus   Do the Academic Focus Scales support your client's career direction? If your client intends to pursue further education, what do the scales suggest your client will experience? Be prepared to discuss the Academic Focus scores in positive terms, since these can easily be misinterpreted by your client. Remember that the Academic Focus scores are **not** measures of intelligence or ability, but indicators of how interested, motivated, and self-confident your client is in academic settings. For example, high-scoring people may simply like to go to the bookstore to smell the new books. Low scoring people, on the other hand, will find many academic demands to be unreasonable or impractical, or may view them merely as hoops to jump through.

Extraversion   Do the scores on the Extraversion Scales support your client's expressed career goals? For example, if your client intends to work closely with others in a job that requires the ability to influence others, such as management or sales, has your client expressed a strong interest in working with others and confidence in this ability?

Step 7: Determine a Preliminary Orientations Code

Take a moment to review the full profile to determine the Orientations code that most accurately summarizes the full array of scores. The Orientations listed on page 2 of the profile may or may not accurately represent the full interest and skills confidence patterns of your client once the scores on the

Basic Scales and Occupational Scales are taken into account. First, notice whether the Occupational Scales labeled Pursue cluster within one, two, or three of the Orientations, and whether those labeled Avoid cluster into other Orientations. Next, determine whether the same patterns are evident across the Basic Scales. Finally, after considering the highlights of all three sections, choose a two- or three-letter Orientation code that best summarizes the highest interest and skill patterns across the entire profile (e.g., HC, PN, ION).

Note any inconsistencies between the Orientations suggested by the Occupational Scales and those suggested by the Orientations and Basic Scales. Be prepared to answer clients' questions about these discrepancies. For example, if a pattern of high scores occurs among the "Creating" Basic Scales but not among the "Creating" Occupational Scales, the "Creating" Orientation may represent hobbies, rather than occupational interests. The client is stating an interest in "Creating" topics, but not in the broader interest patterns, both likes and dislikes, shared among workers in creative careers.

Step 8: Summarize the Important Highlights

Again, you may not have time to review the inventory with the client in all its detail. As a final step in preparing for the interpretation, therefore, try to summarize two or three highlights that you think would be important to stress. For example, you may want to highlight the significance of the Orientations Code or two or three key Basic Interest and Skill Scales that support your client's proposed direction. How does the data in the *CISS* support data gathered from other sources (e.g., the intake interview or other assessments you have used)? Also, look for any inconsistencies or unusual patterns among the scales that may shed light on the client's confusion. Are there particular scales that confirm the client's career plans, or others that raise questions? Keep in mind, however, that all of your hypotheses will need confirmation from the client during the interpretation. Most clients will continue to mull over your points after the session, and one of your goals should be to provide a framework for their further thinking.

If time permits, you may wish to highlight occupations on the counselor's Report Summary page, using, for example, green for Pursues, blue for Develops, and pink for Avoids. This technique can help you get an overview of the profile, and if you are short on time with a client, you can go to this highlighted summary page after a discussion of the Orientations and Basic Scales.

Step 9: Select an Interpretive Sequence

Tentatively decide which sections or scales provide the information that you consider most useful and relevant to your client's concerns. Then develop a tentative plan for how you will apportion your interview time, since not all sections of the inventory will be equally relevant to your counseling goals. Also, consider the order in which you will interpret the inventory. Do you plan to follow a traditional order, as described in the Interpretive Sequence below, or does it make more sense to begin with a particular set of scales that address a particular concern of your client? For example, you may want to reorder pages 4 through 10 to spend more time on Orientations with the greatest number of Pursue and Develop tags.

The Interpretation Sequence

A seven-step model is suggested for interpreting the *CISS*, with some minor modifications based upon the unique characteristics of this instrument (see Rapid Reference 3.10). Although designed for individual interpretations, the same steps can be used for small group interpretations as well. Bear in mind that you may adjust your interpretation to suit your client by focusing on sections that specifically address his or her particular needs. Time is often limited and you may have to make choices about what to emphasize.

Step 1: Introduce the Results

Investigate the client's reactions to completing the CISS   Ask the client what it was like to complete the *CISS*. What thoughts, reactions, or questions occurred? Ask whether the client found it difficult to complete either the Interests or Skills portion of the *CISS* booklet. Remind the client that you will be explaining the meaning of the scores. However, emphasize that a number of factors can influence the results, and you will rely on the client to confirm their degree of accuracy.

<table>
<tr><td colspan="2">

≡Rapid Reference 3.10

Steps to Interpreting the CISS

Step 1: Introduce the Results

Step 2: Explain the Orientations

Step 3: Discuss the Basic Interest and Skill Scales

Step 4: Interpret the Occupational Scales

Step 5: Review the Special Scales

Step 6: Summarize Results

Step 7: Encourage Exploration beyond the Profile

</td></tr>
</table>

CAUTION 5.1

Interpretive Do's

- **Do** clarify clients' expectations for the interpretation.
- **Do** explore clients' previous experiences with assessment, both positive and negative.
- **Do** explain that interests and skills are only two pieces of information needed for good career decision making.
- **Do** remind clients that the *CISS* assesses a full range of life interests and skills, not just career-related interests and skills.
- **Do** clarify that high interest scores suggest similarity in interests to people who enjoy their work and indicate that the client would probably be comfortable in that occupational environment.
- **Do** clarify that high skill scores suggest self-confidence, indicating that the client would probably be confident in performing the tasks in that occupational environment.

Clarify the goals of the interpretation   Review with the client again the goals for the interpretation. Discuss any misconceptions or unrealistic expectations the client may hold, and come to an agreement about the purpose of your interpretation. (Review Cautions 3.1 and 3.2 for tips on reaching a reasonable focus.) Highlight in particular the fact that the *CISS* provides both a measure of interests or attraction for various occupational areas, and an assessment of skills that should be interpreted not as abilities but as a measure of self-confidence in performing well in various areas. Also, remind the client that the *CISS* is a useful tool for getting to know his or her interest and skill patterns better, but it will not tell the client "which career to choose" or "what to do."

Describe the Profile's organization, and how you will proceed   Explain that the *CISS* has four different sections, and that each assesses the client's interests and confidence in skills in a different way. Describe each section briefly and indicate the order in which you will review them. For example, you might say:

"Your CISS profile includes nearly 100 scales (98 total). These scales are organized into four sections; each section addresses a different question about your interests and your confidence in your skills. We will review each of the four sections in turn. First, we will review the section called the Orientations. These seven Orientations summarize your attraction for and confi-

CAUTION 3.2

Interpretive Don'ts

- **Don't** confuse interests with skills or abilities: the CISS assesses interests and confidence in skills separately, providing insights on both.
- **Don't** confuse self-estimates of skills with actual skills or abilities. While research suggests there is a relationship between self-estimates and actual skills, the Skill scales should be interpreted as an estimate of self-confidence in performing in the particular area, not as a measure of actual skill.
- **Don't** forget that a difference of one or two points in scores on different scales is not significant.
- **Don't** over-interpret the tags Pursue, Develop, Explore, and Avoid. Use them as guidelines, rather than prescriptions, for further exploration.
- **Don't** lead clients to believe that the CISS indicates which occupation they "should" pursue.
- **Don't** use the word "test." The CISS is a survey; you cannot pass or fail it.

dence in performing in seven major areas in the working world. Next we will review the section called the Basic Interest and Skill Scales. This section organizes your interests and confidence in skills scores into 29 specific topic areas. In the case of interests, it highlights what you are attracted to or have an aversion for. In the case of skills, it highlights what you are confident or lack confidence in performing. Next we will review the 60 Occupational Scales. These indicate which types of 'happily employed' people, across a wide range of occupations, share with you interests (both likes and dislikes) and a distinctive pattern of confidence. Finally, we will discuss the fourth section, the 2 Special Scales. These measure your general attraction for and confidence in intellectual, scientific, and literary activities, and extraverted activities that may influence your decisions about educational pursuits and work environments."

As with other assessments, structure the interpretation to be a dialogue rather than a lecture. For example, explain that you will describe the meaning of the scales and scores, and will draw attention to the highlights. However, emphasize that you will need the client to explain to you, at each step, how the scores fit or do not fit. Encourage the client to ask questions throughout the interpretation session. At some point relatively early, ask the client directly, "Are you getting out of this session what you hoped for?" and modify your approach accordingly.

Step 2: Explain the Orientations

Introduce the Orientations Explain that the Orientations are used to organize information on the *CISS* and are based on recent research on the underlying structure of interests. If your client has taken the *Strong Interest Inventory* or *Self-Directed Search*, and is already familiar with Holland's constructs, you might mention that the Orientations are similar to Holland's hexagon.

The Orientations are used to organize the client's interests and confidence in skills into seven broad patterns or Orientations. Use the brief descriptions printed on the Profile following each Orientation to introduce them (see Rapid Reference 3.11). Campbell suggests having your clients estimate which of the Orientations will be most descriptive of them at this point in the interpretation, both to get your client more involved in the interpretation and to check the client's comprehension of the Orientations. For more in-depth descriptions of the Orientations, see the *Manual for the Campbell Interest and Skill Survey* (Campbell et al., 1992). You may wish to consider making a handout for your clients of the more in-depth descriptions of the Orientations provided in the manual and on pages 4–10 of the profile (see Rapid Reference 3.12) and

≡ *Rapid Reference 3.11*

Brief Orientation Descriptions

Orientations	Brief Descriptions
Influencing	Influencing others through leadership, politics, public speaking, and marketing
Organizing	Organizing the work of others, managing, and monitoring financial performance
Helping	Helping others through teaching, healing, and counseling
Creating	Creating artistic, literary, or musical productions; designing products or environments
Analyzing	Analyzing data, using mathematics, and carrying out scientific experiments
Producing	Producing products; using "hands-on" skills in farming, construction, and mechanical skills
Adventuring	Adventuring, competing, and risk-taking through athletic, police, and military activities

Adapted from the *Campbell Interest and Skill Survey Individual Profile Report* with permission of NCS.

≡Rapid Reference 3.12

Descriptions of the Orientations

Influencing

The Influencing Orientation covers the general area of leading and influencing others. People who score high are interested in making things happen. They want to take charge and are willing to accept responsibility for results. Influencers are generally confident of their ability to persuade others to their viewpoints, and they enjoy the give and take of verbal jousting. They typically work in organizations and often want to take charge of the specific activities that particularly interest them. They enjoy public speaking and like to be visible in public. Typical high-scoring occupations include company presidents, corporate managers, and school superintendents.

Organizing

The Organizing Orientation includes activities that bring orderliness and planfulness to the working environment, such as managing projects, planning procedures, and directly supervising the work of others. People who score high generally emphasize efficiency and productivity. Organizers are good with details, and usually enjoy solving the day-to-day problems that inevitably appear in organizations. They understand budgets and cash flow and are often good with investments. Typical high-scoring occupations include accountants, financial planners, office managers, and administrative assistants.

Helping

The Helping Orientation involves helping and developing others through activities usually related to personal services, such as teaching, counseling, or healing. People who score high are compassionate and deeply concerned about the well-being of others. Helpers enjoy having close, personal contact with others and are genuinely concerned with helping their students or clients live full, satisfying lives. They readily understand the feelings of others and can provide emotional support. Typical high-scoring occupations include counselors, teachers, and religious leaders.

Creating

The Creating Orientation includes artistic, literary, and musical activities, such as writing, painting, dancing, and working in the theater, and also various design activities such as interior design and fashion design. People who score high are interested in, and confident of, their ability to create new products, new visions, and new concepts within these artistic areas. Creators see the world through innovative eyes and are frequently uncomfortable with traditional organizational constraints. They see themselves as free spirits and are often fluent and expressive. Typical high-scoring occupations include artists, musicians, designers, and writers.

(continued)

aNalyzing

The aNalyzing Orientation involves scientific, mathematical, and statistical activities. People who score high are comfortable with data and numbers and have a strong need to understand the world in a scientific sense. They usually prefer to work alone or in small groups in laboratory or academic settings. aNalyzers have a strong need to be autonomous and like to work through problems for themselves. Typical high-scoring occupations include scientists, medical researchers, and statisticians. This Orientation is labeled with the Letter N because the letter A is used for the Adventuring Orientation below.

Producing

The Producing Orientation covers practical, hands-on, "productive" activities, such as construction, farming, and mechanical activities. People who score high like to work with their hands, generally enjoy being outdoors, and like to be able to see the visible results of their labors. Producers are usually good with tools, and they enjoy taking on new construction projects or repairing mechanical breakdowns. Typical high-scoring occupations include mechanics, veterinarians, and landscape architects.

Adventuring

The Adventuring Orientation covers athletic, police, and military activities involving physical endurance, risk-taking, and competing with others. People who score high enjoy physical activities, and they like to confront competitive situations. They are confident of their physical skills and often seek out excitement. Adventurers enjoy winning, but they also are resilient in defeat. They often like working closely with others in teams. Typical high-scoring occupations include military officers, police officers, and athletic coaches.

have your clients highlight those aspects of the orientations that best describe them.

Since Holland's constructs are the most popular typology of the world of work today (Campbell et al., 1992), if your client is familiar with Holland's work, you may want to differentiate the Orientations from Holland's typology as described earlier (Rapid Reference 3.2). To enrich your own understanding of the definition of the themes, review the specific items that make up the *CISS* Orientation Scales provided in Chapter 5 of the *Manual for the Campbell Interest and Skill Survey* (Campbell et al., 1992).

Remind the client that no one fits any one Orientation perfectly; most people have interests and skills in all seven groups to varying degrees. Emphasize the broad nature of the Orientations. For example, remind clients that in addition to work-related interests, the Orientations can help identify leisure in-

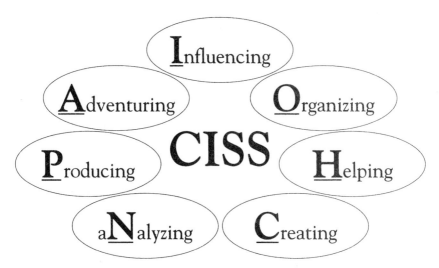

Figure 3.1   A Graphic Representation of the *CISS** Orientations Scales

Note. Copyright © 1989, 1992 David P. Campbell, PhD. Published and distributed exclusively by National Computer Systems, Inc., P.O. Box 1416, Minneapolis, MN 55440. Reproduced with permission by National Computer Systems, Inc.

terests and potential skill areas. Describe how the Orientations are similar and dissimilar to one another: Those adjacent to one another on the Profile have more in common with each other than those that are farther apart. Use Figure 3.1 to demonstrate how the Influencing and Organizing Orientations have a great deal in common with one another and the Helping and Producing Orientations are most dissimilar.

Note that the Orientations are arranged in a slightly different order than Holland's hexagon, with the Influencing Orientation more closely correlated with Adventuring and Organizing Orientations, rather than the Helping Orientation. In Holland's formulation, by contrast, Enterprising is more closely related to Social and Conventional, rather than Realistic types.

Define the scores   Outline the three different ways in which the client's Orientation scores are presented:

1. STANDARD SCORES   *"Two scores are provided for each Orientation, one for Interests and one for Skills. The interest score indicates how appealing the activities in the Orientation are for you and the skill score indicates how confident you feel in performing these activities. The average score is about 50 on each scale; 55 is considered to be a high score, and 45, a low score. Your score on an Interest Scale is a measure of your attraction to this area. A high score*

suggests that you are strongly interested in the activities covered by that scale; a low score suggests that you have an aversion to the activities. Your score on a Skill scale is a measure of how competent you have assessed yourself to be. A high score suggests you have confidence in your ability to perform in these activities and a low score suggests a lack of confidence and/or a lack of experience or opportunity to gain skills in the activities associated with the Orientation." (Although you do not need to discuss this with the client, bear in mind that the raw scores have been converted to standard scores with a mean in the general population of about 50 and a standard deviation of 10).

The distribution of scores on the *CISS* Orientation scales and all other scales is bell-shaped. To help you better understand your client's scores and their relationships in the normal curve, Figure 3.2 provides a reminder of the corresponding values of T scores (standard scores) and percentiles when working with a normal curve.

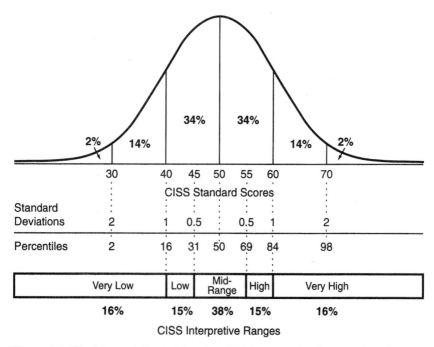

Figure 3.2 The Normal Curve Showing *CISS* Interpretive Ranges, Standard Scores, Standard Deviations and Percentiles

2. STANDARD SCORES PLOTTED TO GRAPHS USING DIAMONDS AND SHADING
One of the particularly appealing aspects of the *CISS* are the graphic design elements. Two scores are plotted for each Orientation. The Interest score is plotted with a solid diamond and the Skill score with a hollow diamond. Campbell suggested a way to remember which diamond is which: Interests tend to be more *solid,* that is, they do not change significantly over time, whereas skills tend to be more *open,* such that skills continue to be acquired over the lifespan. You will note two shaded areas on the profile, with dark shading representing what are described as very high scores of 60 and above and very low scores of 40 or below and light shading representing high scores of 55–59 and low scores of 41–45.

3. INTEREST/SKILL PATTERN TAGS   An interesting innovation with the *CISS* is the comparison that can be made between the level of interest and level of self-reported skill in each of the areas scored on the Orientations, Basic Scales, and Occupational Scales. The resulting patterns can be enlightening and, as Campbell indicates, can be used to suggest further exploratory and career-planning activities. For example, refer to the *CISS* Interest Skill Patterns worksheet (Figure 3.3), that can be used to summarize scales following the interpretation.

Interpretive tags or comments are provided for four particular patterns of combinations of Interest and Skill scores: *Pursue, Develop, Explore,* and *Avoid.* A suggested script for introducing these patterns is offered below:

"A Pursue tag is provided when your Interest and Skill scores are both high (55 or above). Your scores indicate that you have both an attraction to these activities and confidence in your ability to perform them well. A Develop tag is provided when your Interest score is 55 or higher and your Skill score is 54 or lower. Your scores indicate that you enjoy these activities but feel slightly to significantly less certain, depending on the score, about your ability to perform them. An Explore tag is provided when your Skill score is 55 or higher and your Interest score is 54 or lower. Your scores indicate that you are confident in your ability to perform these activities, but have slightly to significantly less attraction, depending on the score, to these activities. The Avoid tag is provided when your Interest and Skill Scales are both low (45 or lower). Your scores indicate that you neither enjoy these activities nor feel confident in your ability to perform them." (Remember that scores of 55 or above are at least 0.5 standard deviation above the mean and scores of 45 or below are at least 0.5 standard deviation below the mean.)

Campbell suggests that the tags can be further interpreted in the following ways (Campbell, 1992, p.6):

Campbell Interest and Skill Survey
Interest/Skill Patterns

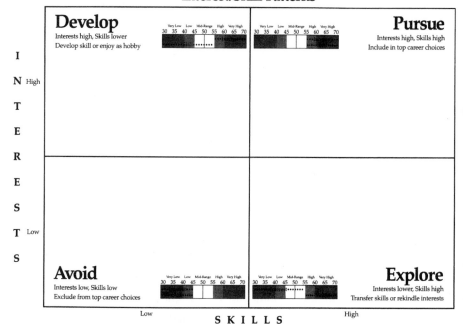

© 1992 David Campbell, Ph.D. All rights reserved.

Figure 3.3 *CISS* Interest/Skill Patterns Worksheet

Note. Copyright © 1989, 1992 David P. Campbell, PhD. Published and distributed exclusively by National Computer Systems, Inc., P.O. Box 1416, Minneapolis, MN 55440. Reproduced with permission by National Computer Systems, Inc.

Pursue: This pattern represents an area that is especially appealing to you and that would be well worth pursuing. It is an area in which you have both interest and confidence in your skills. You are likely to find both significant satisfaction and success here.

Develop: This pattern represents a potential growth area for you or a potential area for leisure or avocational pursuits. You have considerable interest in this area, but feel less talented or experienced in it. If the area is of great enough interest to you, you may want to seek additional education or training, or build your experience, to increase your level of confidence and skill.

Explore: This pattern represents an area in which you have considerable confidence in your skill, but no significant interest. You may want to consider whether it is possible for you to apply these talents to activities that hold greater appeal.

Avoid: This pattern represents an area in which you have neither interest nor confidence in your skills. You probably have no intention to pursue this area. Unless there is a particularly compelling reason to consider it, such as involvement in a family business or some other tradition or expectation, this is an area worth avoiding.

Campbell's innovative combination of interests and skills into these four distinctive patterns provides some useful guidance on how to interpret interest and skill scores for each area. However, the tags can be over-interpreted (see Caution 3.3). As always, check with the client to gain the client's perspective on the value of the information provided, and make adjustments to the suggestions offered to your client accordingly. Be prepared to exercise final judgment, in cooperation with your client, about how the scales should most appropriately be labeled and treated in further investigation in the career planning process.

No interpretive comments, or tags, are attached to scales for which neither the interest nor skill score is 55 or above and one or both falls in the midrange

---

CAUTION 3.3

Interpreting the Interest/Skill Pattern Tags

- Tags, in certain circumstances, can be overly directive or prescriptive (Pugh, 1998).

- Scores that are close to each other and represent no real difference can be labeled quite differently when they occur near cutoffs for different Tag definitions.

- If the scores are within a few points of 55, discuss with the client whether this scale should more appropriately be labeled Pursue, Develop, or Explore.

- When working with younger people, consider both the Pursue and Develop areas, so that your clients don't reject potentially satisfying occupations because they have not yet developed corresponding skills.

- Be careful when interpreting Avoid tags. Clients can obtain low interest scores simply because they have not been exposed to an area, and low skill scores simply because they have not had experience in an area.

(46–54). If the client's profile contains few tags other than Avoid, assist the client in identifying his or her highest scores and help the client develop priorities for further exploring these Orientations.

INDIVIDUALIZED COMMENTS A specific set of computer-generated comments is printed on the lower third of the page for each respondent, summarizing the Orientations according to the Interest/Skill Patterns and suggesting follow-up activities for career and life planning.

Discuss each of the Orientations Beginning with the Influencing Orientation and ending with the Adventuring Orientation, review each of the Orientations, providing the client with a more in-depth explanation of them (see pages 97 and 98). Discuss the client's reactions to each of the interest and skill scores on the Orientations to confirm their degree of accuracy. Usually no one person fits the full prototypical description of any of the Orientations, so ask the client to identify which specific adjectives or descriptors of each Orientation fit them, and which do not. If you have time, this discussion can extend into an exploration of the client's positive and negative past experiences with activities in each of the seven areas.

At the conclusion of your review of the Orientations, discuss whether the Interest/Skill Pattern tags as printed seem appropriate and what, if any, changes should be made. To assist the client in working with this data, as time permits, record the Orientations in the appropriate quadrant on the Interest/Skill Pattern worksheet. One helpful way to do this is to list and underline each of the Orientations placing them in the quadrant—Pursue, Explore, Develop, Avoid—based upon the confirmation of the "best fit" tag that you and your client selected in your earlier discussion. Figures 3.4 and 3.5 illustrate an example of a completed profile for the Orientations section and a sample of a completed Interest/Skill Pattern Worksheet. Alternatively, if time is limited, you may want to assign the worksheet as homework and discuss it in a follow-up session.

Finally, after reviewing all of the Orientations, summarize this section by highlighting those two or three Orientations that the client agrees best describe him or her, by considering both interests and skills in combination or by looking at the highest Interest scores. You can develop an Orientations Code by writing the letter representing each Orientation in priority order (I for Influencing, O for Organizing, H for Helping, C for Creating, N for Analyzing,

CAMPBELL INTEREST AND SKILL SURVEY INDIVIDUAL PROFILE

CASE STUDY C

Orientations

DATE SCORED: 8/04/92

Your CISS profile is organized into seven Occupational Orientations covering important areas of the world of work. Each Orientation is identified by an underlined capital letter. See the back of page 1 for an explanation of your scores.

Influencing - influencing others through leadership, politics, public speaking, and marketing
Organizing - organizing the work of others, managing, and monitoring financial performance
Helping - helping others through teaching, healing, and counseling
Creating - creating artistic, literary, or musical productions and designing products or environments
a**N**alyzing - analyzing data, using mathematics, and carrying out scientific experiments
Producing - producing products, using "hands-on" skills in farming, construction, and mechanical crafts
Adventuring - adventuring, competing, and risk-taking through athletic, police, and military activities

A pair of scores is plotted below for each Orientation. Your Interest score, plotted with a solid diamond (◆), indicates how appealing the activities are for you, and your Skill score, plotted with a hollow diamond (◊), reflects how confident you feel in performing these activities.

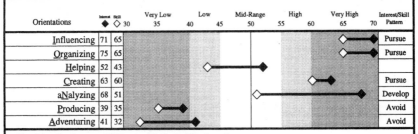

Orientations	Interest	Skill	Very Low 30 35	Low 40 45	Mid-Range 50	High 55 60	Very High 65	70	Interest/Skill Pattern
Influencing	71	65					◊ ◆		Pursue
Organizing	75	65					◊ ◆		Pursue
Helping	52	43		◊	◆				
Creating	63	60				◊ ◆			Pursue
a**N**alyzing	68	51			◊		◆		Develop
Producing	39	35	◊ ◆						Avoid
Adventuring	41	32	◊	◆					Avoid

Your Orientation Interest and Skill scores fall into the following patterns:

Pursue - **I**nfluencing, **O**rganizing, and **C**reating. These are activities that you both enjoy and feel confident about your abilities in performing. Areas where your interests and skills are both high are prime candidates for your future. Definitely include these in your career planning.

Develop - a**N**alyzing. These are activities that you enjoy, but are less confident about your ability to perform. Consider seeking additional education or training to bring your skill level up to your interest level. Or consider adopting some of these activities as hobbies.

Avoid - **P**roducing and **A**dventuring. These are activities that you neither enjoy nor feel confident about in performing. You should avoid these areas in your career planning; they are not likely to provide many satisfying opportunities for you.

Figure 3.4 *CISS* **Case Study C, Profile Page 2** *Orientations*

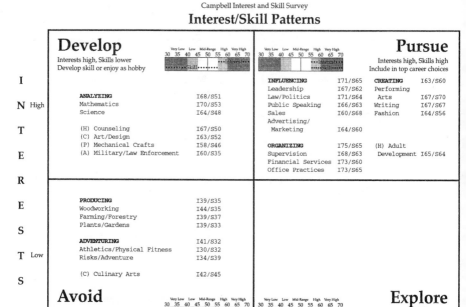

Campbell Interest and Skill Survey
Interest/Skill Patterns

Figure 3.5 Interest/Skill Patterns Worksheet Completed for Case Study C

Note. Copyright © 1989, 1992 David P. Campbell, PhD. Published and distributed exclusively by National Computer Systems, Inc., P.O. Box 1416, Minneapolis, MN 55440. Reproduced with permission by National Computer Systems, Inc.

P for Producing, and A for Adventuring). For example, if the three top interest scores are in the Influencing, Helping, and Creating Orientations, the Orientation code would be IHC. You can note the Orientation code for this section of the profile by writing the code on the profile or circling those Orientation scores and titles.

Step 3: Discuss the Basic Interest and Skill Scales
Provide an overview of the scales   Explain that the Basic Scales are essentially subscales of the Orientations, and that they measure more narrow interests and confidence in skills than do the Orientations. For example, Financial Services and Supervision are subscales of the Organizing Orientation. The 29 pairs of

Basic Scales, one each for interests and skills, help to organize and prioritize your client's preferences and skills confidence in specific areas of activity. Each of the Basic Scales is related to the corresponding Orientation but with a different nuance. A high score on an Interest scale indicates activities to which your client is attracted and a low score indicates strong disinterest in those activities. A high score on a Skill Scale indicates that your client has confidence in his or her ability to perform the activities in that area, and a low score suggests a lack of confidence, experience, or both.

The scores on the Basic Scales are interpreted in a manner similar to the scores on the Orientations (e.g., the standard scores, graphs, and Interest/Skill pattern tags are presented similarly, and have similar meanings). See Figure 3.6 Orientations and Basic Scales for Case Study C, for an example of how the Basic Scales are displayed on the profile. Note that the Orientations are repeated on the page and the corresponding Basic Scales are listed below them. The Orientations are displayed graphically with the large diamonds and the Basic Scales are displayed with the small diamonds.

Although the Orientations are comprised of items taken from each of the Basic Interest and Skill Scales clustered below them, the Basic Scales themselves have additional item content not included on the Orientations. Thus, it is possible to score mid-range or low on an Orientation, but have a Basic Scale listed beneath it with either a high interest or skill score or both, reflecting an attraction for and/or confidence in that particular area of activity without an endorsement for the overall Orientation it is clustered within. For example, it is possible to score mid-range on the Producing Orientation and earn a Pursue tag on the Animal Care Basic Scale clustered within the Producing Orientation. This often occurs for clients who have or wish to own a pet, for example, but have no particular interest in the overall activities associated with the Producing Orientation (farming, construction, mechanical skills).

Explain that the Basic Scales reflect interests that can be fulfilled not only through work tasks or work environments, but also throughout one's general lifestyle—through hobbies or leisure pursuits, friends, family, volunteer activities, or home environment, for example.

Review each scale individually   Review each of the Basic Scales individually, and discuss the client's reactions to the scores. Describe in more detail the content

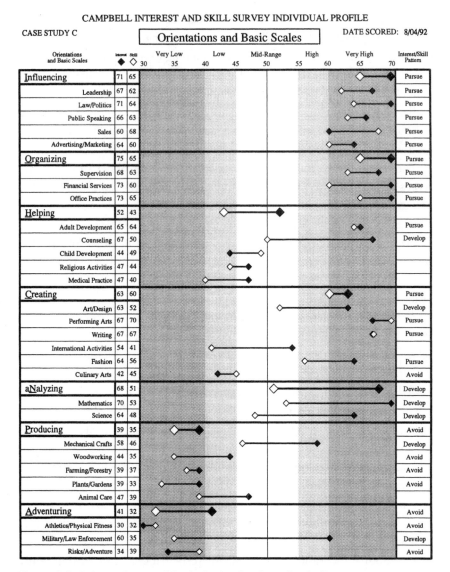

Figure 3.6 Orientations and Basic Scales for Case Study C

Note. Copyright © 1989, 1992 David P. Campbell, PhD. Published and distributed exclusively by National Computer Systems, Inc., P.O. Box 1416, Minneapolis, MN 55440. Reproduced with permission by National Computer Systems, Inc.

of any scale not understandable to the client. (See Rapid Reference 3.9 for a quick descriptive phrase for each.) Ask the client for examples of how the scores might reflect specific interests or disinterests, experience or lack thereof, and the results obtained in these areas.

As you discuss the scales, spend extra time discussing the client's highest scores. You may find it helpful to draw a line down the profile at 60 and at 55 to show more clearly the differentiations in scale scores that led to the Interest/Skill pattern tags. Again, point out the Interest and Skill pattern tags and review their meaning. Give special consideration to those labeled Pursue, or any labeled Develop or Explore where the interest or skill score is within a couple of points of 55. Note also the low scores and confirm with your client whether these are areas he or she wishes to avoid. Low Interest scores typically reflect a dislike of that area. However, be careful with this conclusion, since some clients obtain low scores not because they dislike the area, but because they have never been exposed to that particular Basic Interest area. Low skill scores can be obtained because of experience or lack of experience in that area. Interest and skills both might be developed with additional experience.

Ask the client to identify how his or her highest interests are finding expression through work or non-work related activities. Also, discuss which of these higher interests the client would like to incorporate into a job or career. Take time to discuss any high interest areas that are not finding expression in the client's lifestyle, and help the client strategize how to begin exploring that interest area.

Activities with the Interest/Skill Pattern Quadrant Worksheet   At this point in the interpretation, if time permits, you may wish to continue filling out the Interest/Skill Pattern Quadrant Worksheet (see Figure 3.3) to summarize the results of your interpretation of the Basic Interest and Skill Scales. You can list the Basic Scales in the quadrant that you and your client have agreed is most appropriate beneath the corresponding Orientations. You can also include the standard scores for each scale, for example, I55, S64. You may also wish to include the abbreviation for the Orientation the Basic Scale falls within if the Orientation is not located in that quadrant. See Figure 3.6 to review the Basic Scales for Case Study C and Figure 3.5 to see how the Basic Scales are recorded.

The *CISS* data are so rich that they bear thoughtful consideration. Look at the overall pattern on the worksheet. Are scores plotted in every quadrant? Which quadrant has the most scales? Which has the fewest?

If there are many scales listed in the Pursue quadrant, this may suggest that your client has many interests and confidence in many areas and will need help in identifying which of these are the highest and most important for his or her future career planning. Look at the patterns represented by the Pursue scales. What themes do you see emerging? You might note these in the Pursue quadrant. Assist your client in thinking about how interests might be combined to achieve greater satisfaction in work. You can help your client recognize that some interests can also be met in leisure and volunteer pursuits or through activities with family and friends. Also, help your client think about the sequencing of his or her interests. Given that research shows most people will have 8–10 job changes in their lives, you can help your client think about the ways in which various interests can be met over the lifespan. You can also use the Pursue quadrant to explore how the client's interests relate to his or her current job and to past positions. You may wish to spend additional time generating options that go beyond the profile by brainstorming possible career titles that relate to the Basic Scales in various combinations. You can note these possibilities alongside the quadrant on the worksheet or on a separate worksheet that you create (see Figure 3.7). For example, a client with interests in Law/Politics and International Activities might enjoy a career in International Law, or a client with interests in Medical Practice, Science, and Sales might enjoy a career in pharmaceutical or biotech equipment sales.

If there are several scales listed in the Develop quadrant, it may mean that your client has many interests and less confidence in his or her skills in these areas. This can happen with young people and others who have not yet had much experience or an opportunity to develop skills in their areas of interest. Support your client in deciding whether he or she would like to develop skills in the areas listed or would prefer to maintain these interests as hobbies. If your client would like to develop his or her skills, help your client determine what some options would be for getting further training, education, mentoring, or experience.

If your client has several scores in the Explore quadrant, he or she is reporting high confidence in skills in several areas, but with lower interests. Help your client assess whether these are skills that he or she is tired of using and is ready to leave behind. Campbell has suggested that if there is a 20-point difference between skills and interests and the client is using these skills on the

Interest and Skill Scale Combinations	Career Possibilities
Pursue: *Counseling + Risks/Adventure*	Outward Bound Leader, Recreation Leader, Camp Director, Disaster Counseling, etc.
Pursue: *Science + Sales*	Medical Equipment Sales, Pharmaceutical Sales, Biotech Sales, HMO Group Sales, etc.

Figure 3.7 Worksheet for Brainstorming Career Possibilities from Basic Interest and Skill Scale Combinations Labeled "Pursue"

job, he or she is at high risk for career burnout![2] Are the skills useful to your client in his or her current pursuits or future plans, even if they are not as interesting or attractive as other interest areas? Are there ways the skills could be transferred to other fields or activities that are more interesting to your client? Do these skills play a role in your client's home life or avocational pursuits even though they are not as attractive as other areas your client wishes to pursue in a career?

If many scales are listed in the Avoid quadrant, it may mean that your client has very narrow, focused interests and is neither interested nor confident in his or her skills in other activities. A large number of scales in the Avoid quadrant can also mean that your client has not yet had enough experience with a variety of activities to be able to assess whether he or she enjoys or is good at these areas. If your client feels depressed due to situational or ongoing concerns, his or her depressed mood can contribute to a large number of scores in the Avoid quadrant.

[2] Remarks on the *CISS* at the Mid-Atlantic Career Counseling Association Conference, Lancaster, Pennsylvania, Oct. 1993.

Explore what might be happening with your client. If appropriate, you may want to suggest that your client retake the survey again at a later time. Are the Scales listed in the Avoid quadrant areas that your client would indeed prefer to avoid in his or her work activities or home and personal life? Are there ways these tasks can be delegated to or handled by others? Do these activities relate to things your client must do and would continue to choose to do, that is, required parts of an otherwise well-liked job or home maintenance chores, even though he or she does not feel that these activities are attractive or reflect his or her strengths?

Step 4: Interpret the Occupational Scales

Provide an overview of the Occupational Scales Before reviewing the Occupational Scales with the client, give a brief overview of their construction and purpose. Explain that they differ from the Orientations and the Basic Scales in the following two ways:

1. These scales do not address the content of the client's interests directly; instead they address the question: "With what occupational groups does the client share similar patterns of interests and skills?" The Orientations and the Basic Scales are constructed as homogeneous content scales—the items that comprise each of the scales reflect content obviously related to the scale's label. A client's score can be high only if the client endorses positively weighted responses to such items (i.e., for Interest items: Strongly Like, Like, Slightly Like; and for Skill items: Expert, Good, Slightly Above Average). The Occupational Scales, by contrast, are constructed by empirical methods, using both negatively and positively weighted items for Interest scales. Thus, an occupation's characteristic dislikes as well as likes are included in the scale. (No negatively weighted items appear on the Occupational Skill Scales because the Survey's authors did not intend for users to select careers based upon sharing a similar *lack* of skills with workers in specific areas.) The items that comprise each scale are those that strongly differentiate a particular occupational group from a general reference sample (at least 0.3 standard deviations and usually at least 0.5 standard deviations difference between the Occupational sample and gender-balanced general reference sample). Consequently, the items in the Occupational Scales may have little or no obvious relationship to the scale's label. (For example, a negatively weighted response such as Slightly Dislike, Dislike, or Strongly Dislike to the item

"Sales Techniques" raises one's score on the Medical Researcher Occupational Interest Scale.) A client conceivably could achieve a score in the High range on an Occupational Interest Scale with many negatively weighted item responses (for example, the Commercial Artist or Computer Programmer scales have 1.5–3 times as many negatively as positively weighted items on their scales). The high score would be obtained not because the client shares interests with that occupational group, but because the client dislikes many of the same items that the occupational sample dislikes.

2. The Occupational Scales compare the client's interests to carefully selected samples of men and women in 60 different occupations, rather than the general reference sample. The basic demographics of each of these samples is described in Appendix C-Table 1 of the *Campbell Interest and Skill Survey Manual* (Campbell et al., 1992). These sample sizes range from 35 to 199 individuals with a median sample size of 75. An effort was made to include a minimum of 50 workers in each occupational group; however, a few samples with fewer than 50 respondents were included because their data looked reasonable. The occupational samples include workers who indicated on a checklist item that they enjoyed their work; those who reported that they did not enjoy their work were removed from the criterion samples. Data were also collected on the type of organization the respondents worked in, their level of education, and the percentage of time spent in various activities. These data are also reported in Appendix C, Table 1 of the *CISS Manual* (Campbell et al., 1992). Don't Forget 3.3 and Caution 3.4 highlight the usefulness of the Occupational Scales as well as their limitations.

Describe how the Scales are organized and presented   Begin interpreting the Occupational Scales by pointing out that the occupations are organized according to the Orientations. Begin with the occupations grouped under the Influencing Orientation on page 4 of the profile (see Figure 3.8). Point out that on pages 4–10 of the Profile, the scores on the Orientations and Basic Interest and Skill Scales within them are recapped on the left side of the page. The Occupational Scales that are clustered within each Orientation are presented on the right side of the page.

The Occupational Scale is listed, followed by its one- to three-letter Orientation Code within the IOHCNPA structure (e.g., ski instructor, AP). The Orientation Code is determined by identifying the mean scores of each occupational group on the Orientation scales. If the sample scored 55 or above on

DON'T FORGET 3.3

How the Occupational Scales can be useful:

- The Occupational Scales are the best predictors of what typical, day-to-day work activities the client is likely to enjoy in the fields for which scales have been constructed. Because there are thousands of other occupations beyond those 60 listed on the profile, clients should be encouraged to view these scales as indicators for other possibilities and not as the final list of suggested career options.
- The Occupational Scales:
  —confirm the fit of a client's intended career choice.
  —suggest new occupational fields for the client's consideration.
  —identify types of people the client may enjoy spending time with as co-workers, clients, or friends.

CAUTION 3.4

Limitations of the Occupational Scales

1. The Occupational Scales do not indicate what occupation the client should pursue but indicate only a similarity with people in that occupation.

2. The Occupational Scales represent only 60 occupational areas. The client should use the one- to three-letter Orientation codes assigned to the scale to access a much larger family of occupational titles worth further investigation.

an Orientation Scale, that Orientation's letter was used in the code. If the sample had more than one Orientation score above 55, up to three letters for the Orientations were used, rank-ordered with the highest first. The more similar the Orientation code for the occupational scale is to the highest Orientation scores found on page 2 of the profile, the more your client will likely enjoy working in this occupation.

Next to the Orientation Code are the standard scores for the Occupational Interest and Skill Scales. The standard scores are then plotted to graphs. The range of scores for the middle 50% of the people employed in each occupation (25th to 75th percentile) are represented graphically by the solid bar for Interests and the hollow or open bar for Skills. Your client's Interest and Skill scales are plotted with the solid and hollow diamonds, respectively, to show the

CASE STUDY C | **Influencing Orientation** | DATE SCORED: 8/04/92

Orientation Scale

	Standard Scores	30	35	40	45	50	55	60	65	70	Interest/Skill Pattern
Influencing	I 71								◆		Pursue
	S 65								◊		

Basic Interest and Skill Scales

	Standard Scores	30	35	40	45	50	55	60	65	70	Interest/Skill Pattern
Leadership	I 67								◆		Pursue
	S 62								◊		
Law/ Politics	I 71								◆		Pursue
	S 64								◊		
Public Speaking	I 66								◆		Pursue
	S 63								◊		
Sales	I 60							◆			Pursue
	S 68								◊		
Advertising/ Marketing	I 64							◆			Pursue
	S 60							◊			

Occupational Scales

	Orientation Code	Standard Scores	25	30	35	40	45	50	55	60	65	70	75	Interest/Skill Pattern
Attorney	I	I 54									◆		◊		Explore
		S 70													
Financial Planner	IO	I 66								◆		◊			Pursue
		S 73													
Hotel Manager	IO	I 60							◆			◊			Pursue
		S 68													
Manufacturer's Representative	IO	I 63							◆			◊			Pursue
		S 68													
Marketing Director	IO	I 72								◆		◊			Pursue
		S 69													
Realtor	IO	I 58							◆			◊			Pursue
		S 72													
CEO/President	IOA	I 79							◆			◊			Pursue
		S 67													
Human Resources Director	IOH	I 63							◆		◊				Pursue
		S 66													
School Superintendent	IOH	I 73							◆		◊				Pursue
		S 74													
Advertising Account Executive	IC	I 49						◆				◊			Explore
		S 72													
Media Executive	IC	I 61							◆		◊				Pursue
		S 70													
Public Relations Director	IC	I 58					◆			◊					Pursue
		S 70													
Corporate Trainer	ICH	I 75										◆			Pursue
		S 65									◊				

The Influencing Orientation covers the general area of leading and influencing others. People who score high are interested in making things happen. They want to take charge and are willing to accept responsibility for the results. Influencers are generally confident of their ability to persuade others to their viewpoints, and they enjoy the give and take of verbal jousting. They typically work in organizations, and often want to take charge of the specific activities that particularly interest them. They enjoy public speaking, and like to be visible in public. Typical high-scoring occupations include company presidents, corporate managers, and school superintendents.

You have expressed a strong interest in the area of organizational leadership -- for being in charge and accepting the responsibility for the outcome. You would probably be comfortable in situations where you were responsible for directing the work of others, setting organizational policies and motivating people around you.

Further, you have also reported a high level of confidence in your abilities in leading and motivating other people. You would probably enjoy being in charge of your own department, division, or organization, and are quite confident that you could perform well. Because both your Interest and Skill scores are high, this is an appealing area for you.

Your scores on the Influencing Basic Scales, which provide more detail about your Interests and Skills in this area, are reported above on the left-hand side of the page. Your scores on the Influencing Occupational Scales, which show how your pattern of interests and skills compares with those of people employed in Influencing occupations, are reported above on the right-hand side of the page. Each occupation has a one to three-letter code which indicates its highest Orientation score(s). The more similar the Orientation code is to your highest Orientation scores (which are reported on page 2), the more likely you will find satisfaction working in that occupation.

* Standard Scores: I (◆) = Interests; S (◊) = Skills
** Interest/Skill Pattern: Pursue = High Interests, High Skills; Develop = High Interests, Lower Skills;
  Explore = High Skills, Lower Interests; Avoid = Low Interests, Low Skills
*** Orientation Code: I=Influencing; O=Organizing; H=Helping; C=Creating; N=aNalyzing; P=Producing; A=Adventuring
  Range of middle 50% of people in the occupation: Solid Bar = Interests; Hollow Bar = Skills

Figure 3.8 Campbell Interest and Skill Survey Individual Profile

relationship of your client's scores to the gender-balanced general reference sample, with its standard score mean of 50, and to the occupational samples, whose mean scores are about 65–70 on their own Occupational Scale (about one and one-half to two standard deviations above the general reference sample mean). Since the average person scores about 50 on each Occupational scale, if your client's diamonds fall on or near the solid or hollow bars, this means that your client has interests and/or skills that are similar to those of people who enjoy and are successful in that occupation. For example, the solid bar on the Attorney Interest scale shows where the middle 50% of attorneys in the occupational sample fall on the Attorney Interest Scale. Twenty-five percent of attorneys score lower than the bar and 25% score higher than the bar.

Since occupational sample means are generally in the range of 65–70 and the occupational sample standard deviations are 10, scoring one standard deviation below the mean will generally result in a score of 55–60, which corresponds once again to the shaded portions of the graph. In other words, the shaded portions of the graphs generally represent the majority of workers in the criterion sample.[3] Interest/Skill pattern tags are again provided according to the usual criteria: Pursue (both interest and skill scores are 55 or above); Develop (interest score is 55 or above, skill score is 54 or below); Explore (interest score is 54 or below, skill score is 55 or above); and Avoid (both interest and skill scores are 45 or below). Again, exercise some caution in using the Interest/Skill pattern with the tags as a few points difference around the score of 55—especially given the variability in actual occupational sample means—may not be significant. Again, determine with the client what the "best fit" tag should be.

1. *Similar Interest Scores.* Scores of 55–59 are labeled high scores and scores of 60 and above are labeled very high. These scores indicate that the client and typical individuals from that occupation sample share common interest patterns—both likes and dislikes in the case of the Occupational Interest Scales. A high score indicates that the client may enjoy the work associated with that occupation, since individuals with interest patterns similar to the client enjoy working in that field. There-

[3] Actual occupational sample means can be obtained from Appendix C-Table 2 in the *CISS Manual* (Campbell et al., 1992). For example, the actual occupational sample mean for the Attorney Interest Scale is 67.6 and the actual occupational sample mean for the Attorney Skill Scale is 61.7.

fore, that career field may be worth the client's further exploration. However, the scale does not measure, necessarily, the degree to which the client is interested in the actual tasks of that particular occupation. In fact, an individual may score in the high range on a number of occupations that she or he would not want to pursue. For example, the occupation may require education that the client is not interested in pursuing, or the work tasks may not fit the client's values or lifestyle needs. Nevertheless, the client may enjoy working with individuals from these occupations as clients, or may enjoy spending leisure time with them, given the interests and disinterests they share.

2. *Dissimilar Interest Scores.* Scores of 41–45 are labeled low and scores of 40 or lower are labeled very low scores. These scores indicate little overlap between the client's interests and the interests of that occupational reference sample. In other words, the client and typical individuals from that occupational sample do not share similar interest patterns. Although interest and skill patterns will be labeled "Avoid" when both scores are 45 or lower, take precautions to insure that the client does not interpret dissimilar scores as a directive not to enter or pursue an occupation. Instead, dissimilar scores indicate that the client will find little in common with the typical worker in that occupation. The implications of entering that occupation could be discussed, however, such as the need to find support outside one's work environment, the advantage of bringing to a work environment a different perspective from the typical worker, or the possibility of applying one's interest to the field in a different way (e.g., a veterinarian successfully developing nutritious dog food for a dog food company might have interest patterns different from colleagues in private practice).

3. *Similar Skill Scores.* Scores of 55–59 are labeled high scores and scores of 60 and above are labeled very high. These scores indicate that the client and typical individuals from that occupational sample share common skill patterns; that is, they share common patterns of confidence in skills. A high score indicates that the client has confidence in the skills that differentiate that occupational group from people in general. Therefore, that career field may be worth the client's further exploration. However, the scale does not measure, necessarily, the degree to which the client is actually skilled in performing the required tasks of that particular occupation. In fact, an individual may score in the high range on a number of occupations that she or he would not want

to pursue. For example, the occupation may require skills that the client is confident in using but is not interested in actually performing.

4. *Dissimilar Skill Scores.* Scores of 41–45 are labeled low and scores of 40 or lower are labeled very low scores. These scores indicate little overlap between the client's skills confidence and that of the occupational reference sample. In other words, the client and typical individuals from that occupational sample do not share similar skills confidence patterns. Dissimilar scores indicate that the client will find her/himself having little in common, in terms of the skills he or she feels confident about using with the typical worker in that occupation.

Step 5: Discuss the Special Scales

Provide an overview of the Special Scales (see Figure 3.9). Explain that the scores and graphs for the Special Scales are generally similar to those described earlier for the Orientations, Basic Scales, and Occupational Scales.

CAMPBELL INTEREST AND SKILL SURVEY INDIVIDUAL PROFILE

CASE STUDY C | Special Scales | DATE SCORED: 8/04/92

Academic Focus

Standard Scores	30	Very Low 35	Low 40	45	Mid-Range 50	55	High 60	Very High 65	70
I 64									
S 63									

The Academic Focus Scales reflect your feelings toward the academic world. High scores do not necessarily lead to academic success, nor low scores to failure, but your pattern of scores reflects your degree of comfort in educational settings and can help you plan your educational strategy. High scorers are attracted to intellectual ideas, academic pursuits, and scientific research. Typical high-scoring occupations include university professors, research scientists, technical writers, and other scholars. People who score low usually see themselves as more action-oriented and practical. Business people, especially those in sales and marketing, tend to score low on the Academic Focus scales.

You have expressed both very strong interest for and a high level of confidence in your abilities in academic pursuits, indicating that you would probably be successful in pursuing higher education. You enjoy learning, reading, being in classrooms, interacting with teachers and other students, and working on scientific projects. Because of your high interest and confidence, you should strive to achieve a high level of formal education. Such success is important to you, and you will enjoy the experiences involved in seeking an advanced degree.

Extraversion

Standard Scores	30	Very Low 35	Low 40	45	Mid-Range 50	55	High 60	Very High 65	70
I 66									
S 68									

The Extraversion Scales reflect your attraction for people-oriented activities versus solitary activities. High scorers (such as guidance counselors, hotel managers, and corporate trainers) are energized by frequent social contact and enjoy working closely with others. People who score low prefer more solitary pursuits and are energized by the opportunity for private renewing time. Low-scoring occupations include scientists, skilled craftsworkers, and veterinarians.

You strongly prefer working with other people instead of working alone; you enjoy many social activities. You also feel quite confident in your interpersonal skills, such as starting conversations with others and encouraging other people to talk about themselves. You are most comfortable working in situations requiring a great deal of personal contact with others.

Figure 3.9 Special Scales for Case Study C

Note. Copyright © 1989, 1992 David P. Campbell, PhD. Published and distributed exclusively by National Computer Systems, Inc., P.O. Box 1416, Minneapolis, MN 55440. Reproduced with permission by National Computer Systems, Inc.

Academic Focus The Academic Focus Interest and Skill scales reflect your client's attraction to the academic world (i.e., his or her interest and confidence in performing well in academic settings). If your client has high Interest and Skills scores (55 or higher), he or she will likely enjoy and feel confident in pursuing higher education. If your client has low Interest and Skill Scores (45 or lower), he or she probably does not enjoy or feel confident about performing in academic settings. High scores are not equated with ability and do not guarantee success in higher education. They are simply measures of how interested and self-confident your client is in academic settings. The Academic Focus Interest scale includes positively weighted items in intellectual areas such as science, literature, and the arts, and negatively weighted items in business areas such as marketing, sales, and management. Therefore, a client who is pursuing a graduate degree, such as an MBA, and scores below average (45 or below) will often view higher education as a means to an end, not as a valued goal in and of itself. The mean scores on the Academic Focus Scale by educational level are listed in Rapid Reference 3.13. In contrast to the previous Scales, norms for the Academic Focus Scales have been set so that individuals who have earned a bachelor's degree average about 50.

Clients who score high in Academic Focus Skills confidence but mid-range (46–54) on Academic Focus Interests might be encouraged to consider how they might apply their intellectual talents to specific academic pursuits that particularly interest them. Clients with high academic interests, but lower skills confidence, might be encouraged to consider how they could get assistance from academic support services that would allow them to more confidently pursue the interests they have expressed.

Extraversion Scales The Extraversion Scales reflect your client's attraction for and confidence in working with others versus working alone. If your client has earned a high score (55 or above) on both the Interest and Skill Scales, he or she will prefer work-

≡ Rapid Reference 3.13

Mean Academic Focus Interest and Skill Scale Scores by Educational Level

Degree	Mean Scores	
	Interest	Skill
Doctoral Level	59	56
Some Graduate Work	54	53
College Degree	50	50
Some College	49	47
High School Graduate	47	43
Some High School	45	41

ing with others and will feel quite confident with his or her interpersonal skills, preferring work situations that allow for a high degree of interpersonal interaction. If your client has scored low (45 or lower) on both the Interest and Skill scales, he or she would probably prefer working alone and performing tasks where he or she can succeed through his or her own efforts. With a high Extraversion Interest Scale score and a low Extraversion Skill scale score, your client may enjoy working with others but prefer not to be in situations in which he or she is required to influence or engage others. By contrast, individuals with low interests but high skills on the Extraversion Scale may prefer to work alone, but have confidence in their social skills, which they can likely use when required. These clients will be helped by knowing, however, that they will need time alone for re-energizing themselves after working with others. The norms for the Extraversion Scales were set using the general reference sample so that equally weighted samples of females and males across a variety of occupations equaled 50.

Step 6: Summarize Results

After completing the review of the *CISS* profile, step back with the client to get an overall perspective on the results. Begin by working with the client to develop an overall Orientations Code for the profile. You might wish to use a highlighter to identify the one to three Orientations on page 2 of the Profile that the client feels are most descriptive of him or her (considering both interests and skills in combination, or interests alone). For now, you may also wish to list all of the codes that were tagged as Pursue.

Then, looking at the Basic Scales on page 3, highlight all of those Basic Scales labeled Pursue (different colors could be used to differentiate very high from high scores for the client who has many Pursue tags). Does the number of highlighted Basic Scales within each Orientation support the highest Orientations from page 2? For example, if Influencing was one of the Orientations labeled Pursue, is this Orientation supported by the Basic Scales clustered within the Orientation? In other words, are the majority of the Basic Scales (e.g., four of the five Basic Scales) clustered within Influencing also labeled Pursue? If so, this Orientation is supported. Next, assist the client in determining which Orientation Code or Codes best summarize the highlighted Basic Scales. Note its consistency with, or difference from, the summary code provided in the previous section. For now, you may also wish to list all of the codes for the Orientations that had a predominant number of Basic Scales highlighted within them.

Moving on to the Occupational Scales, highlight or count all of the Occupational Scales labeled Pursue within each Orientation. Remind your client again that these occupations are simply representative of the family of occupations found within each Orientation. Does the number of occupational scales labeled Pursue support the Orientations that were predominant from pages 2 and 3 of the profile? For example, are 11 or 12 of the 13 occupations grouped under Influencing highlighted? If so, this indicates support for the Orientation. Note, also, the Orientation codes for the highlighted occupations. As indicated in the text at the bottom of pages 4–10, the more similar the Orientation code for each occupation is to your client's highest Orientation scores, the more likely he or she will be to find satisfaction working in that occupation. If fewer of the Occupational Scales are indicated, it may mean that your client has a global or general interest in the approach of that Orientation, but is not interested in pursuing typical occupations associated with it. For example, the client who scores high on the Creative Orientation but does not score high on many of the creative occupational scales may have an original, innovative approach to his or her work or be uncomfortable with rigid organizational structures, but may not have a particular interest in or the skills needed to pursue creative occupations in the performing or visual arts. Note the pattern of highlighting to determine which Orientation codes best represent the dominant pattern of highlighting for the Occupational Scales.

Considering the overall pattern of highlighting and the orientations identified across the profile for each of the sections—Orientations, Basic Scales, and Occupational Scales—what one-, two-, or three-letter Orientation code best represents your client's interests and skills confidence? These will be the Orientations that will be most helpful in assisting your client in generating additional occupational options. What Orientations play a supporting role that your client may want to include on a secondary level in his or her career planning, or may want to incorporate into his or her personal or avocational life? Determine with your client which one- to three-letter codes best describe the overall Orientations for the profile and write the Code type on page 2.

To complete your summary, note on the Special Scales clear preferences that confirm the client's Orientation code (e.g., high Extraversion Scales along with a high interest in the Helping Orientation) and explore how apparently inconsistent interests may fit together for the client (e.g., how an individual's pursuit of a graduate business degree may be important for the career he or she wishes to pursue, such as Hospital or Health Care Administration, but the Academic Focus scale may be only mid-range because it is positively weighted toward intellectual areas in science, literature, and the arts and negatively weighted toward business).

Finally, summarize the profile even further by drawing attention to two or three points that appear to be most important. The *CISS* profile includes such a large number of scales and such a variety of information about the client's interest and skill patterns that you may need to help the client focus upon those few pieces of information that will be most useful. Here your clinical judgment and the client's goals will need to guide your choice. For some individuals, for example, you may want to highlight the summary Orientations code to direct occupational information gathering. For others you may want to draw attention to important Basic Interest and Skill Scales that represent areas not finding expression in the client's current job or lifestyle. Alternatively, ask the client to summarize two or three points that appear most important to remember from this array of information. This strategy also can help you address lingering misconceptions, such as a belief that the Occupational Scale with the highest score is the field to pursue.

Step 7: Encourage Exploration beyond the Profile

Conclude the interpretation by reminding the client to read the descriptive information provided in the text of the *CISS* profile. Although the client's next steps will vary depending upon her or his specific career planning needs and goals, many clients will be interested in exploring career options that were generated from the *CISS*.

You may wish to guide the client in developing a finalized list of his or her top five occupations for further exploration. These can be developed from various lists you can assist your client in compiling. For example, you might suggest that your client list all the occupations tagged as Pursue on the profile. To access other possible career options not listed on the profile, the client can consider additional related occupations listed under the appropriate Orientations in the *CISS Career Planner* produced by National Computer Systems. For example, if your client has an Orientations code of HCA, he or she could look at those Related Occupations listed under the Helping, Creating, and Adventuring lists in the Career Planner.

Your client could also list ideas that were generated by brainstorming different combinations of Basic Interest and Skill Scales developed during the activity with the Quadrant Worksheet, Figure 3.7. Finally, your client could access additional occupations by converting the Orientations code to its corresponding Holland code, see Rapid Reference 3.4, and referring to sources such as the *Dictionary of Holland Occupational Codes* or *Occupations Finder* for further ideas. From these lists, guide your client in identifying the five occupations that are most appealing to him or her. These are the possibilities that would then be further assessed in light of other aspects of the career planning process, such as an assessment of your client's priorities, needs, values, educational goals, life stage, and so forth.

Working adults may request help in translating the jobs identified through this process to actual careers in their organizations. You can assist your client in assessing these relationships by having your client first list the top five occupations generated through this process and then review descriptions of the listed occupations in resources such as the *Dictionary of Occupational Titles* or web-based sources such as the *O*NET* (1998). You can have your client list the appealing aspects of the description (leaving out those activities that are not attractive to the client). Then, looking at the core activities of interest, you can compare these to job posting announcements or generic job descriptions that may be available through the organization's web site or employment office. Many organizations have their jobs listed according to job families and you can assist your client in understanding how the Orientations or Holland typologies relate to that organization's system.

Provide your client with some further resources for researching occupational or educational areas suggested by the *CISS*. Library research using the *Occupational Outlook Handbook,* or Internet-based research using the *O*NET* (1998), for example, can be used to explore occupations related to those listed on the *CISS,* and to gather career information about specific career fields, such as day-to-day activities, work environments, salary ranges, or employment prospects for particular career fields.

APPLICATIONS AND STRENGTHS AND WEAKNESSES OF THE *CISS*

The *CISS* was designed specifically for use with individuals who are college bound or are considering careers that require college degrees. The *Survey* is a versatile tool; it can be used with both individuals and groups for a variety of career planning and development tasks. The information presented on the *CISS* profile can be invaluable in helping individuals narrow the range of career options they are willing to explore, or it can help them to discover new occupational areas and roles. Like the *Strong,* the *CISS* was designed as a tool for individual counseling as well as for use in educational institutions, human resource departments, and corporate training or development programs.

The most common application for the *CISS* is in helping people increase self-awareness for career planning. The applications for organizational and educational settings described for the *Strong* apply equally well to the *CISS*. In addition, the authors of the *CISS* encourage users to apply the *Survey* creatively to liven up conferences or retreats, or to improve communication within personal

≡Rapid Reference 3.14

Key Strengths of the *CISS*

- Its psychometric and theoretical foundations are solid.
- Inclusion of scales measuring self-reported skills distinguish the *CISS* from other popular career inventories.
- Well-designed and organized profile and appealing graphics, provides sufficient information to allow an individual to interpret complex information without the aid of a counselor.
- Research supports both its validity and reliability.
- The well-conceived manual lists items comprising various scales, fully explains the construction of the *Survey,* and provides detailed interpretive guidance.
- The six-point response format is user friendly and captures the strength of response better than the three-point format used in many other instruments.
- The comparisons of interest and skill scores for every scale help users prioritize specific areas to Pursue, Explore, Develop, or Avoid.
- The use of unisex scales, instead of separate scales for women and men, simplifies interpretation and helps to avoid unnecessary discussions of gender differences.
- The definitions and labels of the seven Orientations are easier for the user to grasp than are the terms used for Holland's Themes.

and family relationships. For example, during a retreat, all participants can complete the *CISS* and share results on the Basic Scales through small group exercises. This can lead to an appreciation of each other's interests and skills, or to the discovery of common interest areas. Similarly, *Survey* results can be shared between partners or among family members to improve communication, increase understanding, and heighten appreciation of one another. For more detailed suggestions, see Campbell, 1996. Rapid References 3.14 reviews key strengths of the *CISS,* and Rapid References 3.15, key limitations.

≡Rapid Reference 3.15

Key Limitations of the *CISS*

- Important questions still remain about its psychometric properties; it is relatively new compared to many other career interest measures and has not yet accrued a substantial body of research.
- The label "skill" instead of "confidence" may mislead some users, and requires explanation; the relationship between self-reported and actual skills needs further exploration.
- The general reference sample is limited in composition: data were collected by mail, and response percentages are not reported; the group includes almost twice as many men as women; and ethnic and racial group representation is not reported.
- The occupations of the Occupational Scales typically require education beyond high school. Individuals without a college degree or not planning to attend college or pursue other training will find the Occupational Scales of limited value.
- The unisex scales need further examination to evaluate whether important, occupationally relevant gender differences are ignored.
- Further investigation is needed to clarify and confirm the relationships between the seven Orientations and Holland Types.
- Classifying the patterns of scores into four quadrants can be misleading, since different classifications can result from scores that, for practical purposes, are the same.
- The interpretive label "Avoid" may be misleading and overly directive, particularly for individuals with low levels of self-confidence and little work experience.
- The sample sizes for the Occupational Scales are small in some cases (e.g., Athletic Coach, N = 35).

TEST YOURSELF

1. **The *CISS* differs from the *Strong* by:**
   (a) incorporating self-assessed skills
   (b) offering a six-point response format
   (c) combining male and female norms into one reference group
   (d) all of the above

2. **Which of the following Orientations most closely resembles Holland's Realistic type?**
   (a) Producing
   (b) Influencing
   (c) Analyzing
   (d) Organizing

3. **An individual can obtain a scored *CISS* profile directly from the publisher without having to see a counselor for an interpretation.** True or False?

4. **The Occupational Scales of the *CISS* differ from the Basic Scales in that the Occupational Scales:**
   (a) are heterogeneous in content; each scale includes items covering a range of topics
   (b) use only negatively weighted items
   (c) are shorter in length
   (d) all of the above

5. **The Academic Focus Scales were designed primarily to:**
   (a) be an indirect measure of intelligence
   (b) predict an individual's college grade point average
   (c) measure a respondent's interest and confidence in doing well in formal academic pursuits
   (d) help college students choose an academic major

6. **A profile's validity can be assessed by reviewing:**
   (a) the Response Percentage Checks
   (b) the Inconsistency Checks
   (c) the Omitted Items Checks
   (d) all of the above

7. Which Basic Scale covers interest in speaking foreign languages?

(a) International Activities

(b) Law/Politics

(c) Leadership

(d) None of the above

8. A Pursue tag on an Occupational Scale indicates the individual

(a) has interests, but not skills, similar to people in that occupation

(b) has both interests and skills scores similar to people in that occupation

(c) has skills, but not interests, similar to people in that occupation

(d) none of the above

9. When interpreting the *CISS*, it is important to remind the client that the *CISS* measures a full range of life interests and skills, not just career-related interests or skills. True or False?

10. The Adventuring Interest Orientation on the *CISS* measures interests similar to those measured by the *Strong's* Risk Taking/Adventure Scale. True or False?

11. A score of 60 on a Basic Scale is similar to a percentile score of:

(a) 60%

(b) 34%

(c) 98%

(d) 84%

12. If a person has many scales in the Avoid quadrant, it may mean

(a) the person is feeling depressed

(b) the person has narrow, focused interests and skills

(c) The person has not endorsed many interest items as Like or Strongly Like.

(d) all of the above

Answers: 1. d; 2. a; 3. True; 4. a; 5. c; 6. d; 7. a; 8. b; 9. True; 10. True; 11. d; 12. d

Four

SELF-DIRECTED SEARCH

The *Self-Directed Search* (*SDS*) (Holland, 1994) is a simple to use, self-administered, self-scored, and self-interpreted interest inventory. It was one of the first inventories developed to assist individuals without the intervention of a counselor. John Holland published the first edition of the *SDS* in 1970. It was revised in 1977, 1985, and most recently in 1994. The publisher of the *SDS*, Psychological Assessment Resources (PAR), claims that it is the most widely used career interest inventory in the world, completed by more than 22 million persons worldwide over the past 30 years. It has been translated into over 25 languages, and is supported by over 500 research studies. A sample profile for the *SDS* is displayed in Figure 5.3 in Chapter 5.

The instrument consists of an Occupational Daydreams section (up to eight self-identified occupations can be listed) and four sets of scales: Activities (6 scales of 11 items each), Competencies (6 scales of 11 items each), Occupations (6 scales of 14 items each), and Self-Estimates (2 sets of 6 ratings). The paper-and-pencil version requires the user to calculate a three-letter Summary Code using scores from all of the scales except the Occupational Daydreams section. It is recommended that users compare the obtained Summary Code with a code derived from the Occupational Daydreams section, then search for occupational or educational options listed in a variety of support materials. Software and Internet-based administration and scoring options also are available, eliminating the need for the user to calculate scores or search through support materials. Rapid Reference 4.1 provides a brief overview of the *SDS*.

≣Rapid Reference 4.1

Self-Directed Search (*SDS*)—Form R (Regular): 4th Edition

Author: John L. Holland

Publisher: Psychological Assessment Resources, Inc.
P.O. Box 998
Odessa, FL 33556

Copyright Dates: 1970, 1977, 1985, 1994

Age Range: High school students, college students, and adults.

Description: A self-administered, self-scored, and self-interpreted interest inventory designed to assist individuals in finding occupations that suit their interests and abilities.

Profile Summary: The 228-item Assessment Booklet includes four sets of scales (Activities, Competencies, Occupations, and Self-Estimates), and an Occupational Daydream section that measures Holland's six types: Realistic, Investigative, Artistic, Social, Enterprising, and Conventional. A three-letter Holland code is calculated using raw scores, and users are guided toward occupations and educational options with matching codes.

Administration Time: 30–50 minutes

Other Forms:

—Form E for adults and older adolescents with 4th to 6th grade reading levels

—Audiotape Form E for individuals with limited reading skills

—Form CP for adults in organizational settings with occupations requiring upper levels of responsibility and education

—Career Explorer is a form designed for middle-school students

—Interpretive and Professional Reports

—Spanish, English Canadian, and French Canadian Editions

—Software System administration, scoring, and reporting

—Internet-delivered option (www.self-directed-search.com)

Support Materials:

Technical Manual, Professional User's Guide, You and Your Career (8-page booklet), *The Occupations Finder, The Leisure Activities Finder, The Educational Opportunities Finder, Dictionary of Holland Occupational Codes, Position Classification Inventory*

Qualifications: The *SDS* is designed to be self-interpretive; professional qualifications are not necessary for administration or interpretation.

THEORETICAL AND RESEARCH FOUNDATIONS

The Assessment Booklet and the array of classification booklets that form the *SDS* have their roots in Holland's early work in developing the *Vocational Preference Inventory* (Holland, 1985). Holland created the *VPI* as a brief measure of personality based on responses to occupational titles. The *VPI* was revised eight times between 1953 and 1985 and eventually included 160 occupations representing Holland's six personality types. Research with the *VPI* through the 1950s and 1960s led to the refinement of Holland's theory of six types, and to the discovery of their hexagonal structure. In the 1970s Holland extended his research by designing the *SDS*. His goal with the *SDS* was to design an interest tool that would be easy for counselors to use.

Holland designed the *SDS* using homogeneous (theoretically derived) scale construction techniques to measure his personality types and environmental models. Consequently, an understanding of Holland's theory is necessary to understand and use the *SDS*. Rapid Reference 4.2 lists the major assumptions that comprise his theory and Rapid Reference 4.3 provides descriptions of his

≡*Rapid Reference 4.2*

Major Assumptions of Holland's Theory

1. People can be categorized according to the following six personality types: Realistic (R), Investigative (I), Artistic (A), Social (S), Enterprising (E), or Conventional (C).
2. Environments can be categorized according to the same six types.
3. People search for environments that allow them to express their skills, abilities, attitudes, and values and take on agreeable problems and roles.
4. A person's behavior is determined by an interaction between the characteristics of personality and environment.
5. A hexagonal model can estimate the degree of *congruence*, or agreement, between a person and an environment.
6. The typology works more efficiently with people who have a strong *vocational identity*, that is, clarity and stability of goals and self-perceptions.

Note. Adapted and reproduced by special permission of the Publisher, Psychological Assessment Resources, Inc., from *Making Vocational Choices*, Third Edition. Copyright 1973, 1985, 1992, 1997 by Psychological Assessment Resources, Inc. All rights reserved.

≡ Rapid Reference 4.3

Descriptions of the Six Holland Personality Types (RIASEC)

The **Realistic (R)** type likes realistic jobs such as automobile mechanic, aircraft controller, surveyor, farmer, and electrician. Has mechanical abilities, but may lack social skill. Is described as:

Asocial	Genuine	Materialistic	Persistent	Thrifty
Conforming	Hardheaded	Natural	Practical	Uninsightful
Frank	Inflexible	Normal	Self-effacing	Uninvolved

The **Investigative (I)** type likes investigative jobs such as biologist, chemist, physicist, anthropologist, geologist, and medical technologist. Has mathematical and scientific ability but often lacks leadership ability. Is described as:

Analytical	Complex	Intellectual	Precise	Retiring
Cautious	Curious	Introspective	Rational	Unassuming
Critical	Independent	Pessimistic	Reserved	Unpopular

The **Artistic (A)** type likes artistic jobs such as composer, musician, stage director, writer, interior decorator, and actor/actress. Has artistic abilities—writing, musical, or artistic—but often lacks clerical skills. Is described as:

Complicated	Expressive	Impractical	Introspective	Open
Disorderly	Idealistic	Impulsive	Intuitive	Original
Emotional	Imaginative	Independent	Nonconforming	Sensitive

(continued)

The **Social (S)** type likes social jobs such as teacher; religious worker; counselor; clinical psychologist; psychiatric caseworker; and speech therapist. Has social skills and talents, but often lacks mechanical and scientific ability. Is described as:

Ascendant	Friendly	Idealistic	Persuasive	Tactful
Cooperative	Generous	Kind	Responsible	Understanding
Empathic	Helpful	Patient	Sociable	Warm

The **Enterprising (E)** type likes enterprising jobs such as salesperson, manager; business executive, television producer; sports promoter; and buyer. Has leadership and speaking abilities but often lacks scientific ability. Is described as:

Acquisitive	Excitement-seeking	Flirtatious	Optimistic	Sociable
Adventurous	Exhibitionistic	Optimistic	Self-confident	Talkative
Agreeable	Extroverted	Self-confident		

The **Conventional (C)** type likes conventional jobs such as bookkeeper; stenographer; financial analyst, banker; cost estimator; and tax expert. Has clerical and arithmetic ability, but often lacks artistic abilities. Is described as:

Careful	Defensive	Inhibited	Orderly	Prudish
Conforming	Efficient	Methodical	Persistent	Thrifty
Conscientious	Inflexible	Obedient	Practical	Unimaginative

Note. Adapted and reproduced by special permission of the Publisher; Psychological Assessment Resources, Inc., Odessa, FL 33556, from the *Self-Directed Search Professional User's Guide* by John L Holland, PhD. Copyright 1985, 1987, 1994 by PAR, Inc. Further reproduction is prohibited without permission from PAR, Inc.

six types. A more detailed explanation of his theory is provided in the book, *Making Vocational Choices: A Theory of Vocational Personalities and Work Environments* (Holland, 1997).

The interrelationships among the six types can be visually summarized by a hexagonal model in which distances between types are inversely proportional to the size of the correlations between them. (See Figure 4.1). In other words, those types adjacent to each other on the hexagon share the most characteristics in common, and those farthest apart share the least in common. The hexagon is an ideal approximation; actual correlational data show a misshapen, six-sided polygon. However, a substantial number of studies across diverse populations confirm the RIASEC ordering of the types (Rounds & Day, 1998; Tracey & Rounds, 1993; Fouad & Dancer, 1992). Both the Assessment Booklet and the classification booklets are organized according to the hexagonal model to aid in the interpretation of the profile, and to support the search for occupations that are psychologically similar to one another.

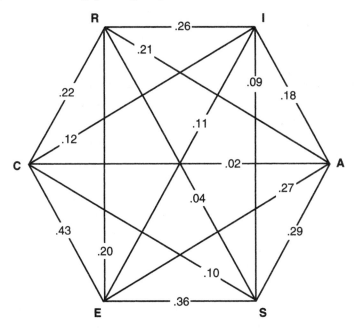

Figure 4.1 Holland's Hexagonal Model

Note. Reproduced by special permission of the Publisher, from the *Self-Directed Search Technical Manual* by John L. Holland, PhD. Copyright 1985, 1987, 1994 by Psychological Assessment Resources, Inc. Further reproduction is prohibited without permission of PAR, Inc.

In addition to the six types, Holland's theory emphasizes the importance of the following three secondary constructs: congruence, consistency, and differentiation. These three constructs in combination with the six types comprise the major elements of Holland's theory and permit considerable complexity for understanding an individual's career or occupational situation.

Congruence is the most widely supported and most important of the three constructs. Congruence refers to the degree of fit between any two Holland codes, such as an individual's Summary Code and the code of the occupation or environment being considered. An example of a high congruence situation is one where the individual's code and the environment's code clearly match, such as an individual coded AIS working in an occupation coded AIS. A low congruence situation is one where the individual's code and the environment's code have little or no match, such as an individual coded AIS working in an occupation coded CER. Between these two extremes lie varying degrees of congruence.

Consistency refers typically to the degree of similarity between the types listed in a three-letter Holland code. Those types that appear adjacent to one another on the hexagon share more in common with each other than do letters that appear farther apart. Types that are opposite one another on the hexagon (e.g., A and C), have the least similarity with one another; instead, their characteristics tend to be opposite of each other. For example, R is highly consistent with I and C, which are adjacent to R on the hexagon. R is less, or moderately, consistent with A and E, which are separated by one type along the perimeter of the hexagon; and R has low consistency with S, which lies opposite on the hexagon.

Differentiation refers to the degree to which a person or environment can be defined clearly by a single type. A person or environment with high differentiation strongly resembles one of the six types and shows little similarity to the other five types. A person or environment with low differentiation resembles all six types in relatively equal amounts.

These three constructs in combination with the six types and six environments comprise the major elements of Holland theory. Using them together permits considerable complexity for understanding an individual's career or occupational situation. However, research support for the constructs of consistency and differentiation has been mixed, and Holland has emphasized reliance on the more empirically supported construct of congruence instead (Holland, 1996a; Holland, 1997).

In his most recent formulations (Holland, Johnston, & Asama, 1993), Holland clarified an additional and important aspect to his theory, the construct of *Vocational Identity*. Vocational Identity refers to the clarity and stability of a person's goals and self-perceptions. Holland also developed a separate inventory, *My Vocational Situation* (*MVS*, Holland, Daiger, & Power, 1980), to measure this indicator, and the *SDS* computer-scored version includes an administration of the *MVS* that results in a vocational identity score. High Vocational Identity indicates relatively untroubled and confident career decision making, even in the context of ambiguous work environments. Low Vocational Identity can indicate unstable interests and difficulty in making career decisions. The higher a person's Vocational Identity, the more powerfully predictive the *SDS* and Holland's typology tend to be (Reardon & Lenz, 1998).

Earlier SDS Editions

The original 1970 edition of the *SDS* demonstrated moderate to good reliability and validity. Internal consistency coefficients ranged from .53 to .88, and test-retest reliabilities ranged from .31 to .87 for periods ranging from three weeks to 10 months. Summary Codes and scales showed greater stability with older respondents. Studies on the 1970 edition also indicated moderately strong predictive validity. Hit rates in predicting eventual college major or career choices, for example, generally were higher than chance.

The 1977 edition of the *SDS* was very similar to the first edition. Sixteen items were replaced and several other items were revised. The scoring procedure was also revised and simplified. The 1977 edition showed similar reliability and validity to the 1971 edition.

The 1985 edition introduced significant changes to the *SDS* to make it more useful to the respondent. Item content was improved and reliability increased slightly (Daniels, 1989). Directions were revised to increase ease and accuracy in completion of the Assessment Booklet.

1994 Edition—Form R (Regular)

The 1994 edition included a number of changes. Items were refined, internal consistency was increased, and norms were updated to reflect the 1990s. The *Occupations Finder* also was updated to reflect changing occupational titles and to simplify use. Validity remained at the same level as previous editions. The largest difference found among all the editions was the mean Realistic Summary Score for males, rising from 22.8 in 1977 to 26.2 in 1994. Although mean Realistic Summary Scores for females also increased (from 12.89 to 14.42), the resulting gender difference remained at one standard deviation, despite efforts in each successive revision to find Realistic items to which females would respond.

Item Selection

The content validity of the *SDS* is obvious: the content of items comprising each scale relate clearly to that scale. For example, items in an Artistic Scale are obviously artistic in nature (e.g., "Sketch, draw or paint," "Write novels or plays," and "Sculptor/Sculptress"). To select items for the 1994 edition, items from the 1985 edition along with 70 new items were administered to a sample of 701 individuals (421 high school students, 160 college students, 99 adults, and 21 unclassifiable others). Items retained for the 1994 edition met the following three criteria:

1. Showed high correlations with their summary scale, and low correlations with other summary scales.
2. Showed acceptable total score correlations for both males and females.
3. Were endorsed by at least 5% of both male and female samples.

The resulting 228 items were administered to a sample of 2,602 students and working adults (1,600 female and 1,002 male) ranging in age from 17-65. The sample population included the following ethnic backgrounds: 75% White, 8% African-American, 7% Hispanic, 4% Asian American, 1% Native American, and 5% "Other." Overall, no substantial differences were found across racial groups. Gender differences were found, however, for Realistic items in particular.

Reliability

Reliability studies with the 1994 Edition indicate both strong internal consistency and test-retest reliability (Holland et al., 1997). Rapid Reference 4.4 summarizes the average internal consistency coefficients for the Activities, Competencies, Occupations, and Summary Scales. KR-20 coefficients are strong and range from .72 to .92. The Summary Scales coefficients are particularly high, ranging from .90 to .94. In addition, the *Technical Manual* (Holland

≡Rapid Reference 4.4

Average Internal Consistency Coefficients (KR-20)

Scale	High School Students (females) n = 475	(males) n = 344	College Students (females) n = 716	(males) n = 399	Adults (females) n = 405	(males) n = 251
Activities	.77–.85	.80–.85	.76–.85	.80–.88	.80–.89	.78–.89
Competencies	.73–.82	.77–.85	.72–.83	.74–.84	.75–.86	.74–.87
Occupations	.83–.90	.86–.92	.82–.92	.84–.90	.82–.91	.86–.91
Summary	.91–.92	.91–.93	.90–.93	.90–.92	.91–.92	.91–.94

Note. Reproduced by special permission of the Publisher, from the *Self-Directed Search Technical Manual* by John L. Holland, PhD. Copyright 1985, 1987, 1994 by Psychological Assessment Resources, Inc. Further reproduction is prohibited without permission of PAR, Inc.

et al., 1997) reports substantial stability of Summary scores over intervals of 4 to 12 weeks; test-retest correlations ranged from .76 to .89.

Validity

Validity studies reported in the *Technical Manual* (Holland et al., 1997) for the 1994 Edition indicate support for the instrument's construct, concurrent, and predictive validity. The authors report Summary Scale intercorrelations to be similar across high school, college, and adult samples of both genders. These data indicate that *SDS* Summary Scales appear to measure Holland's types according to the hexagonal model.

The *Technical Manual* (Holland et al., 1997) also provides additional correlational data for the 24 scales and 12 self-estimates using the 1985 edition. These show clear and strong support for the construct validity of the *SDS*. Only one of the 1,260 correlations failed to correlate according to Holland's theoretical expectations. Interestingly, these data also indicate strong correlations between self-estimates of interests and self-estimates of competencies. This supports the claim that individuals generally enjoy activities in which they are competent.

Table 4.1 Personality Types and Salient Characteristics

	Realistic	Investigative	Artistic	Social	Enterprising	Conventional
Traits	Hardheaded Unassuming Practical Dogmatic Natural Uninsightful	Analytical Intellectual Curious Scholarly Open Broad Interests	Open Nonconforming Imaginative Intuitive Sensitive Creative	Agreeable Friendly Understanding Sociable Persuasive Extroverted	Extroverted Dominant Adventurous Enthusiastic Power-seeking Energetic	Conforming Conservative Unimaginative Inhibited Practical-minded Methodical
Life goals	Inventing apparatus or equipment Becoming outstanding athlete	Inventing valuable product Theoretical contribution to science	Becoming famous in performing arts Publishing stories Original painting Musical composition	Helping others Making sacrifices for others Competent teacher or therapist	Being community leader Expert in finance and commerce Being well liked and well dressed	Expert in finance and commerce Producing a lot of work
Values	Freedom Intellectual Ambitious Self-controlled Docility	Intellectual Logical Ambitious Wisdom	Equality Imaginative Courageous World of beauty	Equality Self-respect Helpful Forgiving	Freedom Ambitious (–) Forgiving (–) Helpful	(–) Imaginative (–) Forgiving

Table 4.1 (continued)

	Realistic	Investigative	Artistic	Social	Enterprising	Conventional
Identifications						
	Thomas Edison	Madame Curie	T. S. Eliot	Jane Addams	Henry Ford	Bernard Baruch
	Admiral Byrd	Charles Darwin	Pablo Picasso	Albert Schweitzer	Andrew Carnegie	John D. Rockefeller
Aptitudes and competencies						
	Technical	Scientific	Arts	Social and educational	Leadership and sales	Business and clerical
				Leadership and sales	Social and educational	
				Interpersonal	Business and clerical	
					Interpersonal	
Self-ratings						
	Mechanical ability	Math ability	Artistic ability	—	—	Clerical ability
		Research ability				
Most competent in						
	Mechanics	Science	Arts	Human relations	Leadership	Business

Note. This incomplete summary was derived from Tables 35–48 in the *SDS* Technical Manual (1994).

Predictive validity has also been demonstrated by examining "hit rates," or prediction of the Holland code of future work environments from Summary Codes measured at a prior time. Hit rates of future vocational choices for high school students, college students, and adults averaged 54.7% of the 1994 edition. (The hit rate was determined by assessing the agreement between the high point code of high school Summary Codes and one-letter occupational code of future work environments.) This rate is relatively high given that most interest inventories have hit rates ranging from 40% to 55% (Holland & Rayman, 1986). This rate is also consistent with similar studies with earlier editions of the *SDS* that indicated higher hit rates for older and more educated populations.

Both the *Technical Manual* (Holland et al., 1997) and the *Professional User's Guide* (Holland, Powell, & Fritzsche, 1997) summarize the extensive research that has investigated the meaning of the *SDS* Scales. A large number of studies have examined the relationship between the *SDS* and *VPI* for a wide range of personality, value, aptitude, competency, and perceptual variables (Gottfredson, Jones, & Holland, 1993; Jin, 1991; Spokane, 1985; Costa, McCrae, & Holland, 1984). These data indicate a range of weak to strong support for the theoretical formulations of each scale (see Table 4.1).

Effects of Completing the SDS

Holland designed the *SDS* not only to be a tool with solid psychometric properties, but also to be a career intervention. Consequently, its effectiveness has been examined from the perspective of its effect upon respondents. The *Technical Manual* (Holland et al., 1997) summarizes the results of 22 experiments that assessed the influence of the *SDS* on those who completed it. The following three findings were reported as the most common:

1. An increase in the number of career options a person considered.
2. An increase in satisfaction with vocational aspiration.
3. An increase in self-understanding.

These effects were found to be independent of age, gender, race, social class, or degree of congruence, consistency, and differentiation.

Influence of Cultural and Demographic Variables

Responses to individual items, scale scores, and *SDS* codes have been shown to relate to a person's age, gender, social class, and intelligence. Individuals respond differently to the inventory as a reflection of their individual, cultural, and contextual differences. Holland interprets these differences in *SDS* scores as outcomes of "the differential treatment of males and females, Blacks and Whites, rich and poor, and so on by parents, schools and society" (Holland et al., 1997, p. 59). Most of these group differences are small, however, except for the notable gender differences on scales measuring the Realistic type.

Assessment Booklet (Form R)

The Assessment Booklet is comprised of five assessment sections: Occupational Daydreams, Activities, Competencies, Occupations, and Self-Estimates.

Occupational Daydreams

The Occupational Daydreams section has respondents list up to eight occupations they have considered or daydreamed about pursuing. Respondents are also instructed to determine a three-letter Holland code for each occupation, using the Occupations finder. This section of the inventory is the result of Holland's finding (Holland, 1968) that an individual's current and recent occupational preferences are good estimates of the career direction that a person will pursue. Evidence supporting this hypothesis is extensive (Borgen & Seling, 1978; Holland, 1992) and indicates that occupational aspirations alone can predict college majors, career plans, and current occupations. In fact, Holland (1996) asserts that the predictive power of the Occupational Daydreams section can exceed that of an interest inventory, particularly when the first two or three occupational aspirations belong to the same RIASEC type.

Activities Scales

This section provides a brief overview of the types of work or leisure activities a client likes and dislikes. The six Activities Scales (RIASEC) assess the individual's level of interest in activities related to each type. Each scale includes 11 items and provides two response options: "L" ("would like to do") or "D" ("would dislike doing, or would be indifferent to"). Some items are correlates of *VPI* and *Strong* scales found in early studies of Holland's theory; other items are taken from nonacademic achievement scales (Richards, Holland, and Lutz, 1967). These scales correlate with other scales of the *SDS* in expected directions and show moderate predictive validity over one- and three-year intervals.

Competencies Scales

The six Competencies Scales (RIASEC), comprised of 11 items each, estimate a person's confidence in competently performing a range of activities. Two response options are offered: "Y" ("can do well or competently") or "N" ("have never performed or perform poorly"). These scales were derived from previous scales developed to predict nonacademic accomplishments (Richards, Holland, and Lutz, 1967). Studies indicate these scales have moderate predictive validity and low but significant correlations with other aptitude tests (Gottfredson & Holland, 1975; Kelso, Holland, & Gottfredson, 1977). These scales can be useful in identifying skills that clients have already developed as well as those they might want to explore in the future. They may reflect an individual's interests, since people tend to develop competencies in areas in which they have interest. However, high competencies may also reflect skills that an individual has developed, but has no interest in pursuing further (e.g., "I learned that skill to please my employer, but don't want to do it any more").

Occupations Scales

The six Occupations Scales (RIASEC), each comprised of 14 items, assess an individual's interest in various kinds of work. Items include two response options, "Y" ("occupations that interest or appeal") and "N" ("occupations that you dislike or find uninteresting"). These scales contain many of the same items as the Occupational Scales of the *Vocational Preference Inventory* (Holland, 1975), since Holland wanted to insure that the *SDS* would measure his occupational types. The Occupations Scales have been shown to discriminate among people who are employed in different occupations (Lacey, 1971) and to correlate in expected directions with other interest inventories (Lee & Hedahl, 1973; Rezler, 1967).

Self-Estimates

The two sets of Self-Estimates ask respondents to rate themselves on various abilities along a scale ranging from 1 (low) to 7 (high). Respondents are instructed to rate themselves "as you really think you are when compared with other persons your own age." Each set includes six scales, one corresponding to each type (RIASEC). For example, one set measures R through a self-estimate of Mechanical Ability; the other set measures R through a self-estimate of Manual Skill. Research indicates that self-ratings have low to moderate predictive and concurrent validity (Abe & Holland, 1965; Gottfredson & Holland, 1975). This set of scales provides a rough measure of an individual's self-efficacy, or confidence, in being able to do certain tasks. Consequently, this section of the *SDS* provides an avenue for discussing past experiences and messages that have shaped an individual's self-view, and for exploring any stereotypes or other factors that may be limiting a person's goals.

Classification Booklets

The classification booklets parallel the Assessment Booklet in employing Holland summary codes to identify and describe the degree to which an environment resembles each of the six types. Three classification booklets have been developed: *The Occupations Finder* (Holland, 1996), *The Educational Opportunities Finder* (Rosen, Holmberg, & Holland, 1997), and *The Leisure Activities Finder* (Holmberg, Rosen, & Holland, 1997).

The Occupations Finder

The Occupations Finder (Holland, 1996) is the product of earlier occupational classifications originally proposed by Holland's theory and later empirically defined using *VPI* profiles. The 1996 Edition is an outgrowth of earlier editions published between 1970 and 1994. Multiple discriminant analysis was used to develop the occupational codes based on descriptions from the *Dictionary of Occupational Titles* (U.S. Department of Labor, 1991) and from ratings of experienced occupational observers. The current edition also includes important occupations from the 1990s and 21st century selected from the *Occupational Outlook Handbook* (U.S. Department of Labor, 1998–99) and other career resources (e.g., Farr, 1994).

The 1996 Edition of *The Occupations Finder* contains a listing of 1,334 occupations representing the most common occupations in the United States. They are organized according to three-letter Holland summary codes. In addition, each listing provides a nine-digit code from the *Dictionary of Occupational Titles,* along with a single digit code indicating the level of education required. The Occupations represent nearly all three-letter subgroups.

An *Alphabetical Occupations Finder* is also available in which the same 1,334 occupations are arranged in alphabetical order. Individuals are referred to the third edition of the *Dictionary of Holland Occupational Codes* (Gottfredson & Holland, 1996) for an expanded listing of 12,860 occupations organized both by three-letter codes and alphabetically.

The Educational Opportunities Finder

The Educational Opportunities Finder (Rosen et al., 1997) was designed to help individuals identify post-secondary educational programs that are consistent with their Holland Summary Code. This classification booklet is an updated edition of the former *College Majors Finder.* It contains a listing of 750 educational programs organized both alphabetically and by three-letter Holland codes. Programs of study include those found in junior and community colleges, four-year colleges and universities, and postgraduate institutions. The programs of study are derived from *Classification of Instructional Programs* (Morgan, 1990).

Holland summary codes were assigned to programs of study by a number of methods. Many were derived from the occupation that is obviously associated with the program. For these programs, the third edition of the *Dictionary of Holland Occupational Codes* and the 1994 edition of *The Occupations Finder* were used to determine most of the codes. Some programs were given codes based on other methods, however, such as the professional judgment of two out of three members on a panel of professional career counselors.

The Leisure Activities Finder

The Leisure Activities Finder (Holmberg et al., 1997) was designed to help individuals locate a range of leisure activities—hobbies, sports, and avocations— that correspond to the first two letters of their Holland Summary Code. The booklet contains over 750 activities organized both by two-letter Holland Summary Codes and alphabetically. Each activity is also identified with a group label such as "Mechanical," "Nature," or "Science" to facilitate searches for leisure activities by general topic area.

Two-letter Holland summary codes were assigned to the activities in several ways using the *Dictionary of Holland Occupational Codes* and *The Occupations Finder* as primary sources of occupational codes. Some codes were taken directly from occupations that were obviously related to the activity; some were generated by inference from similar occupations; and some were based on judgments by two out of three members of a panel of professional counselors. An independent panel of three judges with extensive experience in the Holland system then reviewed all codes. The group labels attached to activities were developed from a basic classification system proposed by Overs (1971).

You and Your Career

In addition to the Assessment Booklet and classification booklets, Holland recommends that people read the booklet *You and Your Career* (Holland, 1994) to enrich the experience of completing the *SDS*. He designed this seven-page booklet to help people learn more about their interests and career choices. It includes detailed information about Holland's typology and provides exercises to help people use their codes and scores. In addition, it offers recommendations for good decision-making.

Other Forms of the SDS

Alternative forms of the *SDS* have been developed for use with specific populations. The *Technical Manual* (Holland et al., 1997) provides data indicating strong support for their use as alternatives to Form R.

Form E

Form E (Holland, 1996c) was developed for use with individuals with limited reading skills (e.g., typically those with less than a high school education). This form includes an Assessment Booklet, a Jobs Finder, and an interpretive booklet, *You and Your Job*. Directions are written in words known by 80% of fourth graders and a number of items were removed or replaced. The scoring procedures also are simplified, and two-letter, instead of three-letter, summary codes are used.

Form CP

Form CP (Holland, 1990) was developed for use in business and organizational settings for adults in professional careers. The Daydreams and Self-Estimates sections were removed, and 88 items were replaced with items oriented to adult workers. This form includes the Assessment Booklet, the *Career Options Finder,* and the interpretive booklet, *Exploring Career Options.*

The Career Explorer

The Career Explorer was developed for use with middle school or junior high school students. Thirty items were replaced or reworded to make them more appropriate for younger people. Two-letter Summary Codes are used. This version includes the Self-Assessment Booklet, the Careers Booklet, and the interpretive booklet, *Exploring Your Future with the* SDS.

SDS *Software*

Many *SDS* versions are available to counselors through the publisher in software format for administration and scoring. This format provides a narrative interpretive report based on the individual's scores. Individuals can also access the *SDS* Form R directly via the Internet (www.self-directed-search.com) to view a copy of an interpretive report or to complete the instrument online.

HOW TO ADMINISTER AND SCORE

The *SDS* can be self-administered through agencies on a drop-in basis, or it can be given through a scheduled appointment. A disadvantage to scheduling the administration is the loss of immediacy. Clients lose the opportunity to receive an immediate intervention. An individual needs to be an interested and active participant for useful completion of the *SDS*. Also, the counselor or organization providing the *SDS* needs to clearly articulate its purpose and how it will be used. Reardon and Lenz (1998) recommend that each setting establish policies and procedures governing the administration and use of the *SDS*. For example, it is important to clarify what materials and information to provide the client and to identify who will interpret the instrument. Completing the instrument in a private setting is recommended as conducive to greater involvement, fewer scoring errors, and more beneficial outcomes. Monitors are recommended for group administrations.

Respondents can hand score their own *SDS* profile by following printed directions in the Assessment Booklet. Software and Internet-based administrations provide automated scoring. Adding the number of items endorsed across all sections results in a summary score for each of the RIASEC codes. For example, an R score is the number of all R items endorsed as "Like" or "Yes" for the Activities, Competencies, and Occupations sections. Hand scoring needs to be checked by respondents and by counselors since scoring errors may occur.

The *Professional User's Guide* (Holland et al., 1997) provides counselors with strategies for calculating indexes of congruence, consistency, differentiation, and aspiration. The *Technical Manual* (Holland et al., 1994) also provides detailed normative data for evaluating each index. However, for most users, the definitions below will suffice for calculating the level of each.

Congruence

Table 4.2 outlines one popular method for calculating congruence, or compatibility, between an individual's three-letter *SDS* Summary Code and three-letter occupational choice. This method can be used to calculate the level of congruence between a person and an environment, or between any two sets of Holland codes. A simpler method to calculate congruence uses only the first letter of each code. Highest congruence occurs when the first letter of the Summary Code matches the first letter of the environment's code (e.g., R and R). The next highest level is when the two letters are not the same, but occur adjacent to one another on the hexagon (e.g., R and I). A lower level of congruence occurs when the first letters are separated along the perimeter of the

Table 4.2 Zener-Schnuelle Index of Agreement between Current Occupational Choice and SDS Summary Code

Degree of agreement		Current choice		Summary Code
6	The two codes are exactly alike.	RIE	and	RIE
5	The first two letters of both codes are the same and in the same order.	RIA	and	RIS
4	The three letters of each code are the same, but they are in a different order.	REI	and	IER
		ERI	and	REI
		RIE	and	EIR
3	The first letter in each code is the same.	SIA	and	SER
2	The first two letters of one code match any two letters in the other.	RIC	and	IER
		CES	and	SCR
		ASE	and	ESI
1	The first letter of either code matches any letter in the other code.	SEA	and	AIR
0	The first letter of each code is not included in the other code.	IRE	and	SEA

Note: From "Effects of the Self-Directed Search on High School Students" by T. B. Zener and L. Schnuelle, 1976, *Journal of Counseling Psychology, 23,* pp. 353–359. Adapted by permission.

hexagon by one letter (e.g., R and A). The lowest congruence between codes occurs when the first letters are opposite each other on the hexagon (e.g., R and S).

Consistency

The degree of consistency or similarity between the first and second letters of a Summary Code is determined by measuring their position along Holland's hexagon. Consistency is coded according to a three-point scale. If these two letters are adjacent on the hexagon, consistency level is scored 3 (high). If they are neither adjacent nor opposite, the consistency level is scored 2 (moderate). If they are opposite each other on the hexagon, the consistency level is 1 (low). High consistency has been linked to greater stability in work history and career choice (Holland, 1997).

Differentiation

Differentiation refers to the degree of definition or distinctiveness of a profile. A client who has strong interests in one of the six types but little interest in the other five is highly differentiated. Conversely, someone interested in all six types in equal amounts is undifferentiated. This construct has received less empirical support than the other indexes, and there is some debate about how best to calculate it. The simplest way to calculate a rough measure of differentiation is simply to subtract the lowest score from the highest score among the RIASEC Summary Scores. The level of differentiation can have particular clinical significance when it is particularly low. Such Profiles are called "undifferentiated" or "flat" (see Rapid Reference 4.10 for examples).

Summary Aspiration Code

An individual's expressed Daydreams can be given a Summary Aspiration Code simply by counting the number of Rs, Is, As, Ss, Es, and Cs among the three-letter codes (ignoring the position of the letters within each three-letter code). The three letters that occur most frequently become the summary code. A weighted procedure is also described in the *Professional User's Guide* (Holland et al., 1997) for more precise ranking.

HOW TO INTERPRET

A primary advantage of the *SDS* is that it does not routinely require counselor interpretation. As a self-administered, self-scored, and self-interpreted instrument it eliminates the need for proctoring, mailing, scoring, or interpreting. Consequently, counseling time can be spent more efficiently addressing the unique needs of the client and providing more detailed interpretative information if necessary. *The SDS Professional User's Guide* (Holland, Powell, & Fritzsche, 1997) and the *SDS Technical Manual* (Holland, Fritzsche, & Powell, 1994) provide detailed recommendations for counselors. In addition, *The Self-Directed Search and Related Holland Career Materials* (Reardon & Lenz, 1998) provides in-depth and practical suggestions for interpreting and using the *SDS* for a range of career interventions. We draw from these particular resources in our recommendations for interpreting the *SDS*.

Holland recommends training for counselors to become proficient in using the *SDS* to help people with career development. Rapid Reference 4.5 lists 14 steps that he recommends for adequate preparation. Holland also recommends the following four counseling strategies when using the *SDS* with clients to encourage clients' independence and continued self-direction:

1. Provide as much information on career development and occupations as the person requests.
2. Provide clear and simple instructional materials about decision-making, self-assessment, job hunting, and employment outlook.
3. Encourage exploration of alternatives.
4. Act more like a consultant than a therapist.

Evaluate the Profile

Before proceeding with an interpretation, check the self-scoring for errors in addition, (unless software scoring was used) and inspect booklets for unanswered items. Next, Holland suggests evaluating several criteria to determine whether the client needs only reassurance and information, or more extensive assistance such as psychotherapy. One to three counseling sessions typically are sufficient, he suggests, if the following positive signs occur on the profile:

1. Congruence is moderate to high.
2. First (or most recent) three vocational daydreams share the same or closely related categories.

≡ Rapid Reference 4.5

Recommendations for Counselor Training in the **SDS**

1. Be trained in measurement theory, interest measurement, and occupational information.

2. Read and master information in the SDS *Professional User's Guide* and SDS *Technical Manual*.

3. Read *Making Vocational Choices: A Theory of Vocational Personalities and Work Environments* (Holland, 1997).

4. Read the article, "Using a Typology of Persons and Environments to Explain Careers: Some Extensions and Clarifications" (Holland & Gottfredson, 1976).

5. Take the SDS yourself.

6. Read and complete the *You and Your Career* booklet.

7. Review your results with a professional user of the SDS.

8. Compare your summary code with your current occupational code and calculate the levels of congruence, consistency, and differentiation for your codes.

9. Retake the SDS two or three weeks later and note differences and similarities.

10. Ask friends to complete it and answer their questions.

11. Give it to a few clients.

12. Begin with individual administrations, working gradually to large group administrations.

13. Learn to use the *Dictionary of Holland Occupational Codes*.

14. Master the sample test in the *Professional User's Guide*.

Note. Reproduced by special permission of the Publisher, from the *Self-Directed Search Technical Manual* by John L. Holland, PhD. Copyright 1985, 1987, 1994 by Psychological Assessment Resources, Inc. Further reproduction is prohibited without permission of PAR, Inc.

3. Consistency is at highest or middle level.
4. Profile shows high differentiation.

Interpret the Profile

Interpreting the *SDS* profile is relatively straightforward, particularly since there are no normative samples or standardized scores to explain. (Normative

≡Rapid Reference 4.6

Steps to a Counselor-Guided Interpretation of the *SDS*

Step 1: Provide a brief description of the *SDS* as a tool for discovering patterns of interests and competencies that many jobs demand.

Step 2: Give a brief description of Holland's types. (Refer to Rapid Reference 4.3 if needed.)

Step 3: Discuss the client's agreement or disagreement with Total Scores and Summary Code; ask client to identify which descriptions fit and which do not.

Step 4: Explain how the three-letter Summary Code can help locate suitable occupations or educational environments (e.g., summarize the explanation on page 11 of Assessment Booklet).

Step 5: Discuss any relevant interests and competencies not assessed by the *SDS*.

Step 6: If you have time, explore past experiences with interests and competencies related to Summary Code.

Step 7: Investigate the influences of family, sex role, race, and social status on client's expressed interests and competencies (e.g., how client's current situation or background helps to explain the pattern of scores and reactions to them).

Step 8: Compare Summary Code with other assessment data you have gathered about client and emphasize patterns that are confirmed by Summary Code.

Step 9: Assess level of congruence between Summary Code and client's Occupational Daydreams or job choices.

Step 10: Point out areas of high and low congruence, and discuss client's experiences and reactions to these.

Step 11: Consider the profile's level of consistency and differentiation and explore any difficulties experienced by clients with low levels of consistency or differentiation.

Step 12: Describe classification booklets and assist client with finding matching occupations or educational programs.

Step 13: Guide client in how to find additional information about occupations or educational programs. (Use relevant support materials listed among Annotated Bibliography, p. 263-269)

Note. Adapted and reproduced by special permission of the Publisher, Psychological Assessment Resources, Inc., Odessa, FL 33556, from the *Self-Directed Search Professional User's Guide* by John L. Holland, PhD. Copyright 1985, 1987, 1994 by PAR, Inc. Further reproduction is prohibited without permission from PAR, Inc.

data are available, however, in the manual and are included with the software-generated interpretive and professional reports). Although the Assessment Booklet leads clients through a basic interpretation, a counselor-directed review of the *SDS* can provide added value in a number of ways. Review the detailed recommendations presented in Chapter 2 (pp. 5–69) for using Holland's theory to interpret the General Occupational Themes of the *Strong Interest Inventory*. The same explanation can be used when introducing Holland's theory with the *SDS*. An informed interpretation of the *SDS* also makes use of his secondary constructs of congruence, consistency, and differentiation. If you are new to Holland's theory, review the relevant sections of this chapter to be sure you understand how to define and calculate each of these secondary constructs. Also refer to the example Profile provided in Chapter 5 (Figure 5.3).

Several Rapid References are provided to offer helpful tips for integrating the *SDS* into your counseling. Follow these guidelines to help your clients gain a deeper understanding of their results. Rapid Reference 4.6 provides a 13-step model for a counselor-guided interpretation of the *SDS*. Don't Forget 4.1 highlights four specific rules that Holland strongly encourages counselors to keep

---

DON'T FORGET 4.1

Holland's Four Rules of Practice

1. **Full Exploration:** Encourage clients to look beyond the occupations coded identical to their own Summary Code for full exploration of alternatives. Search for occupations corresponding to all possible orderings of the three letters.

2. **Rule of Eight:** Given measurement error, assume scores are the same unless they differ by eight points or more.

3. **Rule of Intra-Occupational Variability:** Every occupation includes a variety of people or types or subtypes. Generally only 75% of workers have Summary Codes with a first letter (high point code) that matches their occupational codes.

4. **Rule of Asymmetrical Distribution of Types and Subtypes:** SDS codes are not equally popular. High consistency codes occur much more frequently than low consistency (rare) codes (see Rapid Reference 4.10). People with rare codes may have trouble finding congruent occupations. (See Rapid Reference 4.11 for tips on interpreting rare codes).

≡Rapid Reference 4.7

Four-Category Diagnostic Scheme for using *SDS*

	Illustration	SDS Signs	Treatment
Information Deficit	Lacks information about professional occupations	Low flat profile	Provide information
Skill or Training Deficit	Failing in current job	Discrepancy between aspirations and current education or skills	Provide training or promote access to training
Personality Deficit	Lacks interpersonal skills Lacks clear sense of vocational identity Low self esteem	Low congruence with aspirations Inconsistent profile Low flat profile Aspirations lack coherence Very Low Self Ratings	Group & individual career assistance Referral for specialized help along with career assistance

Note. Adapted and reproduced by special permission of the Publisher, Psychological Assessment Resources, Inc., Odessa, FL 33556, from the *Self-Directed Search Professional User's Guide* by John L. Holland, PhD. Copyright 1985, 1987, 1994 by PAR, Inc. Further reproduction is prohibited without permission from PAR, Inc.

in mind during an interpretation. In addition, Rapid Reference 4.7 summarizes some ways of using the *SDS* to diagnose specific career-related deficits.

An Illustration

The 13-step model indicates how to go about introducing the *SDS* and how to integrate it into a career counseling model. Steps 8 through 11 specifically address interpreting *SDS* scores. For an example of how to implement these steps, see the sample *SDS* scores provided in Table 4.3.

Steps 9 and 10   After the counselor has completed Steps 1 through 8, and before guiding Allison toward educational programs or occupations (Steps 12 and 13), it is important for the counselor to evaluate the *SDS* scores closely. Following Steps 9 and 10, the counselor would evaluate the degree of similarity between Allison's Summary Code, SAE, and the codes of her Occupational Daydreams: SAE, SER, and SEA. Allison's Daydream Codes are very similar to one another. They all share S as a first letter. Such consistent codes typically imply a clear and

Table 4.3: *SDS* Profile of Allison X

Name: Allison X.   Age: 21

Total Scores

R	I	A	S	E	C
8	9	13	28	12	8

Summary Code

Highest	2nd	3rd
S	A	E

Occupational Daydreams	Code
High School Teacher	SAE
Chef	SER
Social Worker	SEA

integrated self-concept. This pattern also indicates a high likelihood that she would maintain Social-type career aspirations in the future as well. If the first letter of each of her Occupational Daydreams instead belonged to different Holland types, the counselor might question whether her self-concept was unclear or conflicted. Not only are Allison's Daydream Codes similar to one another, but they also show high congruence with her Summary Code. In fact, the Zener-Schnuelle Index shows the most recent Daydream Code and Summary Code are exactly alike (a score of 6); the other Daydreams are close behind with scores of 5. The counselor would point out to Allison these similarities and discuss her reactions. If Allison's codes instead showed low congruence, the counselor could explain the Rule of Intra-Occupational Variability (see Don't Forget 4.1) and explore the possible reasons and implications of this disagreement.

If Allison were working and expressed dissatisfaction with her position, the counselor might ask Allison to estimate the likely code type of her position, obtain a summary code from the *Dictionary of Holland Occupational Codes,* or have Allison complete the *Position Classification Inventory* (see Annotated Bibliography). The counselor could then help Allison determine the level of congruence between her Summary Code and her current job. If levels of

≡Rapid Reference 4.8

Tips for Adjusting Person and Job Fit to Increase Congruence

One or More Letters in the Client's Summary Code Do Not Match Job Code

- Restructure the job to include more of the missing activities by reassigning tasks to staff members with expressed preferences for those activities
- Enrich the job through additional projects or assignments
- Seek outlets for interests through committee involvements or special task forces
- Pursue volunteer opportunities in the department or larger organization
- Identify service opportunities outside of work, for example, through professional associations or in the community
- Investigate opportunities for part-time employment including temping, consulting, and starting your own business
- Express interests in hobbies or other avocational pursuits

One or More of the Letters in the Job's Summary Code Are Not Matched by the Client's Code

- Increase competencies and expand interests in required activities through training, further education, mentoring, tutorials, internships, shadowing, individualized learning projects, conferences, workshops, reading, etc.
- Rotate work assignments in less preferred activities among team members
- Delegate tasks to staff members with expressed preferences for those activities
- Restructure the job to include fewer of the required activities, reassigning tasks to staff members with expressed interests in those activities
- Pay temporary workers, contingent work force, students, or interns, or seek volunteers to complete the less preferred tasks

incongruence are small, refer to Rapid Reference 4.8 for suggestions for making adjustments to work and life roles that can lead to greater satisfaction. If levels of incongruence are great, assist clients in exploring the feasibility of pursuing other, more congruent career options.

Steps 11 and 12   Allison's Profile shows a high level of consistency. The first two letters of her Summary Code, SA, are adjacent on the hexagon, demonstrating a high level of consistency (a score of 3). High consistency codes typically reflect stable work histories and stable career choices. Therefore, we would expect Allison to persist with her current aspirations and need little career assistance or intervention. However, if her Summary Code were a low consistency code, such as SRE, she might need more extensive help. Low consistency codes are typically associated with less stable work histories and aspirations. The counselor could turn to Rapid Reference 4.9 for assistance.

Allison's differentiation level could then be calculated by subtracting her highest from her lowest scores. Her profile indicates a separation of 20 points between these scores [28 (S) – 8 (R or C) = 20]. Using the Rule of Eight, described in Don't Forget 4.1, her Social score significantly differs from all other scores, indicating a clearly defined type. The scores of all five other types, however, are similar to one another. Consequently, the counselor could highlight the primary importance of the Social type and the relatively lower importance of her second and third scores. If Allison's scores instead had shown little differentiation (reflecting equal interests across all six types), the counselor could explore the difficulties she may be having in finding a congruent environment. The suggestions for flat profiles listed in Rapid Reference 4.10 would be relevant.

≡Rapid Reference 4.9

Tips for Interpreting Low Consistency Codes

- Explain how client's code includes two seemingly opposite types, and describe each type.
- Explore how client has managed to accommodate or struggle with expressing both types.
- Point out that occupations with low consistency codes are rare but do occur; extra time and effort is usually required to identify them. For example, AC types might find congruence with graphic design, and IE types as research team leaders.
- Be creative in helping client locate sources of occupational information to expand options beyond the few listed in the classification booklets.
- Consider ways to fulfill one type through work activities and the other type through roles outside of work. (Introduce the Leisure Activities Finder to identify non-work options.)
- Try to insure that client does not misinterpret a rare code to signify something negative, deficient, or dysfunctional.

Interpreting "Flat" (Low Differentiation) Profiles

The label "flat profile" refers to those profiles with Summary Codes showing low levels of differentiation (e.g., scores for the majority of the six types are within eight points of one another). Scores for flat profiles can be either uniformly high or uniformly low. Clients with such profiles can especially benefit from a counselor-guided interpretation. As a general rule, discuss possible reasons for such response patterns to determine what action to take. Rapid Reference 4.10 summarizes some common reasons for flat profiles and outlines possible approaches for interpreting them.

≡Rapid Reference 4.10

Suggestions for Working with "Flat" Profiles

Common Reasons for Flat Profiles		Suggestions
Low Flat Profiles		
• Lack of work or life experience	____	Encourage exploration of world of work (e.g., reading, classes, part-time work)
• General indecisiveness or confusion	____	Suggest counseling, career workshop, or class
• Unique or narrowly defined interests	____	Identify these interests and help to extrapolate to other areas
• Depressed mood or disinterest in working	____	Take SDS at another time
High Flat Profiles		
• Multiple, wide ranging interests	____	Discuss ways to integrate different interests across a range of work and life roles
	____	Use values and other non-interest dimensions to help client narrow range of options
	____	Focus on prioritizing interests, for example, filling some today and others in the future
• Uncomfortable saying "No" to items	____	Ask to retake SDS with instructions to endorse more "No" responses
• Afraid of ruling out options	____	Focus on decision-making skills

≡ Rapid Reference 4.11

Number of Occupations with Each Code Appearing Somewhere in the First Three Letters.

Code	Number of Occupations
Realistic	10,708
Investigative	2,551
Artistic	570
Social	6,064
Enterprising	10,405
Conventional	5,999

Note. Reproduced by special permission of the Publisher, Psychological Assessment Resources, Inc., 16102 North Florida Avenue, Lutz, Florida 33549, from the *Dictionary of Holland Occupational Codes,* Third Edition by Gary D. Gottfredson, PhD and John L. Holland, PhD. Copyright 1982, 1989, 1996.

Interpreting Infrequent Codes

Rapid Reference 4.11 summarizes the number of occupations that occur in the workforce for each of Holland's six types. The data summarize listings from the *Dictionary of Holland Occupational Codes* (Gottfredson & Holland, 1996), which has coded the majority of occupations in the U.S. workforce according to Holland's typology. This summary highlights the imbalance of types found in the world of work. For example, only 570 occupations include Artistic among the three letters in their Summary Code, whereas over 10,000 occupations are characterized as Realistic or Enterprising. It is particularly important to highlight this imbalance when interpreting the *SDS* with clients whose Summary Codes include types that occur relatively infrequently in the workforce. Some of these clients may find it reassuring to learn that much of their frustration in finding matching work environments is due to the scarcity of options available to them, rather than to their own limitations.

Interpreting Low Consistency Codes

Another type of "infrequent code" is a low consistency code, a code whose first two letters appear opposite one another on Holland's hexagon. A code of

IE, for example, indicates low consistency. Such codes may require the interpretation of a counselor since they typically indicate conflicting interests, values, or needs. Rapid Reference 4.9 outlines several tips for interpreting such profiles.

APPLICATIONS

The *SDS* can be incorporated easily into individual career counseling and coaching with people of various ages as a tool for increasing the range of career options, for confirming career choices, or for estimating the degree of fit or misfit between an individual's personality and career or educational environment. It is also a tool for increasing self-understanding.

In addition, the *SDS* can be used with groups, such as participants in career courses, seminars, or workshops. It has been successfully used with people ranging in age from middle school through retirement, and in both educational and corporate environments. In high school settings, Holland recommends that the *SDS* be taken individually or, if necessary, in very small groups, to avoid errors in scoring and to encourage involvement. The *SDS* is a popular tool in college settings in both career centers and counseling centers. It is typically used to help students with career indecision and as a guide for job seeking. Among working adults, the *SDS* is used in a variety of ways, such as career planning, staff development, and job classification. Bardsley (1984), for example, outlines an *SDS* workshop model that helps managers understand their current positions and plan their future career directions. Shahnasarian (1996) also has written a resource guide for using the *SDS* in organizational settings in which he outlined ways to use the *SDS* for employee selection, training, and development. Holland also recommends using the *SDS* as a tool to assist individuals in retirement with the transition or movement from an institutionally directed environment to a more self-directed one.

STRENGTHS AND LIMITATIONS

The large research base that underlies both Holland's theory and the development of the *SDS* provides a substantial foundation from which to evaluate the instrument. As a freestanding self-assessment tool and career intervention, it provides the public with invaluable, direct access to guidance from Holland's theory. The use of software or Internet administration insures the accuracy of scores, thus eliminating the minor limitation of the hand-scored version.

Nevertheless, the *SDS* fails to provide a fully self-directed career intervention for everyone. In fact, Holland recommends substantial counselor training for adequate use of the *SDS* in career counseling. Furthermore, his recommendations for counselor-guided use are valuable ingredients for a complete and accurate interpretation. The Interpretive Report incorporates a number of advantages of a counselor-guided interpretation. It explains Holland's theory, provides an explanation of the respondent's results, and cautions users about the limitations of the instrument. In addition, it offers answers to a range of frequently asked questions.

A number of reviews of the *SDS* have been published that detail the strengths and limitations of the inventory (Daniels, 1989; Manuele-Adkins, 1989; Krieshok, 1987; Prediger, 1981). For easy reference, Rapid References 4.12 and 4.13 summarize the central strengths and limitations.

≡ *Rapid Reference 4.12*

Important Strengths of the *SDS*

1. One of the most widely used and researched interest inventories.
2. Provides a direct link between a person's Summary Code and job or educational options.
3. Based on Holland's widely used theory of careers.
4. Practical, easy to use, self-directed inventory—does not require assistance of a counselor.
5. Comprehensive and well designed classification booklets and support materials for finding matching occupational and academic environments.
6. Availability of multiple editions that address needs of different populations.
7. Studies indicate its effects are similar to counselors' interventions.
8. Moderate to strong reliability and validity data support its widespread use.
9. Extensive normative data are available for a range of age groups.
10. Particularly effective with individuals with low indecision and highly differentiated Summary Codes.

≡ Rapid Reference 4.13

Important Limitations of the *SDS*

1. Less effective with individuals with high indecision and undifferentiated Summary Codes.

2. Use of raw scores rather than standard scores results in Summary scores that may be strongly influenced by gender, and possibly culture.

3. Summary Codes rely heavily on self-estimates of ability and may be less valid for respondents with low confidence.

4. Errors in self-scoring are relatively common (though rarely affect the first letter of a code).

5. Procedures to calculate essential constructs of congruence, consistency, and differentiation are unavailable to respondents.

6. Not a fully self-interpreted inventory since some people will need a counselor's assistance after completing it.

7. More research is needed to validate codes assigned to occupations and educational programs listed in classification booklets.

8. Classification booklets provide limited help for rare codes.

9. Little direction given to respondents whose Summary Codes are different from Daydream Codes, even though such disagreements may have significant implications.

10. Current manual does not address the meaning of the absolute elevation of profile.

🐾 TEST YOURSELF 🐾

1. **The "Rule of Eight" refers to the standard error of measurement.** True or False?

2. **Clients with little time should be instructed to search only for occupational or educational environments that are coded identical to their Summary Codes.** True or False?

3. **A Summary Aspiration Code refers to the client's most recent Occupational Daydream.** True or False?

4. **If the first two letters in a Summary Code are adjacent to one another on Holland's hexagon, the code is considered to have high consistency.** True or False?

(continued)

5. **A person's Summary Code reflects not only a person's interests but also some measure of a person's confidence in skills.** True or False?

6. **Scores on the *SDS* are relatively unaffected by an individual's gender, race, or cultural background.** True or False?

7. **All six Holland types are equally popular among the general population.** True or False?

8. **The *SDS* was originally designed to require a counselor-guided interpretation.** True or False?

9. **"Flat" profiles are usually considered invalid and should not be interpreted if possible.** True or False?

10. **High differentiation of an *SDS* Summary Code indicates:**

    (a) A person may closely resemble a single type and show little resemblance to other types

    (b) Little difference between the highest and lowest Summary Scores

    (c) A mistake in scoring probably occurred when subtracting one score from another

    (d) All of the above

11. **Which of the following characteristics does not typically correspond to a Conventional Personality Type?**

    (a) Careful

    (b) Conscientious

    (c) Methodical

    (d) Independent

12. **If an individual's Summary Code shows multiple, wide ranging interests, what suggestion is recommended?**

    (a) Discuss with individual ways to integrate interests across various work and life roles.

    (b) Ask individual to retake *SDS* some other time.

    (c) Do not proceed with interpreting the *SDS*.

    (d) Refer the individual for psychotherapy.

13. **The Occupational Daydreams section of the *SDS***

    (a) Has little interpretive power

    (b) Can be a powerful predictor of future career behavior

    (c) Is typically used to measure skills confidence

    (d) Is a shortened version of the *VPI*

Answers: 1. True; 2. False; 3. False; 4. True; 5. True; 6. False; 7. False; 8. False; 9. False; 10. a; 11. d; 12. a; 13. b

Five

ILLUSTRATIVE CASE REPORT

This chapter presents a case study of Gabrielle Blanc. The purpose of the chapter is twofold. First, it offers an opportunity to view sample profiles for each of the inventories featured in the previous chapters: the *Strong*, the *CISS*, and the *SDS*. Second, it provides a demonstration of the value of administering multiple interest measures concurrently. The previous chapters offered detailed recommendations for interpreting each of the inventories individually. Typically, when administering multiple inventories, one would follow those same guidelines and interpret each profile independently, or sequentially, then discuss their similarities and differences later. An alternative option, however, is to review all profiles in advance of an interpretation, and to provide one interpretation that focuses on those interest patterns that are evident across all instruments.

The focus of this chapter is to demonstrate not only the unique contributions of each inventory to understanding Gabrielle's interest patterns, but also the added value that emerges from the administration of multiple measures. Each of the previous chapters has outlined general guidelines for interpreting the instruments and emphasized the importance of a number of ethical and procedural guidelines, such as checking the validity of profiles, interpreting results within the context of the client's background and goals, and involving the client in determining the accuracy of results. We will not review those in this chapter. Instead, we will focus on providing an example of how the instruments, when used together, can both reinforce and extend the results of one another.

First we will discuss the importance of similarities, or consistencies, that occur across inventories; then we will address differences, or what appear to be contradictions, among them. We will then demonstrate how multiple measures can be used to highlight important summary points.

BACKGROUND FOR GABRIELLE BLANC

Gabrielle is a 33-year-old African American woman who expressed interest in completing the inventories because she would like support in making decisions about her future educational and career goals. She is married and has no children. Gabrielle has been primarily self-supporting since leaving high school and has worked essentially full-time throughout her career. In her current position, she coordinates the administrative operations of an internal career services office for employees in a large organization. She performs very well in the varied administrative tasks of her position, which include budget and facilities management and technology oversight. In addition, she became interested in the career development field, and two years ago completed the Career Development Facilitator (CDF) paraprofessional training program. She provides some job search support to individual clients, maintains the career library, and presents workshops as her schedule permits in her role as a CDF. She reports being satisfied with the content of her current job, but indicates that institutional barriers to advancement are the cause of some dissatisfaction she feels with her career.

Gabrielle has been enrolled for the past seven years in a part-time program in business management for working adults and will complete her undergraduate degree this year. She had previously completed her associate's degree in Accounting, also while working full-time. In earlier jobs, she had worked as a research data associate developing profiles on potential financial donors for a large nonprofit organization, and in retail sales. When her first retail job ended with the closing of the store, Gabrielle attended a two-month Job Training and Partnership Act-supported secretarial training program that prepared her for her first administrative position.

Gabrielle is trying to decide what is next in her career development. With the upcoming completion of her undergraduate business degree, she wishes to clarify both her short- and long-term goals. In the short term, Gabrielle would like to pursue an opportunity for advancement. She is considering some aspect of business management in the institution for which she works; for example, in the budget office, in human resources, or as an administrative manager for a larger department. Gabrielle is also concerned about preparing for longer-term career options. She is considering several options, including financial counseling, the little-known and emerging field of economic psychology (the psychological impact of money and debt), and becoming a lawyer, all of which either require, or would be enhanced by, the completion of a graduate or professional degree. Careers she has previously considered include actuary, accountant, lawyer, and executive coach. A few months ago, Gabrielle was torn between applying to an MBA program and a graduate program in counseling. She recently completed her application and was accepted to an MBA program. In her graduate application, she discussed her interest in establishing a nonprofit organization that provides financial education, counseling, and outreach to the economically disadvantaged. Gabrielle described the career expectations of her family on her intake form as follows: "Find work that makes you happy, but will provide adequate financial compensation. Always be employable and employed. Be independent! Be of service to your community—give back."

EVALUATE SIMILARITIES OF INTERESTS ACROSS PROFILES

Gabrielle completed the *Strong* (Figure 5.1), the *CISS* (Figure 5.2), and the *SDS* (Figure 5.3). First, we will examine the similarities among the profiles to see if the different tools point to the same interest areas. In other words, we will check whether scores on different instruments reinforce one another by showing similar patterns of interests. Such similarities provide evidence for the inventories' convergent validity. More importantly, however, they indicate the importance of particular interests to the client. When the same interests show up across multiple measures, we increase our confidence that we are measuring something real, and decrease the possibility that a particular interest score is due to measurement error.

Gabrielle's three profiles show a remarkable degree of similarity. This is readily apparent from a review of Rapid Reference 5.1, where her highest interest scores for the *Strong, CISS,* and *SDS* are summarized. A predominance of Conventional interests is evident. Conventional is the highest of the RIASEC themes on the *Strong,* and the highest type on the *SDS* as well. The highest Orientation on the *CISS* is Organizing, which corresponds closely to Holland's Conventional type. Similarly, the *Strong's* Basic Interest Scales and the *CISS's* Basic Scales show high scores clustered under the Conventional Theme and Organizing Orientation. Her scores on the Occupational Scales of both inventories also demonstrate strong Conventional interest patterns. Nine out of

Rapid Reference 5.1

Summary of Interest Scores

Strong

General Occupational Themes
Conventional . . . . Very High
Enterprising . . . . High
Social . . . . Average

Basic Interest Scales
Very High Scores:
Office Services 74
Data Management 70
Organizational Management 68
Merchandising 66

CISS

Orientations
Organizing . . . . Very High
Creating . . . . Very High
Influencing . . . . High

Basic Scales
Very High Scores:
Office Practices 73
Financial Services 73
Supervision 70
Fashion 69
Culinary Arts 68
Law Politics 63
Counseling 61
Mathematics 61
Mechanical Crafts 61

SDS

Total Scores
Conventional 50
Enterprising 37
Social 32

Strong

Occupational Scales
Very Similar Scores:

Accountant	64
Credit Manager	63
Human Resources Director	62
Secretary	62
Banker	57
Medical Records Technician	57
Nursing Home Administrator	56
Bookkeeper	55
Business Education Teacher	55
Paralegal	55
Small Business Owner	55

Personal Style Scales

Work Style	(61)	People
Learning Environment	(43)	Practical
Leadership Style	(52)	Mid-range
Risk Taking/Adventure	(43)	Play it safe

CISS

Occupational Scales
Very High Scores:

Bookkeeper	71
Hotel Manager	71
Financial Planner	70
School Superintendent	70
CEO/President	69
Retail Store Manager	67
Hospital Administrator	67
Statistician	66
Bank Manager	64
Secretary	63
Accountant	61
Airline Mechanic	61
Insurance Agent	61
Realtor	60
Translator/Interpreter	60

Special Scales

Academic Focus	(52)	Mid-range
Extraversion-	(63)	Very High

SDS

Daydreams

Accountant	CSR
Budget Officer	ESI
Financial Planner	ESC
Lawyer	ESI
Nursing Home Director	CES
Hotel Manager	ESR
Psychiatrist	ISA

Occupational Finder
Matches Resembling CES

Accountant, Tax
Employment Interviewer
Financial Aid Officer
Personnel Manager

ten highest Occupational Scales on the *Strong* are within the Conventional Theme, and all of the occupations under the *CISS* Organizing Orientation are in the very high interest range.

The strength of Gabrielle's Conventional interests, as reflected in her extremely high scores (e.g. above the 98th percentile on the *SII* and *CISS*) is very consistent with her work experience and provides useful confirmation of her future career aspirations.

Gabrielle has indicated that she very much enjoys the content of her current work, providing administrative oversight to the career services department. Her previous job as a data research associate also included the kind of data management and detailed activities associated with the Conventional theme. Gabrielle's short-term goals under consideration—budget management and department administration—also fit well with the activities of the Office Services and Data Management Basic Interest Scales on the *SII* and the Office Practices Basic Interest and Skill Scales on the *CISS*. There is also support for Gabrielle's tentative long-term career goal to establish a nonprofit organization focusing on financial education and counseling. This goal is also aligned with the Conventional Theme and Organizing Orientation, with their focus on data management, accounting, and financial services activities, topics that will likely be a significant part of the subject matter of her prospective work. In addition, the administrative activities that would be required in operating such a nonprofit also fit well with Gabrielle's very high Conventional interests. Gabrielle's very high skill score on the Organizing Orientation on the *CISS* and the complete endorsement of the Conventional competencies and self-estimates on the *Self-Directed Search* indicate that she feels considerable confidence in performing these activities, which is an indication that she would likely succeed in them.

Gabrielle's results also show clear Enterprising interests across the inventories. Both the *Strong* and the *SDS* show Enterprising as the second ranked theme or type, and the *CISS* ranks Influencing, the closest parallel to Enterprising, as the third highest Interest Orientation. Similarly, the *SII* Basic Interest Scales, the *CISS* Basic Scales, both sets of Occupational Scales, the Occupational Daydream Codes, and the Occupations listed from the Occupations Finder all demonstrate patterns of Enterprising interests.

Gabrielle's high scores on the Enterprising theme also fit well with her stated short-term goal of managing a larger department. Her very high interest in the Organizational Management Basic Interest Scale on the *Strong* lends additional support to this short-term goal, as do the similar scores on the many managerial occupational scales in the Enterprising Theme area of the *SII*. Also of note in the Influencing Orientation is the Financial Planner occupational scale, one of her top three Occupational Interest Scales on the *CISS*. This scale is one more piece of evidence that lends support to Gabrielle's projected long-term career goal.

The skills confidence score of the Influencing Orientation on the *CISS* is of interest, as is the relative level of the interest scores on the Enterprising and Influencing scales on all three inventories. The *CISS* Influencing Skill Scale is 50, which is solidly in the mid-range. On the *SDS,* which is affected by both interest and skill scores, there is a thirteen-point drop from the Conventional to Enterprising scores. There is also a 10-point drop in scores from the Conventional to Enterprising Occupational Themes on the *SII*. All of these data points together raise interesting questions about the relative intra-individual strength of Gabrielle's interest and confidence in this area as compared to the Conventional area. These questions should be discussed with the client.

In the interpretive session, Gabrielle indicated that she has enterprising interests, particularly in leadership and managerial roles, which is well-supported in the many Enterprising and Influencing Occupational Scales with manager, director, or supervisor in or implied in the titles, on which she scored high. Gabrielle feels that because she has many good ideas, classmates and colleagues often ask her to take on leadership roles. However, Gabrielle indicated that she has often experienced a fear of failure and has many times declined such opportunities. She has not necessarily wanted to be in the "hot seat," taking responsibility for difficult issues. However, she indicated that she is increasingly gaining confidence in this role. She is also coming to view leadership in more expansive ways beyond just "success" or "failure," and is recognizing new definitions of leadership that are enabling her to more frequently assume a leadership position, particularly when the issue is important to her. Gabrielle may wish to focus some of her future developmental activities on gaining additional experience and confidence in a leadership role.

Gabrielle also mentioned law as one of her occupational daydreams and included lawyer among the careers she is currently considering. The inventories provide an interesting perspective on this possible career choice. The Law/Politics Basic Interest Scale on the *Strong* has a high interest score and the

Law/Politics Basic Scale on the *CISS* is also strong, having received the Pursue tag. The Lawyer Occupational Scale on the *Strong* and the Attorney Occupational Interest Scale on the *CISS* are both in the similar and high range, respectively. However, in both instances the magnitude of the scores is not nearly as high as those Gabrielle has earned in many other occupations, nor is the magnitude commensurate with that of the Basic Interest Scales. The implications of this should be discussed with Gabrielle. Since the Basic Interest Scales measure specific interests in the area, and the Occupational Scales measure the broad range of likes and dislikes of employed lawyers, this suggests that Gabrielle may be interested in the content of the field of law, but would not enjoy as well the day-to-day activities of lawyers.

In the interpretive discussion with Gabrielle, this point was raised. Gabrielle indicated that she is less interested in practicing law, and more interested in understanding the law and its applications to financial planning and counseling. She also indicated that she believes she would gain credibility in her professional life if she also had a law degree, and for this reason would still consider pursuing it. It is important to stress that the scores on the scales do not imply that Gabrielle should not pursue law, but simply suggest that she does not look as much like lawyers in her broad range of interests (though she does in her skills confidence scale on the *CISS*) as she does other professional groups. If she would like to pursue this possibility further at some future point, Gabrielle might wish to look into law school training programs that would be particularly aligned with her interests in financial planning and organizational management and that might be designed especially for working adults who are interested in business and other practical applications of the law.

At this point, Gabrielle's preference for Learning Environments was also brought up. Gabrielle's score on the practical learning pole of the Learning Environment Personal Style Scale on the *Strong* and the mid-range interest and skill scores on the Academic Focus Special Scales on the *CISS* indicate that Gabrielle prefers practical learning environments focused on achieving a specific goal. These results support her choice to pursue the MBA program. Her learning environment preferences may fit less well with some of the advanced degree programs she was also considering. For example, psychologist and lawyer are among the top five occupations of 15 highest scoring occupations on the *Strong* in their preference for academic environments versus practical learning environments. Again, these scores do not imply that Gabrielle should not pursue graduate programs in psychology or law. However, they suggest she might prefer to select, from among those options, programs that have a more applied orientation. Alternatively, she might recognize that she would need to tolerate some of the more abstract, theoretical, or esoteric aspects of these programs as an acceptable means to an end, should she decide to pursue future schooling in either of these fields.

A third area of interest, Social, occurs across the profiles, but this pattern is less pronounced. Both the *Strong* and *SDS* show Social as a tertiary interest pattern; however, the *CISS* does not show Helping as a high interest. There appears to be high interest on specific Basic Interest scales worthy of note: high interest on the Social Service Basic Interest Scale on the *Strong* and very high interest on the Counseling Basic Interest Scale on the *CISS*. In addition, the *Strong's* Occupational Scales show a cluster of occupations in the similar range, and several of her most similar Occupational Scales have Social included in their codes. Likewise, on the *SDS,* all of the occupations Gabrielle listed for Occupational Daydreams and from the Occupations Finder include Social in their three-letter codes. The *CISS* shows high skills confidence on the Helping Orientation. Similarly, on the *SDS,* Gabrielle rates her Competencies and Self-Estimates high in the Social areas.

Gabrielle indicated that she would like to have a variety of activities in her work. She said the ideal mix would be about one-third activities working in some sort of a helping role with people and the remaining in a variety of other tasks, which is consistent with the average interest score she has earned on the Social Theme on the *SII,* the Mid-range Interest Score she has earned on the Helping Orientation of the *CISS,* and the mix of average or midrange and high scores on the Basic Interest Scales and Basic Scales within the *SII* and *CISS.* In the case of the *CISS* Basic Scales on Adult Development and Counseling, two areas that would have impact on her long-term goals, the skills confidence scores are higher than the interest scores, a reversal of the pattern we saw with the Influencing Basic Scales. Gabrielle confirmed that she is very confident in her social and interpersonal skills, and would want to be protective of her time so that she did not become overly involved in providing direct service to the detriment of other goals she would like to accomplish. Also of note is that Gabrielle did obtain a similar score on the High School Counselor scale on the *SII* and a tag of Pursue on the Guidance Counselor scale on the *CISS.* However, she did not score high on other helping occupations on the *CISS,* such as the social worker or psychologist scale. When asked about this, Gabrielle concluded that her interest in counseling would be as a tool in providing financial counseling or planning assistance. This clarification helped Gabrielle feel more confident about the decision she had made to pursue her MBA over a counseling graduate degree. At the same time, Gabrielle indicated that she would enjoy the opportunity to learn more about counseling approaches that could be utilized as techniques in her future practice. To that end, she would also be interested in opportunities to take advanced coursework in the counseling area.

Also, the Community Service Organization Director Occupational Scale came up as a high score under the Social Theme on the *SII,* supporting Gabrielle's long-term goal of establishing a nonprofit organization. Several of the teaching Occupational Scales under the Social Theme on the *SII* came up as similar or very similar, which would support Gabrielle's interest in providing financial *education* to the economically disadvantaged. There were, however, some inconsistencies in her interests in teaching. She scored average on the Teaching Basic Interest Scale on the *SII,* similar on the Corporate Trainer Occupational Scale on the *SII,* and the Corporate Trainer on the *CISS* was tagged Explore due to the very high skills confidence score and mid-range interest score. When asked about these apparent discrepancies, Gabrielle responded that she did not have a love of teaching per se. She has gained a great deal of confidence in her abilities to present information and connect with an audience. She cited her recent success in designing and delivering workshops on managing personal finances as an example. However, she would want to use teaching and training as a means to get her message out to large numbers of people, that is, as a means to an end.

One of the most interesting similarities among her scores is the recurrence of the occupation of Accounting across the inventories. Gabrielle's most similar occupational scale on the *Strong* is Accountant; one of her top listed Occupational Daydreams on the *SDS* is Accountant; the first Occupation she lists from the Occupational finder is Tax Accountant; and Accountant occurs again among the very high scores of the *CISS* Occupational Scales. Similar, though less striking, parallels occur with occupations involving finance, banking, administration, and management. These combinations of scores, along with Gabrielle's high Mathematics Basic Interest Scale on the *SII* and Basic Interest and Skill Scales on the *CISS,* add additional strength to Gabrielle's short-term goal in budget administration and long-term goal of establishing a nonprofit focused on helping others with financial management. Another similarity occurs with Gabrielle's scores on the *Strong*'s Work Style and the *CISS*'s Extraversion Scales. On both scales she scores in the direction of liking to work in people-oriented environments.

Another way to view the similarities among the instruments is to review the patterns of low scores to confirm Gabrielle's areas of disinterest. Notice that across all three instruments, and within all types of scales, Gabrielle shows little Realistic interest. This appears to be her lowest interest area, particularly when all instruments are viewed together. Realistic is the lowest type on the *SDS* and next to lowest on the *Strong*'s General Occupational Themes. Similarly, she scores lowest on the *CISS* Orientations that correspond most closely to Realistic, the Adventuring and Producing Orientations. With the exception of a Very High score on Mechanical Crafts, she shows low to mid-range interest in all the related Basic Interest Scales on the *CISS.*

Similarly, Gabrielle shows no similar interests to any of the Realistic occupations on the *Strong* or to the Adventuring occupations on the *CISS.* She shows only one high interest score (Airline Mechanic) among the Producing Orientation. Similarly, her skills confidence is lowest for the Producing and Adventuring Orientations, and her Competencies and Self-Estimates ratings are lowest for Realistic. Gabrielle confirmed that she has little interest in Realistic types of activities, aside from having some understanding of how to select, set up, and troubleshoot technology (including computers, projection systems, etc.), reflected in the Mechanical Crafts score on the *CISS* Basic Interest Scale. She felt the low midrange skills confidence score on Mechanical Crafts on the *CISS* was an accurate reflection of how she views her current skills and indicated that she hoped to develop additional skills in this area by pursuing a training opportunity offered at work to become certified as a network technician.

One other way to review similarities across the profiles is to check whether a particular inconsistency or unusual pattern of scores found within one inventory recurs on a different instrument. For example, Gabrielle shows an unusual combination of scores on the *Strong.* She shows a pattern of high Enterprising interests, yet she scores towards the "Plays it safe" pole on the Risk Taking/Adventure Personal Style Scale. Typically, individuals who have strong Enterprising interests score toward the "Takes chances" pole instead.

This seemingly inconsistent pattern might indicate her unique combination of interests, or it may represent conflicts she has encountered. If we were using the *Strong* in isolation of other assessment tools, we might question the accuracy of these scores, and look to Gabrielle for confirmation or help in explaining them. However, her *CISS* scores indicate a similar pattern of interests. She shows relatively high scores on a range of Influencing scales but relatively low scores on the Risks/Adventure Basic Scales. Since both inventories reflect the same atypical pattern, we can increase our confidence that it reflects her actual interests, and may point to conflicts she has experienced. However, we still need to discuss this pattern with Gabrielle directly to verify and explore its meaning. In the interpretive session, Gabrielle indicated that she only likes calculated risk-taking, which makes sense in the context of the combination of her high Enterprising and low risk-taking interest and skill scores.

CHECK FOR CONTRADICTIONS BETWEEN SCORES ACROSS PROFILES

An important advantage of administering multiple measures is the opportunity to find contradictions, or differences, between scores where you would expect to find similarity.

For example, you would expect to find similar scores among the Strong Artistic General Occupational Theme, the *SDS* Artistic Summary score, and the *CISS* Creating Orientation, since these scales attempt to measure similar constructs. When you find differences, however, it is not typically a sign of measurement error. Rather, it is due usually to the differences in the construction of the scales. Consequently, the challenge to the interpreter is to understand the different ways each of the scales work. Each measures a different nuance of the construct, and each measures the construct by a different method. Helping the client to understand these differences then becomes the task for the interpretation.

For example, Gabrielle scores Very High on the *CISS* Creating Interest Orientation, yet only Average on the *Strong* Artistic General Occupational Theme. Artistic also does not occur in her *SDS* summary code or in the first two letters of any of her Occupational Daydream codes. This does not mean that the *CISS* score is an error. However, it provides an opportunity for a discussion with Gabrielle about her Artistic interests and experiences. Such an exploration might not have occurred if the *Strong* or *SDS* had been assigned independently. One explanation that may account for the scores, for example, is the different way each of the inventories calculates and presents scores. The *CISS* uses a combined male and female reference group, the *Strong* uses a female reference group, and the *SDS* uses no reference group. One would expect some degree of difference among scores as a result. Also, the *CISS* Orientations are comprised of a few items from each of the Basic Scales clustered below them. There are some additional Basic Scales on the *CISS*, Fashion and International Activities, that do not appear on the *SII*. Gabrielle has scored Very High and High on these scales, which is probably contributing to her higher score on the Creating Orientation on the *CISS*. It is also important to note that the actual point difference between the Artistic and Social Themes on the *SII* and *SDS* are small. Thus, the Artistic Themes on the *SII* and *SDS* would typically be considered as a part of the three-letter code, routinely written as CES/A. In that respect, there continues to be continuity between the three instruments.

Artistic or Creating should be considered as an element in the overall picture of Gabrielle's interests. The interpreter can help Gabrielle understand these differences, then ask her to elaborate on the how this information fits her self-image. For example, she may point out a number of specific Artistic interests that are personally enjoyable to her, such as fashion, cooking, and performing arts, yet see other interests as more important to pursue as a career. The *CISS* may reinforce an important area, and the discussion may lead her to inject more creativity into her day-to-day work tasks. In the interpretive session, Gabrielle indicated that Creating is in fact an important part of her work, particularly in regard to being able to create new programs, services, and resources. To that end, this interest is again supportive of her longer-term career goal of creating a nonprofit organization and the services and resources that would go with it.

SUMMARY AND NEXT STEPS

Gabrielle's primary concerns about her future educational and career directions have been neatly addressed by the inventories, individually and in combination. In summary, Gabrielle has been concerned about whether to pursue a degree in business or counseling. Her choice to pursue an MBA is confirmed by both the Conventional and Enterprising themes and their related orientations, and by the associated interest scales and occupational scales across the inventories. The Learning Environment and Academic Focus scales also confirm this choice. At the same time, the inventories also suggest that she may want to build in a sub-concentration or elective focus in her graduate program of counseling and/or training skills, if possible, since those interests are also strong, though less so than the administrative, financial, and management aspects of her interests. As often is the case, one particularly satisfying solution to the dilemma of competing interests is to find ways to combine them in work, as well as in educational preparation, whenever feasible. Gabrielle is encouraged to find ways through her selection of elective courses, additional graduate certification courses, or professional study to do this.

After completing her MBA program, Gabrielle may feel that she would still like to pursue the law school option. In that event, she would be encouraged to check into the curriculum of law schools she might wish to attend, to see which among them might be the best fit with her more practical, business-related interests.

The inventories all have been very confirming of Gabrielle's long-term goal to establish a nonprofit for financial education, counseling, and outreach. The next steps for her in moving forward with this goal would be to follow the "4 P's," which are outlined in more detail in the section on DISCOVER in Chapter 6. These steps include: (a) reading *profiles* of people who have done related work, (b) talking with *people* who are already directors of nonprofits, (c) attending *programs* that will teach her more about how she needs to prepare for this future goal, and (d) *participating* in the field by gaining volunteer, part-time, or internship-type experiences in organizations with related missions to continue building her skills set, people networks, and experience.

With regard to Gabrielle's short-term goals, budget management or administrative management could be a good next step, providing the advancement opportunity she seeks in an area of interest and skill. Because of the discrepancy in her interest scores on the Human Resources Director scales on the *SII* and *CISS,* she may want to take a closer look at the HR area before pursuing it further. In addition, if the institutional advancement issues of her current job could be reconciled, she could also potentially stay in her current administrative role. The short-term choice might best be made as a strategic decision. That is, Gabrielle may wish to assess which of her potential options will position her best for her future long-term goal. Gabrielle will want to determine which of the available opportunities will provide her the chance to learn more about administration and financial management. She will also want to assess which of these opportunities provide her the greatest access to resources and opportunities for her educational pursuits in business and the further development of her training and counseling skills.

Finally, Gabrielle is encouraged to pursue additional leadership opportunities in her department through task force or committee assignments in her organization, or through volunteer work to further develop her skill base and confidence in her leadership abilities. She is encouraged, as well, to attend training sessions to increase her skills set and confidence in technology so that she can further develop the skills she needs to support her interests in technology and meet the demands for those skills in her current job.

While Gabrielle must ultimately make the choices that will determine the path of her current and future career, the assessments, both individually and in combination, provide rich resources she can draw upon now and in the future to help support her in the decisions she will make.

STRONG INTEREST INVENTORY™

Profile report for **XXXXX**
ID: **XXXXX**
Age: **33**
Gender: **Female**

Date tested:
Date scored: **4/21/00**

Page 1 of 6

SNAPSHOT: A SUMMARY OF RESULTS FOR
XXXXX

VH	=	very high interest
H	=	high interest
A	=	average interest
L	=	little interest
VL	=	very little interest

VS	=	very similar
S	=	similar
M-R	=	mid-range
D	=	dissimilar
VD	=	very dissimilar

GENERAL OCCUPATIONAL THEMES

The General Occupational Themes describe interests in six very broad areas, including interest in work and leisure activities, kinds of people, and work settings. Your interests in each area are shown at the right in rank order. Note that each Theme has a code, represented by the first letter of the Theme name.

You can use your Theme code, printed below your results, to identify school subjects, part-time jobs, college majors, leisure activities, or careers that you might find interesting.

THEME CODE	THEME	VL	L	A	H	VH	TYPICAL INTERESTS
C	CONVENTIONAL	☐	☐	☐	☐	☑	Accounting, processing data
E	ENTERPRISING	☐	☐	☐	☑	☐	Selling, managing
S	SOCIAL	☐	☐	☑	☐	☐	Helping, instructing
A	ARTISTIC	☐	☐	☑	☐	☐	Creating or enjoying art
R	REALISTIC	☐	☐	☑	☐	☐	Building, repairing
I	INVESTIGATIVE	☐	☐	☑	☐	☐	Researching, analyzing

Your Theme code is CES—(see explanation at left).
You might explore occupations with codes that contain any combination of these letters.

BASIC INTEREST SCALES

The Basic Interest Scales measure your interests in 25 specific areas or activities. Only those 5 areas in which you show the *most* interest are listed at the right in rank order. Your results on all 25 Basic Interest Scales are found on page 2.

To the left of each scale is a letter that shows which of the six General Occupational Themes this activity is most closely related to. These codes can help you to identify other activities that you may enjoy.

THEME CODE	BASIC INTERESTS	VL	L	A	H	VH	TYPICAL ACTIVITIES
C	OFFICE SERVICES	☐	☐	☐	☐	☑	Performing clerical and office tasks
C	DATA MANAGEMENT	☐	☐	☐	☐	☑	Analyzing data for decision making
E	ORGANIZATIONAL MANAGEMENT	☐	☐	☐	☐	☑	Managing or supervising others
E	MERCHANDISING	☐	☐	☐	☐	☑	Selling retail or wholesale products
S	SOCIAL SERVICE	☐	☐	☐	☑	☐	Helping people

OCCUPATIONAL SCALES

The Occupational Scales measure how similar your interests are to the interests of people who are satisfied working in those occupations. Only the 10 scales on which your interests are *most* similar to those of these people are listed at the right in rank order. Your results on all 211 of the Occupational Scales are found on pages 3, 4, and 5.

The letters to the left of each scale identify the Theme or Themes that most closely describe the interests of people working in that occupation. You can use these letters to find additional, related occupations that you might find interesting.

THEME CODE	OCCUPATION	VD	D	M-R	S	VS
CE	ACCOUNTANT	☐	☐	☐	☐	☑
CE	CREDIT MANAGER	☐	☐	☐	☐	☑
EAS	HUMAN RESOURCES DIRECTOR	☐	☐	☐	☐	☑
CES	SECRETARY	☐	☐	☐	☐	☑
CE	BANKER	☐	☐	☐	☐	☑
C	MEDICAL RECORDS TECHNICIAN	☐	☐	☐	☐	☑
CES	NURSING HOME ADMINISTRATOR	☐	☐	☐	☐	☑
C	BOOKKEEPER	☐	☐	☐	☐	☑
CES	BUSINESS EDUCA-TION TEACHER	☐	☐	☐	☐	☑
CE	PARALEGAL	☐	☐	☐	☐	☑

PERSONAL STYLE SCALE
measure your levels of comfort regarding Work Style, Learning Environment, Leadership Style, and Risk Taking/Adventure. This information may help you make decisions about particular work environments, educational settings, and types of activities you would find satisfying. Your results on these four scales are on page 6.

CONSULTING PSYCHOLOGISTS PRESS, INC. • 3803 E. Bayshore Road, Palo Alto, CA 94303

Figure 5.1 SII Results

Note. Modified and reproduced by special permission of the publisher, Consulting Psychologists Press, Inc., Palo Alto, CA 94303, from the 2000 CPP Catalog © 2000 by CPP, Inc.

STRONG INTEREST INVENTORY™

Profile report for   XXXXX
ID: XXXXX

Page 2 of 6

GENERAL OCCUPATIONAL THEMES

BASIC INTEREST SCALES

Female
Male

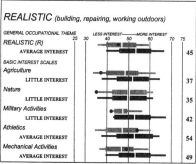

REALISTIC (building, repairing, working outdoors)

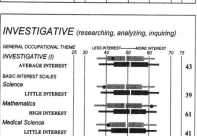

INVESTIGATIVE (researching, analyzing, inquiring)

ARTISTIC (creating or enjoying art, drama, music, writing)

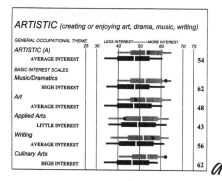

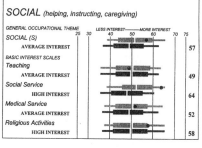

SOCIAL (helping, instructing, caregiving)

ENTERPRISING (selling, managing, persuading)

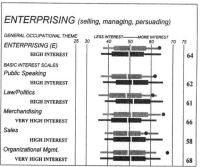

CONVENTIONAL (accounting, organizing, processing data)

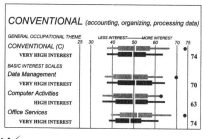

CPP CONSULTING PSYCHOLOGISTS PRESS, INC. • 3803 E. Bayshore Road, Palo Alto, CA 94303

Figure 5.1 (continued)

OCCUPATIONAL SCALES

NOTES

REALISTIC (building, repairing, working outdoors)

THEME CODES FEMALE MALE			YOUR SCORES FEMALE	MALE	DISSIMILAR INTERESTS————————SIMILAR INTERESTS 15 20 30—MID-RANGE—40 50 55
RIS	(SIR)	Athletic Trainer	20	(SIR)	
R	R	Auto Mechanic	16	14	
RIA	REA	Carpenter	14	22	
RIA	RIC	Electrician	27	10	
RCI	RI	Emergency Medical Technician	31	26	
RI	RI	Engineer	35	23	
(CSE)	RC	Farmer	(CSE)	19	
RI	RI	Forester	1	1	
RC	RE	Gardener/Groundskeeper	25	14	
REI	REI	Horticultural Worker	10	5	
(CRE)	RCE	Military Enlisted Personnel	(CRE)	37	
REI	REC	Military Officer	37	29	
*	R	Plumber	*	18	
RE	R	Police Officer	28	16	
RIS	RI	Radiologic Technologist	30	27	
(CE)	RE	Small Business Owner	(CE)	30	
RSI	RSE	Vocational Agriculture Teacher	4	18	

INVESTIGATIVE (researching, analyzing, inquiring)

THEME CODES FEMALE MALE			YOUR SCORES FEMALE	MALE	DISSIMILAR INTERESTS————————SIMILAR INTERESTS 15 20 30—MID-RANGE—40 50 55
IS	IA	Audiologist	25	33	
IRA	IA	Biologist	4	1	
IR	IR	Chemist	14	14	
IR	IRA	Chiropractor	29	34	
IAR	IAS	College Professor	21	31	
IR	IAR	Computer Progr./Systems Analyst	31	15	
IRA	IR	Dentist	11	11	
IES	(SEC)	Dietitian	24	(SEC)	
IRA	IA	Geographer	33	20	
IRA	IRA	Geologist	12	-6	
IRC	ICA	Mathematician	5	-1	
IRC	IRE	Medical Technician	26	20	
IRC	IRC	Medical Technologist	21	26	
IR	IR	Optometrist	25	21	
ICR	ICE	Pharmacist	19	33	
IAR	IAR	Physician	0	15	
IRA	IRA	Physicist	6	6	
IA	IA	Psychologist	25	27	
IR	IRC	Research & Development Manager	16	19	
IRA	IRS	Respiratory Therapist	24	25	
IRS	IRS	Science Teacher	15	16	
IAR	(AI)	Sociologist	29	(AI)	
IRA	IR	Veterinarian	-3	4	

Figure 5.1 (continued)

STRONG INTEREST INVENTORY™

Profile report for **XXXXX**
ID: **XXXXX**

OCCUPATIONAL SCALES (continued)

NOTES

ARTISTIC (creating or enjoying art, drama, music, writing)

THEME CODES FEMALE MALE		Occupation	YOUR SCORES FEMALE MALE		DISSIMILAR INTERESTS 15	20	30—MID-RANGE— 40	SIMILAR INTERESTS 50	55
AE	AE	Advertising Executive	28	34			●		
ARI	ARI	Architect	6	11	●				
ARI	A	Artist, Commercial	0	9	●				
AR	A	Artist, Fine	-9	0	●				
ASE	AS	Art Teacher	7	19	●				
AE	AE	Broadcaster	39	36				●	
AES	AES	Corporate Trainer	47	57				●	
ASE	ASE	English Teacher	43	42				●	
(EA)	AE	Interior Decorator	(EA)	40				●	
A	A	Lawyer	42	46				●	
A	A	Librarian	39	41				●	
AIR	AIR	Medical Illustrator	-21	11	●				
A	A	Musician	31	37			●		
ARE	ARE	Photographer	21	21		●			
AER	ASE	Public Administrator	40	47				●	
AE	AE	Public Relations Director	29	39			●		
A	A	Reporter	30	31			●		
(IAR)	AI	Sociologist	(IAR)	34			●		
AIR	AI	Technical Writer	24	33		●			
A	AI	Translator	28	39			●		

SOCIAL (helping, instructing, caregiving)

THEME CODES FEMALE MALE		Occupation	YOUR SCORES FEMALE MALE		DISSIMILAR INTERESTS 15	20	30—MID-RANGE— 40	SIMILAR INTERESTS 50	55
(RIS)	SIR	Athletic Trainer	(RIS)	17	●				
S	*	Child Care Provider	25	*		●			
SE	SE	Community Serv. Organization Dir.	51	48				●	
(IES)	SEC	Dietitian	(IES)	52				●	
S	S	Elementary School Teacher	20	31		●			
SAE	SA	Foreign Language Teacher	41	42				●	
SE	SE	High School Counselor	46	49				●	
SE	*	Home Economics Teacher	45	*				●	
SAR	SA	Minister	30	45			●		
SCE	SCE	Nurse, LPN	36	47				●	
SI	SAI	Nurse, RN	23	28		●			
SAR	SA	Occupational Therapist	18	27	●				
SE	SE	Parks and Recreation Coordinator	40	47				●	
SRC	SR	Physical Education Teacher	24	21		●			
SIR	SIR	Physical Therapist	26	30		●			
SEA	SEC	School Administrator	49	45				●	
SEA	SEA	Social Science Teacher	52	53				●	
SA	SA	Social Worker	34	41			●		
SE	SEA	Special Education Teacher	23	36		●			
SA	SA	Speech Pathologist	21	41	●				

CPP CONSULTING PSYCHOLOGISTS PRESS, INC. • 3803 E. Bayshore Road, Palo Alto, CA 94303

Figure 5.1 (continued)

| STRONG INTEREST INVENTORY™ | | Profile report for   XXXXX | Page 5 of 6 |
| | | ID: XXXXX | |

OCCUPATIONAL SCALES (continued)

NOTES

ENTERPRISING (selling, managing, persuading)

THEME CODES FEMALE MALE			YOUR SCORES FEMALE MALE		DISSIMILAR INTERESTS —————— SIMILAR INTERESTS 15 20 30—MID-RANGE— 40 50 55
*	ECR	Agribusiness Manager	*	30	
EC	EC	Buyer	38	46	
ERA	ER	Chef	32	46	
EIS	*	Dental Hygienist	44	*	
EAS	ESA	Elected Public Official	42	37	
EAS	EAS	Flight Attendant	47	58	
EAC	EAC	Florist	26	38	
EC	EA	Hair Stylist	50	44	
ECS	ECS	Housekeeping & Maintenance Supr.	50	44	
EAS	ES	Human Resources Director	62	56	
EA	(AE)	Interior Decorator	19	(AE)	
EIR	ECI	Investments Manager	33	32	
E	E	Life Insurance Agent	45	39	
EA	EA	Marketing Executive	32	41	
ECR	ER	Optician	49	36	
ECR	ECR	Purchasing Agent	51	48	
E	E	Realtor	37	44	
ECR	ECR	Restaurant Manager	52	45	
ECA	ECS	Store Manager	52	47	
ECA	ECA	Travel Agent	49	58	

CONVENTIONAL (accounting, organizing, processing data)

THEME CODES FEMALE MALE			YOUR SCORES FEMALE MALE		DISSIMILAR INTERESTS —————— SIMILAR INTERESTS 15 20 30—MID-RANGE— 40 50 55
CE	CE	Accountant	64	57	
CI	CI	Actuary	40	38	
CE	CE	Banker	57	55	
C	C	Bookkeeper	55	53	
CES	CES	Business Education Teacher	55	60	
CE	CE	Credit Manager	63	57	
CSE	*	Dental Assistant	44	*	
CSE	(RC)	Farmer	35	(RC)	
CES	CES	Food Service Manager	54	50	
CIR	CIS	Mathematics Teacher	35	24	
C	C	Medical Records Technician	57	55	
CRE	(RCE)	Military Enlisted Personnel	52	(RCE)	
CES	CES	Nursing Home Administrator	56	58	
CE	CA	Paralegal	55	54	
CES	*	Secretary	62	*	
CE	(RE)	Small Business Owner	55	(RE)	

Figure 5.1 (continued)

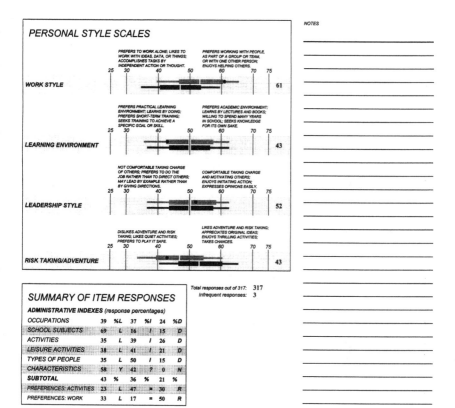

PERSONAL STYLE SCALES

Female
Male

PERSONAL STYLE SCALES

NOTES

WORK STYLE

PREFERS TO WORK ALONE; LIKES TO WORK WITH IDEAS, DATA, OR THINGS; ACCOMPLISHES TASKS BY INDEPENDENT ACTION OR THOUGHT.

PREFERS WORKING WITH PEOPLE, AS PART OF A GROUP OR TEAM, OR WITH ONE OTHER PERSON; ENJOYS HELPING OTHERS.

25 30 40 50 60 70 75 — 61

LEARNING ENVIRONMENT

PREFERS PRACTICAL LEARNING ENVIRONMENT; LEARNS BY DOING; PREFERS SHORT-TERM TRAINING; SEEKS TRAINING TO ACHIEVE A SPECIFIC GOAL OR SKILL.

PREFERS ACADEMIC ENVIRONMENT; LEARNS BY LECTURES AND BOOKS; WILLING TO SPEND MANY YEARS IN SCHOOL; SEEKS KNOWLEDGE FOR ITS OWN SAKE.

25 30 40 50 60 70 75 — 43

LEADERSHIP STYLE

NOT COMFORTABLE TAKING CHARGE OF OTHERS; PREFERS TO DO THE JOB RATHER THAN TO DIRECT OTHERS; MAY LEAD BY EXAMPLE RATHER THAN BY GIVING DIRECTIONS.

COMFORTABLE TAKING CHARGE AND MOTIVATING OTHERS; ENJOYS INITIATING ACTION; EXPRESSES OPINIONS EASILY.

25 30 40 50 60 70 75 — 52

RISK TAKING/ADVENTURE

DISLIKES ADVENTURE AND RISK TAKING; LIKES QUIET ACTIVITIES; PREFERS TO PLAY IT SAFE.

LIKES ADVENTURE AND RISK TAKING; APPRECIATES ORIGINAL IDEAS; ENJOYS THRILLING ACTIVITIES; TAKES CHANCES.

25 30 40 50 60 70 75 — 43

SUMMARY OF ITEM RESPONSES

Total responses out of 317: 317
Infrequent responses: 3

ADMINISTRATIVE INDEXES (response percentages)

OCCUPATIONS	39	%L	37	%I	24	%D
SCHOOL SUBJECTS	69	L	16	I	15	D
ACTIVITIES	35	L	39	I	26	D
LEISURE ACTIVITIES	38	L	41	I	21	D
TYPES OF PEOPLE	35	L	50	I	15	D
CHARACTERISTICS	58	Y	42	?	0	N
SUBTOTAL	43	%	36	%	21	%
PREFERENCES: ACTIVITIES	23	L	47	=	30	R
PREFERENCES: WORK	33	L	17	=	50	R

CONSULTING PSYCHOLOGISTS PRESS, INC. • 3803 E. Bayshore Road, Palo Alto, CA 94303

Figure 5.1 (continued)

CAMPBELL INTEREST AND SKILL SURVEY INDIVIDUAL PROFILE REPORT

GABRIEL BLANC

DATE SCORED: 2/15/2000

| Orientations |

Your CISS profile is organized into seven Orientation Scales covering important areas of the world of work. Each Orientation is identified by an underlined capital letter.

Influencing - influencing others through leadership, politics, public speaking, sales, and marketing
Organizing - organizing the work of others, managing, and monitoring financial performance
Helping - helping others through teaching, healing, and counseling
Creating - creating artistic, literary, or musical productions and designing products or environments
a**N**alyzing - analyzing data, using mathematics, and carrying out scientific experiments
Producing - producing products, using "hands-on" skills in farming, construction, and mechanical crafts
Adventuring - adventuring, competing, and risk taking through athletic, police, and military activities

A pair of scores is plotted below for each Orientation. Your interest score, plotted with a solid diamond (♦), indicates how appealing the activities are to you, and your skill score, plotted with a hollow diamond (◊), reflects how confident you feel in performing these activities.

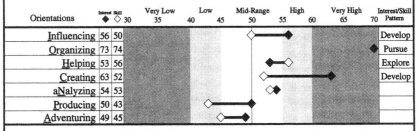

Orientations	Interest	Skill	Very Low 35	Low 45	Mid-Range 50	High 60	Very High 70	Interest/Skill Pattern
Influencing	56	50						Develop
Organizing	73	74						Pursue
Helping	53	56						Explore
Creating	63	52						Develop
aNalyzing	54	53						
Producing	50	43						
Adventuring	49	45						

Your Orientation interest and skill scores fall into the following patterns:

Pursue - **O**rganizing. These are activities that you enjoy and feel confident about your abilities in performing. Areas for which your interests and skills are both high are prime candidates for your future. Pursue these areas in your career planning.

Develop - **I**nfluencing and **C**reating. These are activities that you enjoy, but you are less confident about your ability to perform them. Consider seeking additional education or training to bring your skill level up to your interest level. Or consider adopting some of these activities as hobbies.

Explore - **H**elping. These are activities that you do not particularly enjoy, but you are confident of your ability to perform them. Consider how you might transfer these skills to other occupational areas to open up new possibilities.

Figure 5.2 *CISS* Results

CAMPBELL INTEREST AND SKILL SURVEY INDIVIDUAL PROFILE REPORT

GABRIEL BLANC

DATE SCORED: 2/15/2000

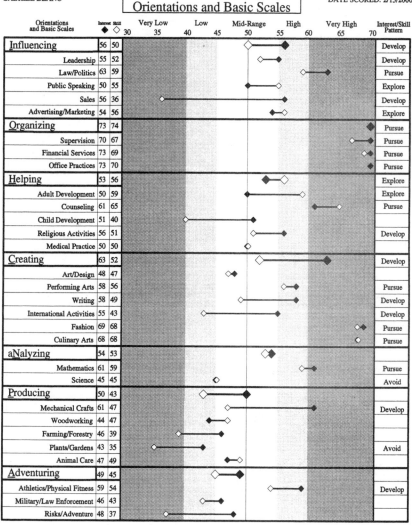

Orientations and Basic Scales

Orientations and Basic Scales	Interest ◆	Skill ◇	Very Low 30	Low 35 40	Mid-Range 45 50	High 55 60	Very High 65 70	Interest/Skill Pattern
Influencing	56	50						Develop
Leadership	55	52						Develop
Law/Politics	63	59						Pursue
Public Speaking	50	55						Explore
Sales	56	36						Develop
Advertising/Marketing	54	56						Explore
Organizing	73	74						Pursue
Supervision	70	67						Pursue
Financial Services	73	69						Pursue
Office Practices	73	70						Pursue
Helping	53	56						Explore
Adult Development	50	59						Explore
Counseling	61	65						Pursue
Child Development	51	40						
Religious Activities	56	51						Develop
Medical Practice	50	50						
Creating	63	52						Develop
Art/Design	48	47						
Performing Arts	58	56						Pursue
Writing	58	49						Develop
International Activities	55	43						Develop
Fashion	69	68						Pursue
Culinary Arts	68	68						Pursue
aNalyzing	54	53						
Mathematics	61	59						Pursue
Science	45	45						Avoid
Producing	50	43						
Mechanical Crafts	61	47						Develop
Woodworking	44	47						
Farming/Forestry	46	39						
Plants/Gardens	43	35						Avoid
Animal Care	47	49						
Adventuring	49	45						
Athletics/Physical Fitness	59	54						Develop
Military/Law Enforcement	46	43						
Risks/Adventure	48	37						

Figure 5.2 (continued)

CAMPBELL INTEREST AND SKILL SURVEY INDIVIDUAL PROFILE REPORT

GABRIEL BLANC

DATE SCORED: 2/15/2000

Influencing Orientation

The Influencing Orientation focuses on influencing others through leadership, politics, public speaking, sales, and marketing. Influencers like to make things happen. They are often visible because they tend to take charge of activities that interest them. They typically work in organizations where they are responsible for directing activities, setting policies, and motivating people. Influencers are generally confident of their ability to persuade others and they usually enjoy the give-and-take of debating and negotiating. Typical high-scoring individuals include company presidents, corporate managers, school superintendents, sales representatives, and attorneys.

Your Influencing interest score is high and your skill score is mid-range. People who have this pattern of scores typically report strong interest but moderate confidence in leading, negotiating, marketing, selling, and public speaking.

Develop your Influencing skills through education, training, and experience, or simply enjoy these activities as hobbies.

Your scores on the Influencing Basic Scales, which provide more detail about your interests and skills in this area, are reported above on the left-hand side of the page. Your scores on the Influencing Occupational Scales, which show how your pattern of interests and skills compares with those of people employed in Influencing occupations, are reported above on the right-hand side of the page. Each occupation has a one-, two-, or three-letter code that indicates its highest Orientation score(s). The more similar the Orientation code is to your highest Orientation scores (which are reported on page 2), the more likely it is that you will find satisfaction working in that occupation.

* Standard Scores: I (♦) = Interests; S (◊) = Skills
** Interest/Skill Pattern: Pursue = High Interests, High Skills; Develop = High Interest, Lower Skills;
Explore = High Skills, Lower Interests; Avoid = Low Interest, Low Skills
*** Orientation Code: I= Influencing; O= Organizing; H= Helping; C= Creating; N=aNalyzing; P= Producing;
A= Adventuring
▬▬▬▬ Range of middle 50% of people in the occupation: Solid Bar = Interests; Hollow Bar = Skills

Figure 5.2 (continued)

CAMPBELL INTEREST AND SKILL SURVEY INDIVIDUAL PROFILE REPORT

GABRIEL BLANC

DATE SCORED: 2/15/2000

| Organizing Orientation |

Orientation Scale

	Standard Scores	30	35	40	45	50	55	60	65	70	Interest/Skill Pattern
Organizing	I 73 S 74										Pursue

Occupational Scales

	Orientation Code	Standard Scores	25	30	35	40	45	50	55	60	65	70	75	Interest/Skill Pattern
Secretary	O	I 63 S 81												Pursue
Bank Manager	OI	I 64 S 61												Pursue
Insurance Agent	OI	I 61 S 58												Pursue
Retail Store Manager	OI	I 67 S 65												Pursue
Hospital Administrator	OIH	I 67 S 60												Pursue
Accountant (CPA)	ON	I 61 S 80												Pursue
Bookkeeper	ON	I 71 S 67												Pursue

Basic Interest and Skill Scales

	Standard Scores	30	35	40	45	50	55	60	65	70	Interest/Skill Pattern
Supervision	I 70 S 67										Pursue
Financial Services	I 73 S 69										Pursue
Office Practices	I 73 S 70										Pursue

The Organizing Orientation includes activities that bring efficiency, productivity, and organization to the work environment. Organizers typically prefer to work in structured settings where they are responsible for planning, scheduling, supervising, and working with details. Organizers are seen as methodical, steady, reliable workers who display sensible judgment and enjoy solving the day-to-day problems that inevitably appear in organizations. Typical high-scoring individuals include accountants, financial planners, office managers, and administrative assistants.

Your Organizing interest and skill scores are both very high. People who have scores as high as yours typically report very strong interest and very substantial confidence in planning, scheduling, supervising, budgeting, and monitoring.

Pursue some of these Organizing activities in your career.

Your scores on the Organizing Basic Scales, which provide more detail about your interests and skills in this area, are reported above on the left-hand side of the page. Your scores on the Organizing Occupational Scales, which show how your pattern of interests and skills compares with those of people employed in Organizing occupations, are reported above on the right-hand side of the page. Each occupation has a one-, two-, or three-letter code that indicates its highest Orientation score(s). The more similar the Orientation code is to your highest Orientation scores (which are reported on page 2), the more likely it is that you will find satisfaction working in that occupation.

*   Standard Scores: I (♦) = Interests; S (◊) = Skills
**   Interest/Skill Pattern: Pursue = High Interests, High Skills; Develop = High Interest, Lower Skills;
    Explore = High Skills, Lower Interests; Avoid = Low Interest, Low Skills
***   Orientation Code: I= Influencing; O= Organizing; H= Helping; C= Creating; N=aNalyzing; P= Producing;
    A= Adventuring
    ▬▬▬ Range of middle 50% of people in the occupation: Solid Bar = Interests; Hollow Bar = Skills

Figure 5.2 *(continued)*

CAMPBELL INTEREST AND SKILL SURVEY INDIVIDUAL PROFILE REPORT

GABRIEL BLANC

Helping Orientation

DATE SCORED: 2/15/2000

The Helping Orientation covers teaching, counseling, medical services, and religious activities. Helpers are seen as supportive, nurturing, trusting individuals who value compassion, interpersonal harmony, and service to others. Helpers enjoy solving human problems and are genuinely concerned with improving the lives of others. Helping occupations usually involve a good deal of close contact with others. Typical high-scoring individuals include counselors, teachers, social workers, and religious leaders.

Your Helping interest score is mid-range and your skill score is high. People who have this pattern of scores typically report moderate interest but substantial confidence in counseling, teaching, supporting, healing, and caring for others.

Explore how your Helping skills could be transferred to more appealing areas.

Your scores on the Helping Basic Scales, which provide more detail about your interests and skills in this area, are reported above on the left-hand side of the page. Your scores on the Helping Occupational Scales, which show how your pattern of interests and skills compares with those of people employed in Helping occupations, are reported above on the right-hand side of the page. Each occupation has a one-, two-, or three-letter code that indicates its highest Orientation score(s). The more similar the Orientation code is to your highest Orientation scores (which are reported on page 2), the more likely it is that you will find satisfaction working in that occupation.

---

   *   Standard Scores: I (♦) = Interests; S (◊) = Skills
  ** Interest/Skill Pattern: Pursue = High Interests, High Skills; Develop = High Interest, Lower Skills;
       Explore = High Skills, Lower Interests; Avoid = Low Interest, Low Skills
*** Orientation Code: I= Influencing; O= Organizing; H= Helping; C= Creating; N=aNalyzing; P= Producing;
     A= Adventuring
▬▬▬▬ Range of middle 50% of people in the occupation: Solid Bar = Interests; Hollow Bar = Skills

Figure 5.2 (*continued*)

CAMPBELL INTEREST AND SKILL SURVEY INDIVIDUAL PROFILE REPORT

GABRIEL BLANC

DATE SCORED: 2/15/2000

| Creating Orientation |

Orientation Scale

	Standard Scores	Very Low 30 35	Low 40 45	Mid-Range 50	High 55 60	Very High 65 70	Interest/Skill Pattern
Creating	I 63				♦		Develop
	S 52			◊			

Basic Interest and Skill Scales

	Standard Scores	Very Low 30 35	Low 40 45	Mid-Range 50	High 55 60	Very High 65 70	Interest/Skill Pattern
Art/Design	I 48		♦				
	S 47		◊				
Performing Arts	I 58				♦		Pursue
	S 56				◊		
Writing	I 58				♦		Develop
	S 49			◊			
International Activities	I 55			♦			Develop
	S 43		◊				
Fashion	I 69					♦	Pursue
	S 68					◊	
Culinary Arts	I 68					♦	Pursue
	S 68					◊	

Occupational Scales

	Orientation Code	Standard Scores	Very Low 25 30 35	Low 40 45	Mid-Range 50	High 55 60	Very High 65 70 75	Interest/Skill Pattern
Commercial Artist	C	I 35	♦					
		S 52			◊			
Fashion Designer	C	I 49		♦				Explore
		S 55			◊			
Liberal Arts Professor	C	I 45		♦				
		S 50		◊				
Librarian	C	I 51			♦			
		S 49		◊				
Musician	C	I 48		♦				Explore
		S 64				◊		
Translator/Interpreter	C	I 60				♦		Develop
		S 48		◊				
Writer/Editor	C	I 34	♦					Explore
		S 57			◊			
Restaurant Manager	CO	I 65				♦		Pursue
		S 60				◊		
Chef	CP	I 58				♦		Pursue
		S 60				◊		

The Creating Orientation includes artistic, literary, and musical activities such as writing, painting, dancing, and working in the theater. Creators are described as imaginative, clever, inventive, and original. Creators tend to be sources of new and different ideas and enjoy acting, thinking, and speaking in fresh and unusual ways. They tend to be uncomfortable with traditional organizational constraints and prefer work that allows for self-expression. Typical high-scoring individuals include artists, musicians, writers, interior designers, and chefs.

Your Creating interest score is very high but your skill score is only mid-range. People who have this pattern of scores typically report very strong interest but moderate confidence in designing, writing, performing, and other creative activities.

Develop your Creating skills through education, training, and experience, or simply enjoy these activities as hobbies.

Your scores on the Creating Basic Scales, which provide more detail about your interests and skills in this area, are reported above on the left-hand side of the page. Your scores on the Creating Occupational Scales, which show how your pattern of interests and skills compares with those of people employed in Creating occupations, are reported above on the right-hand side of the page. Each occupation has a one-, two-, or three-letter code that indicates its highest Orientation score(s). The more similar the Orientation code is to your highest Orientation scores (which are reported on page 2), the more likely it is that you will find satisfaction working in that occupation.

* Standard Scores: I (♦) = Interests; S (◊) = Skills
** Interest/Skill Pattern: Pursue = High Interests, High Skills; Develop = High Interest, Lower Skills;
   Explore = High Skills, Lower Interests; Avoid = Low Interest, Low Skills
*** Orientation Code: I= Influencing; O= Organizing; H= Helping; C= Creating; N=aNalyzing; P= Producing;
    A= Adventuring
━━━ Range of middle 50% of people in the occupation: Solid Bar = Interests; Hollow Bar = Skills

Figure 5.2 *(continued)*

CAMPBELL INTEREST AND SKILL SURVEY INDIVIDUAL PROFILE REPORT

GABRIEL BLANC   DATE SCORED: 2/15/2000

| aNalyzing Orientation |

Orientation Scale

	Standard Scores	Very Low 30 35	Low 40 45	Mid-Range 50 55	High 60	Very High 65 70	Interest/Skill Pattern
aNalyzing	I 54 / S 53				♦ / ◊		

Basic Interest and Skill Scales

	Standard Scores	Very Low 30 35	Low 40 45	Mid-Range 50 55	High 60 65	Very High 70	Interest/Skill Pattern
Mathematics	I 61 / S 59				◊ ♦		Pursue
Science	I 45 / S 45		♦ ◊				Avoid

Occupational Scales

	Orientation Code	Standard Scores	Very Low 25 30 35	Low 40 45	Mid-Range 50 55	High 60	Very High 65 70 75	Interest/Skill Pattern
Physician	N	I 41 / S 42	♦ ◊					Avoid
Chemist	NP	I 46 / S 52		♦ ◊				
Medical Researcher	NP	I 45 / S 53		♦ ◊				
Engineer	NP	I 50 / S 51			♦ ◊			
Math/Science Teacher	NPH	I 46 / S 55			♦ ◊			Explore
Computer Programmer	NO	I 51 / S 64			♦		◊	Explore
Statistician	NO	I 66 / S 64					◊ ♦	Pursue
Systems Analyst	NOP	I 54 / S 66			♦		◊	Explore

(This Orientation is labelled with the letter "N" because the letter "A" is used for the Adventuring Orientation below.) The aNalyzing Orientation involves scientific, mathematical, statistical, and research activities. People who score high are comfortable with data and numbers and have a strong need to understand the world in a scientific sense. They usually prefer to work alone or in small groups in laboratory or academic settings, solving problems and designing experiments. ANalyzers are generally autonomous and like to work through problems for themselves. Typical high-scoring individuals include scientists, medical researchers, statisticians, computer programmers, and physicians.

Your aNalyzing interest and skill scores are both mid-range. People who have this pattern of scores typically report moderate interest and confidence in analyzing data, using mathematics, and conducting scientific research.

Your scores on the aNalyzing Basic Scales, which provide more detail about your interests and skills in this area, are reported above on the left-hand side of the page. Your scores on the aNalyzing Occupational Scales, which show how your pattern of interests and skills compares with those of people employed in aNalyzing occupations, are reported above on the right-hand side of the page. Each occupation has a one-, two-, or three-letter code that indicates its highest Orientation score(s). The more similar the Orientation code is to your highest Orientation scores (which are reported on page 2), the more likely it is that you will find satisfaction working in that occupation.

    *   Standard Scores: I (♦) = Interests; S (◊) = Skills
  **   Interest/Skill Pattern: Pursue = High Interests, High Skills; Develop = High Interest, Lower Skills;
        Explore = High Skills, Lower Interests; Avoid = Low Interest, Low Skills
***   Orientation Code: I= Influencing; O= Organizing; H= Helping; C= Creating; N=aNalyzing; P= Producing;
        A= Adventuring
    ━━━ Range of middle 50% of people in the occupation: Solid Bar = Interests; Hollow Bar = Skills

Figure 5.2 (continued)

CAMPBELL INTEREST AND SKILL SURVEY INDIVIDUAL PROFILE REPORT

GABRIEL BLANC **Producing Orientation** DATE SCORED: 2/15/2000

Orientation Scale

	Standard Scores	Very Low 30	Low 35	40	Mid-Range 45	50	High 55	60	Very High 65	70	Interest/Skill Pattern
Producing	I 50				◊		♦				
	S 43										

Basic Interest and Skill Scales

	Standard Scores	Very Low 30	Low 35	40	Mid-Range 45	50	High 55	60	Very High 65	70	Interest/Skill Pattern
Mechanical Crafts	I 61							♦			Develop
	S 47				◊						
Wood-working	I 44		♦								
	S 47			◊							
Farming/ Forestry	I 46		♦								
	S 39	◊									
Plants/ Gardens	I 43		♦								Avoid
	S 35	◊									
Animal Care	I 47			♦							
	S 49				◊						

Occupational Scales

	Orientation Code	Standard Scores	Very Low 25	30	Low 35	40	Mid-Range 45	50	High 55	60	Very High 65	70	75	Interest/Skill Pattern
Carpenter	P	I 39		♦			◊				▬▬▬			Avoid
		S 45												
Electrician	PN	I 51						◊	♦		▬▬			
		S 44												
Veterinarian	PN	I 35		♦			◊				▬▬▬			Avoid
		S 43												
Airline Mechanic	PNA	I 61					◊			♦ ▭▭▭				Develop
		S 45												
Agribusiness Manager	PO	I 45					♦			▬▬				
		S 47					◊							
Landscape Architect	PNC	I 35		♦			◊			▬▬				
		S 46												
Architect	PC	I 43			♦		◊			▬▬▬				
		S 47												

The Producing Orientation covers practical, hands-on, "productive" activities such as construction, farming, skilled crafts, and mechanical crafts. People who score high like to work with their hands, generally enjoy being outdoors, and like to be able to see visible results of their labors. Producers are usually good with tools, and they enjoy taking on construction projects, repairing mechanical breakdowns, or managing large outdoor operations. They tend to be rugged, practical, and down-to-earth people. Typical high-scoring individuals include mechanics, farmers, veterinarians, landscape architects, electricians, and carpenters.

Your Producing interest score is mid-range and your skill score is low. People who have this pattern of scores typically report moderate interest but little confidence in using "hands-on" skills in farming, construction, and mechanical crafts.

Your scores on the Producing Basic Scales, which provide more detail about your interests and skills in this area, are reported above on the left-hand side of the page. Your scores on the Producing Occupational Scales, which show how your pattern of interests and skills compares with those of people employed in Producing occupations, are reported above on the right-hand side of the page. Each occupation has a one-, two-, or three-letter code that indicates its highest Orientation score(s). The more similar the Orientation code is to your highest Orientation scores (which are reported on page 2), the more likely it is that you will find satisfaction working in that occupation.

---

   * Standard Scores: I (♦) = Interests; S (◊) = Skills
  ** Interest/Skill Pattern: Pursue = High Interests, High Skills; Develop = High Interest, Lower Skills;
      Explore = High Skills, Lower Interests; Avoid = Low Interest, Low Skills
*** Orientation Code: I= Influencing; O= Organizing; H= Helping; C= Creating; N=aNalyzing; P= Producing;
     A= Adventuring
   ▬▬▬ Range of middle 50% of people in the occupation: Solid Bar = Interests; Hollow Bar = Skills

Figure 5.2 (continued)

CAMPBELL INTEREST AND SKILL SURVEY INDIVIDUAL PROFILE REPORT

GABRIEL BLANC   DATE SCORED: 2/15/2000

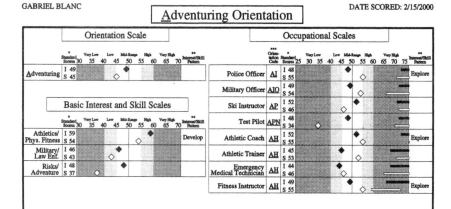

The Adventuring Orientation focuses on athletic, police, and military activities involving physical endurance, risk taking, and teamwork. People who score high are robust and vigorous, enjoying both physical challenges and competitive outlets. Adventurers are active, energetic, and confident in strenuous or dangerous situations. They also enjoy the opportunity to work with others in skilled, disciplined groups such as athletic teams or military units. Typical high-scoring individuals include military officers, police officers, athletic coaches, emergency medical technicians, and fitness instructors.

Your Adventuring interest score is mid-range and your skill score is low. People who have this pattern of scores typically report moderate interest but little confidence in physically active, adventurous, and competitive activities, such as athletics, police work, and military activities.

Your scores on the Adventuring Basic Scales, which provide more detail about your interests and skills in this area, are reported above on the left-hand side of the page. Your scores on the Adventuring Occupational Scales, which show how your pattern of interests and skills compares with those of people employed in Adventuring occupations, are reported above on the right-hand side of the page. Each occupation has a one-, two-, or three-letter code that indicates its highest Orientation score(s). The more similar the Orientation code is to your highest Orientation scores (which are reported on page 2), the more likely it is that you will find satisfaction working in that occupation.

  *   Standard Scores: I (♦) = Interests; S (◊) = Skills
 **   Interest/Skill Pattern: Pursue = High Interests, High Skills; Develop = High Interest, Lower Skills;
      Explore = High Skills, Lower Interests; Avoid = Low Interest, Low Skills
***   Orientation Code: I= Influencing; O= Organizing; H= Helping; C= Creating; N=aNalyzing; P= Producing;
      A= Adventuring
 ▄▄▄▄ Range of middle 50% of people in the occupation: Solid Bar = Interests; Hollow Bar = Skills

Figure 5.2 (*continued*)

CAMPBELL INTEREST AND SKILL SURVEY INDIVIDUAL PROFILE REPORT

GABRIEL BLANC   DATE SCORED: 2/15/2000

Special Scales

Academic Focus

Standard Scores	30	Very Low 35	Low 40	Mid-Range 45	50	55	High 60	Very High 65	70
I 52					◆				
S 50			◇						

The Academic Focus Scales reflect your feelings toward the academic world. High scores do not necessarily lead to academic success, nor low scores to failure, but your pattern of scores reflects your degree of comfort in educational settings and can help you plan your educational strategy. High scorers are attracted to intellectual ideas, academic pursuits, and scientific research. Typical high-scoring individuals include university professors, research scientists, technical writers, and other scholars. People who score low usually see themselves as more action-oriented and practical. Business people, especially those in sales and marketing, tend to score low on the Academic Focus Scales.

Your Academic Focus interest and skill scores are both mid-range. People who have this pattern of scores typically report moderate interest and confidence in academic activities, such as studying, conducting research, and writing scientific papers.

Extraversion

Standard Scores	30	Very Low 35	Low 40	Mid-Range 45	50	55	High 60	Very High 65	70
I 63								◆	
S 51					◇				

The Extraversion Scales indicate level of interest and confidence working with all types of people in many different occupational settings. High scores reflect an attraction to a wide range of people-oriented activities. Lower scores may suggest a narrower focus, such as an interest in working with children but not adults, or confidence in counseling others but not selling. Low scores may indicate a preference for less contact with people on the job.

Occupational Extraverts (such as guidance counselors, hotel managers, corporate trainers, and realtors) are energized by frequent social contact and enjoy working closely with others. People who score low on the Extraversion Scales may prefer more independent work assignments and the opportunity for private time and space. Low-scoring individuals include scientists, skilled craftsworkers, and veterinarians.

Your Extraversion interest score is very high but your skill score is only mid-range. People who have this pattern of scores typically report very strong interest but moderate confidence in work situations requiring a great deal of personal contact with others. You may want to work closely with others only in particular situations, or you may wish to expand your social skills to match your high interest level

Procedural Checks

The Procedural Checks are designed to detect possible problems in the administration, completion, or processing of answer sheets. See the CISS manual for details.

All Procedural Checks are VALID.

Interest Items

Topic	STRONGLY LIKE	Like	slightly like	slightly dislike	Dislike	STRONGLY DISLIKE			
Response Percentage Check - **Valid**							Inconsistency Check - **Valid**		
							# Inconsistent Pairs		0
Occupations	7	22	32	22	14	2			
School Subjects	19	28	35	19	0	0			
Varied Activities	7	31	36	22	4	0	Omitted Items Check - **Valid**		
Overall Percentage	10	27	34	22	8	1	# Omitted Items		0

Skill Items

	EXPERT	Good	above average	below average	Poor	NONE			
Response Percentage Check - **Valid**							Inconsistency Check - **Valid**		
							# Inconsistent Pairs		1
Varied Activities	18	14	23	23	10	11			
							Omitted Items Check - **Valid**		
							# Omitted Items		0

Figure 5.2 (continued)

CAMPBELL INTEREST AND SKILL SURVEY INDIVIDUAL PROFILE REPORT

GABRIEL BLANC
DATE SCORED: 2/15/2000
Female
Age 33

Orientations and Basic Scales

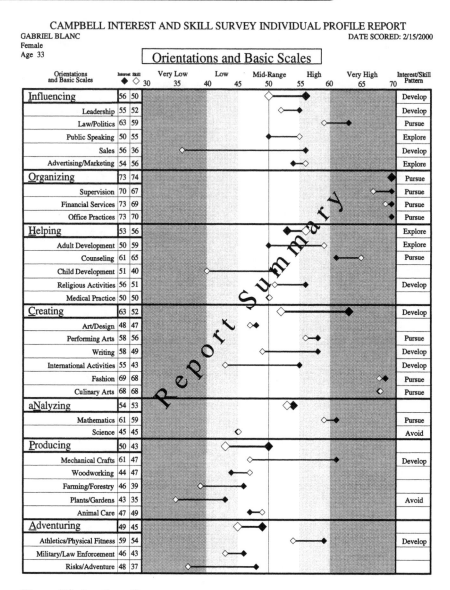

Orientations and Basic Scales	Interest	Skill	Very Low 30	35	Low 40	45	Mid-Range 50	55	High 60	Very High 65	70	Interest/Skill Pattern
Influencing	56	50										Develop
Leadership	55	52										Develop
Law/Politics	63	59										Pursue
Public Speaking	50	55										Explore
Sales	56	36										Develop
Advertising/Marketing	54	56										Explore
Organizing	73	74										Pursue
Supervision	70	67										Pursue
Financial Services	73	69										Pursue
Office Practices	73	70										Pursue
Helping	53	56										Explore
Adult Development	50	59										Explore
Counseling	61	65										Pursue
Child Development	51	40										
Religious Activities	56	51										Develop
Medical Practice	50	50										
Creating	63	52										Develop
Art/Design	48	47										
Performing Arts	58	56										Pursue
Writing	58	49										Develop
International Activities	55	43										Develop
Fashion	69	68										Pursue
Culinary Arts	68	68										Pursue
aNalyzing	54	53										
Mathematics	61	59										Pursue
Science	45	45										Avoid
Producing	50	43										
Mechanical Crafts	61	47										Develop
Woodworking	44	47										
Farming/Forestry	46	39										
Plants/Gardens	43	35										Avoid
Animal Care	47	49										
Adventuring	49	45										
Athletics/Physical Fitness	59	54										Develop
Military/Law Enforcement	46	43										
Risks/Adventure	48	37										

Report Summary

Figure 5.2 (*continued*)

CAMPBELL INTEREST AND SKILL SURVEY INDIVIDUAL PROFILE REPORT

GABRIEL BLANC
Female
Age 33

DATE SCORED: 2/15/2000

Occupational Scales

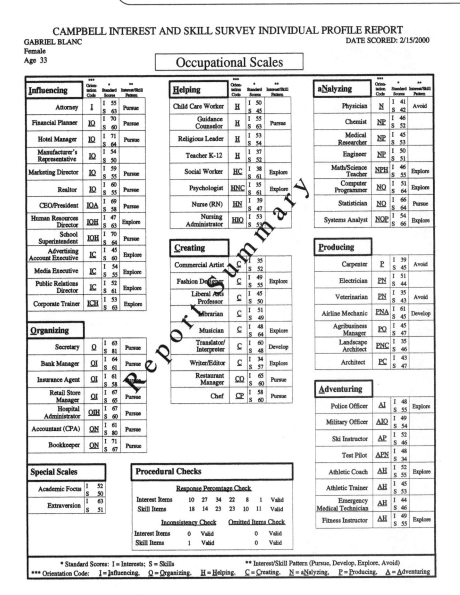

Influencing

	Orientation Code	Standard Scores	Interest/Skill Pattern
Attorney	I	I 55 / S 63	Pursue
Financial Planner	IO	I 70 / S 60	Pursue
Hotel Manager	IO	I 71 / S 64	Pursue
Manufacturer's Representative	IO	I 54 / S 50	
Marketing Director	IO	I 59 / S 55	Pursue
Realtor	IO	I 60 / S 55	Pursue
CEO/President	IOA	I 69 / S 58	Pursue
Human Resources Director	IOH	I 47 / S 63	Explore
School Superintendent	IOH	I 70 / S 64	Pursue
Advertising Account Executive	IC	I 45 / S 60	Explore
Media Executive	IC	I 54 / S 55	Explore
Public Relations Director	IC	I 52 / S 61	Explore
Corporate Trainer	ICH	I 53 / S 63	Explore

Organizing

	Orientation Code	Standard Scores	Interest/Skill Pattern
Secretary	O	I 63 / S 81	Pursue
Bank Manager	OI	I 64 / S 61	Pursue
Insurance Agent	OI	I 61 / S 58	Pursue
Retail Store Manager	OI	I 67 / S 65	Pursue
Hospital Administrator	OIH	I 67 / S 60	Pursue
Accountant (CPA)	ON	I 61 / S 80	Pursue
Bookkeeper	ON	I 71 / S 67	Pursue

Special Scales

	Standard Scores
Academic Focus	I 52 / S 50
Extraversion	I 63 / S 51

Helping

	Orientation Code	Standard Scores	Interest/Skill Pattern
Child Care Worker	H	I 50 / S 45	
Guidance Counselor	H	I 55 / S 63	Pursue
Religious Leader	H	I 53 / S 54	
Teacher K-12	H	I 37 / S 52	
Social Worker	HC	I 38 / S 61	Explore
Psychologist	HNC	I 35 / S 61	Explore
Nurse (RN)	HN	I 39 / S 47	
Nursing Administrator	HIO	I 53 / S 53	

Creating

	Orientation Code	Standard Scores	Interest/Skill Pattern
Commercial Artist	C	I 35 / S 52	
Fashion Designer	C	I 49 / S 55	Explore
Liberal Arts Professor	C	I 45 / S 50	
Librarian	C	I 51 / S 49	
Musician	C	I 48 / S 64	Explore
Translator/Interpreter	C	I 60 / S 48	Develop
Writer/Editor	C	I 34 / S 57	Explore
Restaurant Manager	CO	I 65 / S 60	Pursue
Chef	CP	I 58 / S 60	Pursue

Procedural Checks

Response Percentage Check

Interest Items	10	27	34	22	8	1	Valid
Skill Items	18	14	23	23	10	11	Valid

Inconsistency Check   Omitted Items Check

Interest Items	0	Valid	0	Valid
Skill Items	1	Valid	0	Valid

aNalyzing

	Orientation Code	Standard Scores	Interest/Skill Pattern
Physician	N	I 41 / S 42	Avoid
Chemist	NP	I 46 / S 52	
Medical Researcher	NP	I 45 / S 53	
Engineer	NP	I 50 / S 51	
Math/Science Teacher	NPH	I 46 / S 55	Explore
Computer Programmer	NO	I 51 / S 64	Explore
Statistician	NO	I 66 / S 64	Pursue
Systems Analyst	NOP	I 54 / S 66	Explore

Producing

	Orientation Code	Standard Scores	Interest/Skill Pattern
Carpenter	P	I 39 / S 45	Avoid
Electrician	PN	I 51 / S 44	
Veterinarian	PN	I 35 / S 43	Avoid
Airline Mechanic	PNA	I 61 / S 45	Develop
Agribusiness Manager	PO	I 45 / S 47	
Landscape Architect	PNC	I 35 / S 46	
Architect	PC	I 43 / S 47	

Adventuring

	Orientation Code	Standard Scores	Interest/Skill Pattern
Police Officer	AI	I 48 / S 55	Explore
Military Officer	AIO	I 49 / S 54	
Ski Instructor	AP	I 52 / S 46	
Test Pilot	APN	I 48 / S 34	
Athletic Coach	AH	I 52 / S 55	Explore
Athletic Trainer	AH	I 45 / S 53	
Emergency Medical Technician	AH	I 44 / S 46	
Fitness Instructor	AH	I 49 / S 55	Explore

* Standard Scores: I = Interests; S = Skills   ** Interest/Skill Pattern (Pursue, Develop, Explore, Avoid)
*** Orientation Code: I = Influencing, O = Organizing, H = Helping, C = Creating, N = aNalyzing, P = Producing, A = Adventuring

Figure 5.2 (continued)

Figure 5.3 *SDS* Results

This booklet may help you explore what occupation to follow. If you have already made up your mind about an occupation, it may support your idea or suggest other possibilities. If you are uncertain about what occupation to follow, the booklet may help you to locate a small group of occupations for further consideration. Most people find that filling out this booklet is helpful and fun. If you follow the directions carefully, page by page, you should enjoy the experience. Do not rush; you will gain more by approaching the task thoughtfully. Use a lead pencil, so you can erase easily.

Name   _Gabrielle Blanc_

Age   _33_   Sex _Female_   Date _2/16/2000_

Years of education completed   _15 (Bachelor's degree expected May 2000)_

Figure 5.3 (continued)

Occupational Daydreams _____

1. List below the occupations you have considered in thinking about your future. List the careers you have daydreamed about as well as those you have discussed with others. Try to give a history of your daydreams. Put your most recent choice on Line 1 and work backwards to the earlier jobs you have considered.

Occupation   **Code**

1. *Financial Planner* | E | S | C |
2. *Accountant* | C | S | I |
3. *Budget Officer* | E | S | I |
4. *Lawyer* | E | S | I |
5. *Nursing Home Administrator* | S | E | R |
6. *Hotel or Motel Manager* | E | S | R |
7. *Psychiatrist* | I | S | A |
8. _____ | | | |

2. Now use The Occupations Finder. Locate the three-letter code for each of the occupations you just wrote down. This search for occupational codes will help you learn about the many occupations in the world. This task usually takes from 5 to 15 minutes. The Alphabetized Occupations Finder, which is available separately, may make your search easier.

If you can't find the exact occupation in The Occupations Finder, use the occupation that seems most like your occupational aspiration.

If you're in a hurry, do the coding after you complete this booklet.

Figure 5.3 (continued)

Activities

Blacken under **L** for those activities you would like to do. Blacken under **D** for those things you would dislike doing or would be indifferent to.

R

	L	D
Fix electrical things	■	☐
Repair cars	■	☐
Fix mechanical things	■	☐
Build things with wood	☐	■
Take a Technology Education (e.g., Industrial Arts, Shop) course	☐	■
Take a Mechanical Drawing course	☐	■
Take a Woodworking course	☐	■
Take an Auto Mechanics course	■	☐
Work with an outstanding mechanic or technician	■	☐
Work outdoors	☐	■
Operate motorized machines or equipment	☐	■

Total No. of Ls ⟦5⟧

I

	L	D
Read scientific books or magazines	☐	■
Work in a research office or laboratory	☐	■
Work on a scientific project	☐	■
Study a scientific theory	☐	■
Work with chemicals	☐	■
Apply mathematics to practical problems	■	☐
Take a Physics course	☐	■
Take a Chemistry course	☐	■
Take a Mathematics course	■	☐
Take a Biology course	☐	■
Study scholarly or technical problems	☐	■

Total No. of Ls ⟦2⟧

A

	L	D
Sketch, draw, or paint	■	☐
Design furniture, clothing, or posters	■	☐
Play in a band, group, or orchestra	■	☐
Practice a musical instrument	■	☐
Create portraits or photographs	■	☐
Write novels or plays	■	☐
Take an Art course	■	☐
Arrange or compose music of any kind	■	☐
Work with a gifted artist, writer, or sculptor	■	☐
Perform for others (dance, sing, act, etc.)	■	☐
Read artistic, literary, or musical articles	■	☐

Total No. of Ls ⟦11⟧

Figure 5.3 (continued)

S

	L	D
Meet important educators or therapists	■	☐
Read sociology articles or books	☐	●
Work for a charity	☐	●
Help others with their personal problems	☐	●
Study juvenile delinquency	☐	●
Read psychology articles or books	☐	●
Take a Human Relations course	■	☐
Teach in a high school	☐	●
Supervise activities for mentally ill patients	●	☐
Teach adults	■	☐
Work as a volunteer	■	☐

Total No. of Ls [6]

E

	L	D
Learn strategies for business success	●	☐
Operate my own service or business	☐	●
Attend sales conferences	☐	●
Take a short course on administration or leadership	●	☐
Serve as an officer of any group	●	☐
Supervise the work of others	●	☐
Meet important executives and leaders	■	☐
Lead a group in accomplishing some goal	■	☐
Participate in a political campaign	☐	●
Act as an organizational or business consultant	●	☐
Read business magazines or articles	●	☐

Total No. of Ls [8]

C

	L	D
Fill out income tax forms	●	☐
Add, subtract, multiply, and divide numbers in business or bookkeeping	●	☐
Operate office machines	●	☐
Keep detailed records of expenses	●	☐
Set up a record-keeping system	●	☐
Take an Accounting course	●	☐
Take a Commercial Math course	●	☐
Take an inventory of supplies or products	●	☐
Check paperwork or products for errors or flaws	■	☐
Update records or files	●	☐
Work in an office	●	☐

Total No. of Ls [11]

Figure 5.3 (*continued*)

Competencies

Blacken under **Y** for "Yes" for those activities you can do well or competently. Blacken under **N** for "No" for those activities you have never performed or perform poorly.

R

	Y	N
I have used wood shop power tools such as a power saw, lathe, or sander	☐	■
I can make a scale drawing	☐	■
I can change a car's oil or tire	☐	■
I have operated power tools such as a drill press, grinder, or sewing machine	☐	■
I can refinish furniture or woodwork	☐	■
I can make simple electrical repairs	☐	■
I can repair furniture	☐	■
I can use many carpentry tools	☐	■
I can make simple plumbing repairs	☐	■
I can build simple articles of wood	☐	■
I can paint rooms of a house or an apartment	■	☐

Total No. of Ys $\boxed{1}$

I

	Y	N
I can use algebra to solve mathematical problems	■	☐
I can perform a scientific experiment or survey	☐	■
I understand the "half-life" of a radioactive element	☐	■
I can use logarithmic tables	■	☐
I can use a computer to study a scientific problem	■	☐
I can describe the function of the white blood cells	☐	■
I can interpret simple chemical formulae	☐	■
I understand why man-made satellites do not fall to earth	☐	■
I can write a scientific report	☐	■
I understand the "Big Bang" theory of the universe	☐	■
I understand the role of DNA in genetics	☐	■

Total No. of Ys $\boxed{3}$

A

	Y	N
I can play a musical instrument	☐	■
I can participate in two- or four-part choral singing	■	☐
I can perform as a musical soloist	☐	■
I can act in a play	■	☐
I can do interpretive reading	■	☐
I can do a painting, watercolor, or sculpture	☐	■
I can arrange or compose music	☐	■
I can design clothing, posters, or furniture	☐	■
I write stories or poetry well	■	☐
I can write a speech	■	☐
I can take attractive photographs	☐	■

Total No. of Ys $\boxed{5}$

Figure 5.3 (*continued*)

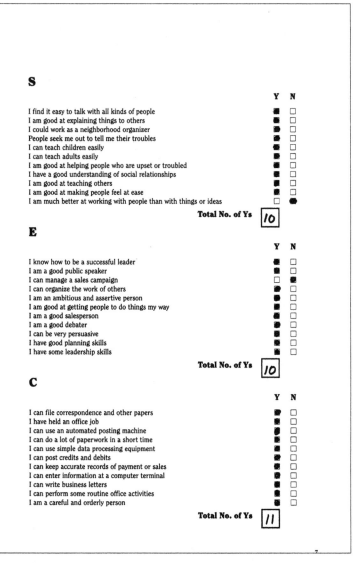

S

	Y	N
I find it easy to talk with all kinds of people	■	☐
I am good at explaining things to others	■	☐
I could work as a neighborhood organizer	■	☐
People seek me out to tell me their troubles	■	☐
I can teach children easily	■	☐
I can teach adults easily	■	☐
I am good at helping people who are upset or troubled	■	☐
I have a good understanding of social relationships	■	☐
I am good at teaching others	■	☐
I am good at making people feel at ease	☐	■
I am much better at working with people than with things or ideas	☐	●

Total No. of Ys `10`

E

	Y	N
I know how to be a successful leader	■	☐
I am a good public speaker	■	☐
I can manage a sales campaign	☐	■
I can organize the work of others	■	☐
I am an ambitious and assertive person	■	☐
I am good at getting people to do things my way	■	☐
I am a good salesperson	■	☐
I am a good debater	■	☐
I can be very persuasive	■	☐
I have good planning skills	■	☐
I have some leadership skills	■	☐

Total No. of Ys `10`

C

	Y	N
I can file correspondence and other papers	■	☐
I have held an office job	■	☐
I can use an automated posting machine	■	☐
I can do a lot of paperwork in a short time	■	☐
I can use simple data processing equipment	■	☐
I can post credits and debits	■	☐
I can keep accurate records of payment or sales	■	☐
I can enter information at a computer terminal	■	☐
I can write business letters	■	☐
I can perform some routine office activities	■	☐
I am a careful and orderly person	■	☐

Total No. of Ys `11`

Figure 5.3 (continued)

Occupations

This is an inventory of your feelings and attitudes about many kinds of work. Show the occupations that *interest* or *appeal* to you by blackening under Y for "Yes." Show the occupations that you *dislike* or find *uninteresting* by blackening under N for "No."

	Y	N		Y	N
Airplane Mechanic	☐	■	Career Counselor	■	☐
Auto Mechanic	■	☐	Sociologist	☐	■
Carpenter	☐	■	High School Teacher	☐	■
Truck Driver	■	☐	Substance Abuse Counselor	☐	■
Surveyor	☐	■	Juvenile Delinquency Expert	☐	■
Construction Inspector	☐	■	Speech Therapist	☐	■
Radio Mechanic	☐	■	Marriage Counselor	■	☐
Locomotive Engineer	☐	■	Clinical Psychologist	☐	■
Machinist	☐	■	Social Science Teacher	☐	■
Electrician	☐	■	Personal Counselor	■	☐
Farmer	☐	■	Youth Camp Director	☐	■
Helicopter Pilot	☐	■	Social Worker	☐	■
Electronic Technician	☐	■	Rehabilitation Counselor	☐	■
Welder	☐	■	Playground Director	☐	■

Total R Ys 2   **Total S Ys** 3

	Y	N		Y	N
Meteorologist	■	☐	Buyer	■	☐
Biologist	☐	■	Advertising Executive	☐	■
Astronomer	■	☐	Manufacturer's Representative	☐	■
Medical Laboratory Technician	☐	■	Business Executive	■	☐
Anthropologist	☐	■	Master of Ceremonies	■	☐
Chemist	☐	■	Salesperson	☐	■
Independent Research Scientist	☐	■	Real Estate Salesperson	☐	■
Writer of Scientific Articles	☐	■	Department Store Manager	■	☐
Geologist	☐	■	Sales Manager	☐	■
Botanist	☐	■	Public Relations Executive	■	☐
Scientific Research Worker	☐	■	TV Station Manager	■	☐
Physicist	☐	■	Small Business Owner	☐	■
Social Science Researcher	☐	■	Legislator	■	☐
Environmental Analyst	☐	■	Airport Manager	■	☐

Total I Ys 2   **Total E Ys** 8

	Y	N		Y	N
Poet	■	☐	Bookkeeper	■	☐
Musician	■	☐	Budget Reviewer	■	☐
Novelist	■	☐	Certified Public Accountant	■	☐
Actor/Actress	■	☐	Credit Investigator	■	☐
Free-Lance Writer	■	☐	Bank Teller	■	☐
Musical Arranger	☐	■	Tax Expert	■	☐
Journalist	☐	■	Inventory Controller	■	☐
Artist	■	☐	Computer Operator	■	☐
Singer	■	☐	Financial Analyst	■	☐
Composer	☐	■	Cost Estimator	■	☐
Sculptor/Sculptress	☐	■	Payroll Clerk	■	☐
Playwright	☐	■	Bank Examiner	■	☐
Cartoonist	☐	■	Accounting Clerk	■	☐
Entertainer	■	☐	Audit Clerk	■	☐

Total A Ys 8   **Total C Ys** 14

Figure 5.3 (continued)

Self-Estimates

1. Rate yourself on each of the following traits *as you really think you are when compared with other persons your own age.* Give the most accurate estimate of how you see yourself. Circle the appropriate number and *avoid rating yourself the same in each ability.*

	Mechanical Ability	Scientific Ability	Artistic Ability	Teaching Ability	Sales Ability	Clerical Ability
High	7	7	7	(7)	7	(7)
	6	6	6	6	6	6
	5	5	5	5	(5)	5
Average	4	4	4	4	4	4
	3	3	(3)	3	3	3
	2	(2)	2	2	2	2
Low	(1)	1	1	1	1	1
	R	I	A	S	E	C

	Manual Skills	Math Ability	Musical Ability	Under-standing of others	Managerial Skills	Office Skills
High	7	(7)	7	7	7	(7)
	6	6	6	(6)	(6)	6
	5	5	5	5	5	5
Average	4	4	4	4	4	4
	3	3	(3)	3	3	3
	(2)	2	2	2	2	2
Low	1	1	1	1	1	1
	R	I	A	S	E	C

Figure 5.3 (continued)

How To Organize Your Answers _____

Start on page 4. Count how many times you said L for "Like." Record the number of **Ls** or **Ys** for each group of Activities, Competencies, or Occupations on the lines below.

Activities (pp. 4-5)

$$\frac{5}{R} \quad \frac{2}{I} \quad \frac{11}{A} \quad \frac{6}{S} \quad \frac{8}{E} \quad \frac{11}{C}$$

Competencies (pp. 6-7)

$$\frac{1}{R} \quad \frac{3}{I} \quad \frac{5}{A} \quad \frac{10}{S} \quad \frac{10}{E} \quad \frac{11}{C}$$

Occupations (p. 8)

$$\frac{2}{R} \quad \frac{2}{I} \quad \frac{8}{A} \quad \frac{3}{S} \quad \frac{8}{E} \quad \frac{14}{C}$$

Self-Estimates (p. 9)
(What number did you circle?)

$$\frac{1}{R} \quad \frac{2}{I} \quad \frac{3}{A} \quad \frac{7}{S} \quad \frac{5}{E} \quad \frac{7}{C}$$

$$\frac{2}{R} \quad \frac{7}{I} \quad \frac{3}{A} \quad \frac{6}{S} \quad \frac{6}{E} \quad \frac{7}{C}$$

Total Scores
(Add the five R scores, the five I scores, the five A scores, etc.)

$$\frac{11}{R} \quad \frac{16}{I} \quad \frac{30}{A} \quad \frac{32}{S} \quad \frac{37}{E} \quad \frac{50}{C}$$

The letters with the three highest numbers indicate your Summary Code. Write your Summary Code below. (If two scores are the same or tied, put both letters in the same box.)

Summary Code

C	E	S
Highest	2nd	3rd

Figure 5.3 (*continued*)

What Your Summary Code Means _____

Your Summary Code is a simple way of organizing information about people and jobs. It can be used to discover how your special pattern of interests, self-estimates, and competencies resembles the patterns of interests and competencies that many occupations demand. In this way, your Summary Code locates suitable groups of occupations for you to consider.

It is vital that you search The Occupations Finder for every possible ordering of your three-letter code. For example, if you are an **ESC**, search for all the **ESC**, **ECS**, **SEC**, **SCE**, **CES**, and **CSE** occupations by completing Steps 1 and 2.

Step 1. Find the occupations whose codes are *identical* with yours and list those occupations that are of interest to you. If your code is **SEI**, occupations with codes **SEI** are identical. Go to Step 2, whether or not you find an occupation with a code identical to yours.

Summary Code   _CES_

Occupation	Education	Occupation	Education
None of interest			

Step 2. Make a list of occupations whose Summary Codes *resemble* yours. Search The Occupations Finder for the five arrangements of your code. For example, if your code is **IRE**, search for occupations with codes of **IER**, **RIE**, **REI**, **EIR**, and **ERI**. Start by writing down the five possible letter arrangements of your Summary Code. (If your Summary Code includes a tie such as **RIEA**, you must look up more letter combinations and their arrangements.)

Similar Codes   _CSE_   _ESC_   _ECS_   _SEC_   _SCE_

	Occupation	Education	Occupation	Education
ECS	Accountant-Tax	5		
SCE	Employment Interviewer	5		
SEC	Financial Aids Officer	5		
SEC	Personnel Manager	5		

Go to the Next Page

Figure 5.3 (*continued*)

Six

OTHER TYPES OF INTEREST ASSESSMENT

The previous chapters reviewed three of the most commonly used print inventories for interest assessment: the *SII, CISS,* and *SDS.* This chapter will provide an overview of instruments that can be used to assess interests in three different types of formats: (a) computer-assisted career guidance systems, (b) Internet-based career assessments, and (c) card sorts. One assessment tool in each type of format will be profiled and references will be provided for other examples.

DISCOVER, developed through ACT, Inc., will be profiled because it is one of the most commonly used computer-assisted career guidance systems and has recently been released with multimedia features in test administration and interpretation. *Careerhub,* a new career assessment site offered through Consulting Psychologists Press, will be highlighted as a state-of-the-art Internet assessment site. *Talent Sort 2000* (formerly *Deal Me In),* distributed by Mastery Works, will be summarized as an example of a card sort based on interest sorting.

Because Internet sites and card sorts are relatively new innovations and there is little research to date on these types of assessments, the review of *Careerhub* and *Talent Sort 2000* will focus primarily on the administration and interpretation of the instruments.

DISCOVER and *Careerhub* include additional assessments beyond the interest inventories of particular importance to our purposes here. While an overview of these resources will be provided, the primary focus of the discussion will be on the use of the interest assessment components of these more comprehensive tools.

DISCOVER, A COMPUTER-ASSISTED CAREER GUIDANCE SYSTEM

Computer-assisted career guidance systems are now in their third decade of popular use. A brief comparison of 15 computer-assisted career guidance systems can be found in *A Counselor's Guide to Career Assessment Instruments* (Kapes et al., 1994). DISCOVER is one of the most popular systems in use in a variety of settings, including high school, college and university, and community and organizational career centers. DISCOVER is a comprehensive software system designed to aid users in making career and educational decisions. It has versions appropriate for individuals from high school through adult.

We are highlighting DISCOVER, Windows version because of its exciting new multimedia capabilities for delivering career assessments and providing career information. Macintosh and MS-DOS platforms are also available. The multimedia features are available on the Macintosh, and in such cases many of the comments below are relevant to the Macintosh version as well. However, to simplify our discussion, the Windows version of DISCOVER will be our primary focus and all future references to DISCOVER will concern the Windows version.

The new Windows version uses several features, including videos, slides, graphics, and audio screen directions that allow users to enjoy a multimedia experience while learning about themselves, work, and careers through both visual and auditory learning styles. DISCOVER includes over 110 minutes of video presentations and 5,000 slides that enhance the user's experience and understanding of the applications throughout the program.

DISCOVER uses a graphic symbol for its "World-of-Work Center" (Figure 6.1) and organizes all of the information and activities in the software program into four "Halls": (1) Learn about Self and Career, (2) Choose Occupations, (3) Plan My Education, and (4) Plan for Work. See Figure 6.2 for a map of DISCOVER's interior "Halls."

In Hall 1, DISCOVER allows users to complete assessments of interests, abilities, and job values or to enter scores from other print tests or inventories. DISCOVER then will immediately score and interpret test results by plotting the results of the assessments to the World-of-Work Map. In Hall 2, users can view narrated videos on job families they have identified and access extensive databases to learn about occupations selected according to the inventories they have completed, by job families of interest identified in the World-of-Work Map, by job characteristics, or by a look-up feature. In Hall 3, users can identify majors based upon their selection of occupations or their location in the World-of-Work Map, find appropriate schools, and identify sources of financial aid. Finally, in Hall 4, users can gain information about apprenticeship or internship opportunities, learn how to conduct a job search, develop appropriate corre-

Figure 6.1 World-of-Work Center Building

The graphics, "World of Work Center Directory" and "World of Work Center Building," appear in "DISCOVER Career Guidance and Information System Overview" Copyright 1998 by ACT, Inc. All rights reserved.

spondence for the search, and prepare for interviewing. An innovative feature of DISCOVER Windows version is its access to the Internet via hyperlinks to related websites, such as schools, occupational information, job banks, etc.

For more information on DISCOVER, refer to Rapid Reference 6.1. The remainder of our discussion will focus on DISCOVER's Interest Inventory, UNIACT.

UNIACT, DISCOVER's Interest Inventory

The UNIACT is a well-developed interest inventory with over 20 years of research behind it. The UNIACT consists of 90 items which can be taken in

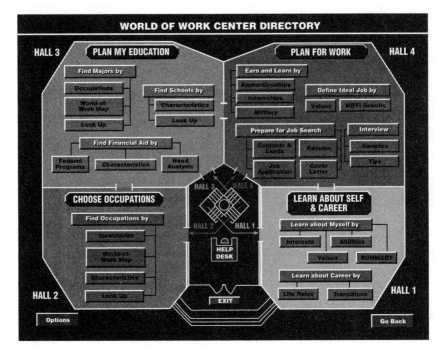

Figure 6.2 Map of DISCOVER'S Halls

The graphics, "World of Work Center Directory" and "World of Work Center Building," appear in "DISCOVER Career Guidance and Information System Overview" Copyright 1998 by ACT, Inc. All rights reserved.

They are reproduced here with permission. No further reproduction is authorized without explicit permission from ACT, Inc.

DISCOVER online or in paper-and-pencil formats. When taken online in DISCOVER Windows version, each item is accompanied by an illustrative visual and audio presentation. There are two versions of UNIACT, Level 1 for 8th–12th grade students and Level 2 for college students and adults. Each version has different norms that are appropriately utilized based upon the demographic data the user enters at sign-on. According to the test's publisher, ACT, Inc., UNIACT is taken each year by approximately 3.2 million junior high and high schools students and by 1 million college students and adults, making it the most used inventory in the world (Swaney, 1995). The UNIACT-R (1989 revised edition) is intended for persons in the early stages of career planning or re-planning, as in the case of career changers. It is designed to assist clients

≋Rapid Reference 6.1

DISCOVER

Authors: ACT, Inc.

Publisher: ACT, Inc.
Educational Services
P.O. Box 168
Iowa City, IA 52243-0168
1-800-498-6068
http://www.act.org/discover/
discover@act.org

Copyright Date: 2000

Description: DISCOVER is a comprehensive computer-based career guidance and information system that assists users in making important career and educational decisions. DISCOVER includes inventories for interests, abilities, and values assessment; linkages between these assessments and ACT's World-of-Work Map; extensive occupational information databases; comprehensive databases on educational information including majors, schools, training institutions, and financial aid; and information on methods for gaining career-related experience and preparing for the job search.

DISCOVER's Interest Inventory is the UNIACT, the Unisex Edition of the ACT Interest Inventory. UNIACT is accessible via DISCOVER and in other assessment services offered by ACT.

Age Range: DISCOVER, Windows Version, High School to Adult

Other Forms: DISCOVER for Colleges and Adults, 2000
DISCOVER for High Schools, 2000

Administration Time: 15–30 minutes for the UNIACT Interest Inventory
5–15 minutes for the Inventory of Work-Related Abilities
15–30 minutes for the Inventory of Work-Related Values

Qualifications: DISCOVER is designed to be self-interpreted. Research on DISCOVER and other computer-assisted career guidance systems indicates that use of computer-based career planning systems alone provides gains for individuals in the usual career planning process. The best outcomes, however, are achieved when a user has the benefits of both the computer program and counselor support (*DISCOVER Professional Manual,* 1999).

in "focused exploration," that is, it is intended to point to regions of the world of work that clients may want to explore, rather than to suggest one specific occupation to pursue (Swaney, 1995).

History and Development

Development of ACT's various interest inventories first began when John Holland, as ACT's Vice President for Research, headed ACT's Research and Development Division in the late 1960s. The ACT Guidance Profile (1968) provided the foundation for the initial (1971) edition of the ACT Interest Inventory. The unisex edition (UNIACT) was first published in 1977 and then

≡ *Rapid Reference 6.2*

History of the Development of the UNIACT

1968	ACT Guidance Profile
1971	Vocational Interest Profile (ACT VIP)
1973	ACT Interest Inventory (ACT-IV)
1977	Unisex Edition of the ACT Interest Inventory (UNIACT)
1989	Revised Edition of UNIACT, Levels 1 and 2

Note. Adapted with permission of ACT, Inc. from Technical Manual: Revised Unisex Edition of the ACT Interest Inventory (UNIACT), 1995, p. 8.

revised in 1989. The latest revision of the UNIACT involved research on item/scale functioning for over 15,000 people ranging from 8th grade to adult, resulting in approximately 40% of the items being revised or replaced. See Rapid Reference 6.2 for a brief history of the development of the UNIACT. The UNIACT continues to be based upon Holland's theory of careers, most recently explicated by Holland in 1997 (Holland, 1997).

Theoretical and Research Foundations

Holland developed his Hexagon while he was at ACT in the late 1960s. He then developed the ACT Guidance Profile, which was the foundation for the initial edition of the ACT Interest Inventory. Today's UNIACT (Unisex Edition of the ACT Interest Inventory) contains 90 items total, 15 items for each of the six scales corresponding to Holland's (1997) occupational types. Rapid Reference 6.3 describes the UNIACT scales and their related Holland types and abbreviations.

The World-of-Work Map   The World-of-Work Map (WWM) is an empirically-based structure used in DISCOVER to explain how occupations are organized and to link assessment results to career options. The WWM was developed through the work of Dale Prediger in ACT's Research Division, who began to extend Holland's hexagon in the early 1970s. In research that has spanned 25 years, Prediger and others have identified the WWM's two underlying dimensions, which allow all occupations to be organized according to their involvement with four work tasks: data, ideas, things, and people. Rapid Reference 6.4 describes the data, ideas, things, and people work tasks, which form the poles of these two dimensions.

The relationship between these two bipolar dimensions and Holland's Hexagon are illustrated in Figure 6.3.

≡ Rapid Reference 6.3

UNIACT Basic Interest Scales and Corresponding Holland Types and Abbreviations

Science (Investigative—I)	Investigating and attempting to understand phenomena in the natural sciences through reading, research, and discussion.
Arts (Artistic—A)	Expressing oneself through activities such as painting, designing, singing, dancing, and writing; artistic appreciation of such activities (e.g., listening to music, reading literature).
Social Service (Social—S)	Helping, enlightening, or serving others through activities such as teaching, counseling, working in service-oriented organizations, engaging in social/political studies.
Business Contact (Enterprising—E)	Persuading, influencing, directing or motivating others through activities such as sales, supervision, and aspects of business management.
Business Operations (Conventional—C)	Developing and/or maintaining accurate and orderly files, records, accounts, etc.; designing and/or following systematic procedures for performing business activities.
Technical (Realistic—R)	Working with tools, instruments, and mechanical or electrical equipment. Activities include designing, building, repairing machinery, and raising crops/animals.

Note. Adapted with permission of ACT, Inc., from the Technical Manual: Revised Unisex Edition of the ACT Interest Inventory (UNIACT), 1995, p. 2. Reproduced by permission of ACT, Inc.

≡Rapid Reference 6.4

Descriptions of the Data/Ideas and Things/People Bipolar Dimensions

Data (facts, records, files, numbers, systematic procedures).

Data tasks are *impersonal* tasks that expedite goods/services consumption by people (for example, by organizing or conveying facts, instructions, products, etc.). Purchasing agents, accountants, and air traffic controllers work mainly with data.

Ideas (abstractions, theories, knowledge, insights, new ways of expressing something—for example, with words, equations, or music).

Ideas tasks are *intrapersonal* tasks such as creating, discovering, interpreting, and synthesizing abstractions or implementing applications of abstractions. Scientists, musicians, and philosophers work mainly with ideas.

Things (machines, tools, living things, materials such as food, wood, or metal).

Things tasks are *non-personal* tasks such as producing, transporting, servicing, and repairing. Bricklayers, farmers, and machinists work mainly with things.

People (no alternative terms).

People tasks are *interpersonal* tasks such as caring for, educating, servicing, entertaining, persuading, or leading others—in general, producing a change in human behavior. Teachers, salespeople, and speech pathologists work mainly with people.

Note. Adapted with permission of ACT, Inc., from the Technical Manual: Revised Unisex Edition of the ACT Interest Inventory (UNIACT), 1995, pp. 2–3. Reproduced by permission of ACT, Inc.

Prediger (1976) has suggested that all occupations have some involvement with each of these work tasks, but usually only one or two best describe the primary purpose. For example, scientists work with data, but they are *primarily* concerned with creating or utilizing scientific knowledge or ideas. In the latest revision of the WWM, Prediger and others evaluated job analysis data of 12,099 occupations in the fourth edition of the *DOT* and utilized interest inventory scores of 991 educational and occupational groups to determine the locations of jobs on the World-of-Work Map (ACT, 1988). Figure 6.4 provides a graphic representation of the World-of-Work Map (WWM).

The WWM consists of the four compass points–data, ideas, things, and people–that determine an occupation's location in the WWM. The six Basic Interest Scales and the related Holland Types form the outer ring of the map

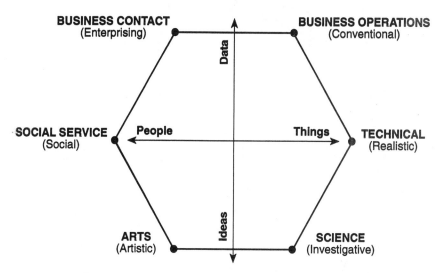

Figure 6.3 Relationship between UNIACT-R Basic Interest Scales and the Data/Ideas and Things/People Work Task Dimensions.

Note. Technical Manual: Revised Unisex Edition of the ACT Interest Inventory (UNIACT), 1995, p. 6. Reproduced with permission of ACT, Inc.

and are further subdivided into regions that are associated with the four different basic work tasks. For example, regions 9 and 10 are both involved in working predominantly with ideas, with Region 9 having some involvement with things tasks and Region 10 having some involvement with people tasks. Within the 12 regions, 23 job families, or groups of similar jobs, are located that represent various combinations of data, ideas, things, and people work tasks. The further toward the outer circle a job family is located, the greater its involvement in the work tasks associated with that particular region. The closer it is to the center of the WWM, the more the job family includes combinations of all four work task dimensions (data, ideas, people, and things). The data base in DISCOVER and Job Family Charts available from ACT list over 500 occupations by job family that cover more than 95% of the labor force (*DISCOVER Professional Manual*, 1999).

Item Content and Format   Two aspects of the selection of item content of the UNIACT are worthy of mention. One is the use of everyday, work-relevant activities (e.g., plan a monthly budget, conduct a meeting, etc.) rather than occupational titles or job duties as items. As Kuder (1977) pointed out, those who need

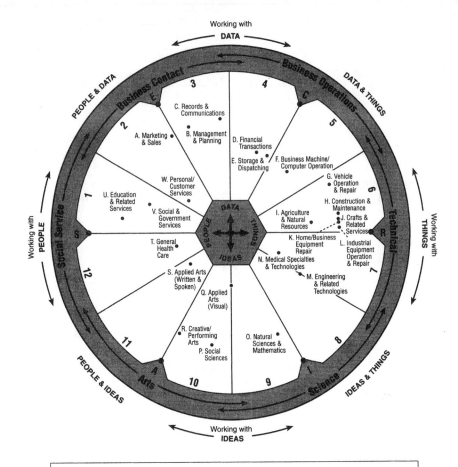

ABOUT THE MAP

- The World-of-Work Map arranges job families (groups of similar jobs) into 12 regions. Together, the job families cover nearly all U.S. jobs. Although the jobs in a family differ in their locations, most are located near the points shown.

- A job family's location is based on its primary work tasks. The four primary work tasks are working with—

  DATA: Facts, numbers, files, accounts, business procedures.
  IDEAS: Insights, theories, new ways of saying or doing something—for example, with words, equations, or music.
  PEOPLE: People you help, serve, inform, care for, or sell things to.
  THINGS: Machines, tools, living things, and materials such as food, wood, or metal.

- Six general areas of the work world and related Holland types are indicated around the edge of the map. Job Family Charts (available from ACT) list over 500 occupations by general area, job family, and preparation level.

Figure 6.4 ACT's World-of-Work Map

Research Support for DISCOVER Assessment Components

Reproduced with permission of ACT, Inc.

assistance with making career decisions are not as likely as others to have knowledge about various career options or may have misconceptions about jobs. Therefore, using career titles in inventories is not particularly useful to them. In addition, he suggested, interest inventory items with occupational titles are likely to stimulate unwanted response biases that do not contribute to the clarification of interest patterns, a finding validated in Prediger's (1982, 1998) research. Therefore, the use of "activity" items that individuals have experienced either directly or vicariously is intended to minimize the effects of such response biases. Because of the use of Likert response scales (e.g., Like, Indifferent, Dislike), Prediger found that response styles have an impact on the overall score level of UNIACT and most other interest inventories. He suggests addressing this in the interpretive process by responding to profile shape (e.g., the three letter code obtained to identify WWM regions) rather than score levels.

Special efforts were also taken in the selection of the UNIACT items so that gender-related differences in item responses would be minimized. Prediger and Johnson's (1979) research suggested that gender differences in responses to various items were primarily the result of gender-related connotations associated with different activities (*DISCOVER Professional Manual,* 1999). The elimination of items with male-female response differences (e.g., "Would you like to operate a power shovel?" "Would you like to raise young children?") was an effort to minimize obtaining results that were stereotypic for both sexes. Prediger (1981) showed that females are more likely to score low on traditionally male scales (e.g., Holland's Type R) when sex-divergent raw scores rather than sex-balanced normed scores are used. To combat this problem, sex differences were minimized at the item level by identifying sex-balanced items on which females and males obtained similar distributions of scores on the resulting scales. Sex-balanced items then permitted the use of combined sex norms, yielding sex-balanced reports. Swaney (1995) summarized the results of 14 validity studies that indicated the validity of such sex-balanced scores is equal to and often higher than that of sex-divergent scores (*DISCOVER Professional Manual,* 1999).

Reliability   Test-retest reliability coefficients are reported for a sample of 453 11th grade students who took the UNIACT at some point during the 1989–90 school year, and again one to eight months later. With an average test-retest interval of 4.5 months, obtained reliability coefficients ranged from .68 to .78 with a median of .75 for males, and from .69 to .82 with a median of .78 for females (*Research Support for DISCOVER Assessment Components,* 1999).

Validity   Criterion-related validity has been evaluated through measuring "hit rates," as described earlier for the *Strong* and *SDS*. Several studies of both concurrent and predictive validity are summarized in the *Technical Manual* (1995) and the publication *Research Support for DISCOVER Assessment Components* (1999). The summary of the studies indicates that for a total of 616 groups, including high school students, college students, and adults, DISCOVER's UNIACT high-point code matched the Holland type of the group (criteria included college majors and occupations) with an average hit rate of 73%. The hit rate expected by chance alone is 17% (1 out of 6). The results of the studies demonstrate substantial criterion-related validity.

How to Administer and Score

Administration   DISCOVER is essentially a self-administered, computer-based career guidance and information system. If you are using DISCOVER, Windows version, it is most helpful to provide clients with a brief orientation to the World-of-Work Center Directory and explain how the user can access any part of the program by clicking the mouse on the menu tab for each module. Instructions on how to navigate through DISCOVER are also useful. For example, a panel of icons appears at the bottom of each screen, giving clients direct access to the main menu, help function, and their career plan. Icons also permit them to add or delete data in their lists of favorites, print information, repeat an audio portion, view a video, and move to the previous or next screen.

By clicking on the Interests menu tab in Hall 1, "Learn About Self and Career," the user will be able to take the inventory online. Each item is presented online with a full multimedia presentation including text, audio reading of the text, and photo illustrations. Clients will click on the Dislike, Indifferent, or Like button to select their response options. The UNIACT Interest Inventory can also be taken in a paper-and-pencil format and the responses can be entered for scoring.

In addition, DISCOVER provides the unique feature of being able to enter scores from a variety of non-ACT interest inventories to generate suggested job families and regions in the World-of-Work map. DISCOVER will, for example, accept scores from the *Strong Interest Inventory* and *Self-Directed Search,* as well as seven other interest inventories to generate job families.

Scoring   Fifteen items comprise each of the six Basic Interest Scales. Users respond to each of the 90 activity items with a three-point, free-response format, selecting either the Like, Indifferent, or Dislike response. Raw scores are based on response weights where Like = 3, Indifferent = 2, and Dislike = 1. The total raw score is determined for each of the six, 15-item Basic Interest Scales by summing the item scores, dividing by the number of items answered, and multiplying this response average by 15. Raw scores are converted to percentile ranks based on age-appropriate norm tables, and then are converted to stanines. The three highest stanines are used in rank order to determine the "three-letter code." Scores of 4, 2, and 1 are applied to the first, second, and third Holland types in rank order and used in Data/Ideas (D/I) and Things/People (T/P) formulas to obtain work task scores. The D/I and T/P scores are then translated into regions and associated job families in the World-of-Work Map. Further details on scoring procedures are available in the UNI-ACT *Technical Manual* (Swaney, 1995).

The user is provided his or her results through the World-of-Work Map, which identifies job families suggested by the inventory results in three regions—the obtained region and the two adjacent regions—enabling clients to more readily explore occupations in the identified and related fields. The results can also be provided in a summary printout. Job families can be used to identify selected occupations among the 500 included in DISCOVER's database. Clients can view narrated videos and generate a list of occupations for each job family. Clients can further investigate each occupation on their list by clicking on tabs in the Lookup option. Users can view a narrated slide show for each occupation by selecting the video icon. Information in all the folders on an occupation, such as description, salary/outlook, and training, can be viewed, printed, and saved to the user's personal diskette.

How to Interpret

UNIACT is essentially interpreted for DISCOVER, Windows Version, online through the use of narrated videos that describe each of the job families that have been identified and through narrated slide shows that review each of the occupations within the job families that the user selects to explore further. In addition, as described above, the user can access detailed information on any of the occupations within the identified job families by selecting any or all of its lookup features. DISCOVER is particularly valuable for its ability to integrate results of multiple inventories, including interests, abilities, and values, into the World-of-Work map so that users can see how their interests, values, and abilities relate to one another and the various career options.

Counselors are needed in many instances, particularly in working with high school students, to verify that users understand their printouts and results. Counselors are often needed, as well, to provide additional support in the review and interpretation of these results by helping clients understand how to make sense of results when different job families are recommended by two or more inventories, which is often the case. For example, the client who has interests in Marketing and Sales and abilities in Financial Transactions can be assisted by the counselor in understanding how he or she may be able to acquire some of the abilities, through education, training, or experience, needed for the career of interest. This can be done by referring to the "Training" and "Desirable Qualities" information topics for that career or by examining the abilities related to the job clusters in the *Professional Manual* (1999). Counselors are also often needed to support clients in narrowing the occupations in the job families to a shorter list and helping them research the options further, sorting them by criteria such as the client's highest priority values.

Counselor support for interpreting the UNIACT Interest Inventory will most often be needed when a client does not show a clear pattern of interests. With the UNIACT inventory, this occurs when three or more of the ACT/Holland clusters are tied or because an unusually high number of items have the same response, that is, Like, Indifferent, or Dislike. When this occurs, users will view their Basic Interest Scales on the screen, displayed by stanines. The counselor can recommend that the user explore job families represented by the highest Basic Interest Scales. However, when the profile is clearly flat, the best approach is often to take advantage of the unique multimedia capabilities of DISCOVER and have the client click on any job family of potential interest to view its videos. The videos quickly provide exposure to many fields, enabling clients to begin the process of forming opinions about what does and does not interest them. Having the client take the Inventory again, attempting to differentiate more between their responses, is another alternative. If the client has many high scores (a high, flat profile), the counselor can assist the client in sorting the careers into highest priority options by evaluating which job families and specific career options they have the greatest talents for, which would enable them to fulfill their most important values, and which are in greatest alignment with their resources (e.g., time and finances needed to accomplish the goal). If the client has many low scores (a low, flat profile), the counselor may want to explore whether the client has had enough experience to assess his or her interests at this time or if other factors, such as a depressed mood, may have had an impact on the test results. As discussed in previous chapters, clients can also be encouraged to explore the world of work through classes, part-time work, or other experiential activities.

Another problem where counselor assistance is sometimes needed is in the case of split profiles, where two scores are tied for highest, and two split regions are reported (e.g., regions 1 and 6 or 2 and 7). The results will simply identify job families in both regions. The counselor can help the client assess which job families and jobs are most appropriate, once the other assessments for abilities and values have been completed, by looking for job families that were suggested by two or three inventories. The counselor can also assist the client in identifying ways in which interests might be combined. For example, in the case of a client for whom Job Family U., Education and Related Services (Region 1) and Job Family I., Agriculture and Natural Resources (Region 6) were suggested, the counselor could encourage the client to think about options that would combine both interest areas, such as teaching and consulting in his or her state's Natural Resources Department. Alternatively, the counselor might recommend that the functions of one job family could be applied to the environment of the other. For example, if the client had two high scores yielding the job families Marketing and Sales (Region 2) and Medical Specialties and Technologies (Region 7), the counselor might suggest a career like Market Research applied to a medical equipment or pharmaceutical company.

Since DISCOVER is used primarily to assist clients with career exploration, your most important role is to help your client understand how to actively learn more about the career options that have been identified. Career exploration tasks beyond the very effective videos and slide shows integrated into DISCOVER can be framed as four "P's": Profiles, People, Programs, and Participation. You can assist your client in (a) obtaining further *profiles* of the occupations by identifying additional information sources (print or electronic); (b) identifying *people* for information interviews or job shadowing; (c) identifying informational *programs* to attend, such as those sponsored by professional associations, university departments, student organizations, etc.; and (d) *participating* in internship, volunteer, or part-time work opportunities that can help him or her gain real-world experience that will be helpful in further narrowing the career options under consideration. Rapid Reference 6.5 reviews types of counselor support that can be of use in working with DISCOVER.

Counselor Support for DISCOVER

DISCOVER can be used as a stand-alone system. However, counselor support can enhance the use of the instrument in the following ways.

Needs/Concerns	Suggestions
Evaluating careers within job families. **Resolving discrepancies between job families identified by two or more of the assessment inventories.**	Once careers of high interest have been identified, assist your client in evaluating the abilities needed and guide the client toward preliminary choices that match his or her current skills or potential to develop the required abilities. Next, evaluate which of those occupations has the greatest potential for satisfying your client's highest priority work values.
Split regions	Help clients evaluate which careers of high interest they are best suited for in terms of their abilities and needs. Help clients consider how they might integrate qualities in each region into new career possibilities or how they might select one career field and apply it to the other environment. Assist clients in understanding how some of their work-related interests might be met in other life roles (refer your client to the Career Rainbow section in Hall 1).
High, flat profile	Help your client prioritize several high interest options based upon which of these best match their abilities, values, and resources.
Low, flat profile	Encourage clients to gain work experience, view job family videos of interest, explore the world of work, or take DISCOVER at a later time. If more general confusion or depressed affect is evident, consider referring your client for counseling.
Next steps	Encourage your client to work toward developing a "short list" of occupations by engaging in exploratory activities that complement information available in the DISCOVER databases and Internet links. Appropriate activities include taking relevant coursework and participating in information interviews, job shadowing, internships, and part-time jobs.

Strengths and Limitations

The Strengths of DISCOVER's Interest Inventory, UNIACT, is the strong research base upon which the instrument has been built. In addition, over 25 years of research have gone into creating the World-of-Work Map, a valuable interpretive aid that extends Holland's theory to two bipolar dimensions into which all of the occupations in the *Dictionary of Occupational Titles* can be arranged. The use of the interest assessment in conjunction with the World-of-Work Map allows the test results to be immediately converted to suggested WWM job families and occupations. DISCOVER, Windows Version, is a stimulating tool for completing the Interest Inventory and educates the user about the suggested job families and occupations in exciting multimedia formats that take advantage of multiple learning styles.

One of the limitations of taking the UNIACT online in DISCOVER is that the user does not receive a copy of the completed assessment, nor does the user obtain scores on the Basic Interest Scales or Data/Ideas and Things/People work task dimensions. Rather, the scores are automatically converted into WWM job families. It is therefore not possible to know what the actual scores were, their magnitude, or how differentiated the scores were. Consequently, it can be useful to suggest that the client complete the inventory via the Career Planning Guidebook and then enter the responses online. The Career Planning Guidebook can be retained as a record of the responses. The UNIACT *Technical Manual* (1995) provides a scoring key that allows the interested counselor to gain an understanding of how his or her client's responses were scored and translated to the suggested job families, methods which can be helpful if there are any questions about the results obtained. Rapid References 6.6 and 6.7 provide a summary of key strengths and limitations for DISCOVER's Interest Inventory.

Applications

Our primary focus has been on UNIACT, DISCOVER's Interest Inventory. The following comments apply both to the Interest Inventory and DISCOVER as a whole. DISCOVER, Windows Version, is intended for users from high school through adulthood who are in the early stages of career planning or replanning. It is particularly useful in the full range of its features (all of the assessments; linkages to job families, majors, school and financial aid databases, etc.) for high school students and for college students who are in the early stages of selecting a major or career.

≡Rapid Reference 6.6

Strengths of DISCOVER's Interest Inventory, UNIACT

1. UNIACT has a long and distinguished history of research behind it, beginning with Dr. John Holland's work on the Hexagon when he was Vice President of Research at ACT in the late 1960s.
2. DISCOVER utilizes the World-of-Work Map, another outstanding product of ACT's Research Division, and includes an extensive database of over 500 occupations representing 95% of the labor force.
3. The results of the UNIACT are directly linked to the World-of-Work Map.
4. DISCOVER allows the integration of results from several assessments, including interests, abilities, and values, by plotting them all to the WWM.
5. Once job families have been identified, users can move directly into career exploration by accessing extensive databases of occupational information that link them to other important databases such as those on majors, schools, and sources of financial aid, and to other relevant Internet hyperlinks.
6. Highly appropriate for individuals beginning the career planning process or for adults considering a career change.
7. Multimedia effects provide a stimulating test administration and the ability to educate users about job families and occupations using multiple learning modalities (visual and auditory).
8. Items have been carefully selected. They are gender-balanced and reflect work activities rather than the occupations they are intended to identify.

Its greatest utility with adult users is for those who are either trying to select a career for the first time or are considering a major career change. For example, an adult who has been in a "job" and is now seeking a "career" that would be more personally rewarding or fulfilling, or that would make greater use of his or her abilities, would find DISCOVER very helpful in linking him or her to potentially more rewarding career options. The career changer who is similarly motivated would be supported in the use of DISCOVER as well. An employee who has lost a job or wishes to find a lateral opportunity can also be supported by DISCOVER, by plotting his or her last two or three jobs on the World-of-Work Map and then exploring careers in job families in the identified and adjacent regions. These careers would likely satisfy the same interests and require the same skills (with a search performed at the same educational level).

≡ *Rapid Reference 6.7*

Limitations of DISCOVER's Interest Inventory, UNIACT

1. The UNIACT is intended for users in the early stages of career planning or replanning and is less suitable for many adult users who are less concerned about initial career choice and more concerned about ongoing career management or mobility.

2. DISCOVER's UNIACT results lead to the identification of job families, but the program does not offer additional guidance in the selection of specific occupations within job families.

3. The Interest Inventory scores in DISCOVER, Windows Version, are not available for counselor or client use. Therefore, questions about how the job families were identified are difficult to answer unless the client has completed the inventory in the Career Planning Guide and the counselor is familiar with the scoring process in the *Technical Manual*.

4. Multi-interested individuals do not have the opportunity to see their results plotted to the WWM, since only the three highest scores are used in plotting the results of the Inventory to job families.

5. Useful raw scores on the Basic Interest Scales are not available to the counselor or client to aid in other important career decision-making tasks, such as role change, advancement, or job enrichment issues.

6. More research is needed to determine the best weighting of the Basic Interest Scales for translation to locations on the WWM.

7. Little guidance is offered to the user on how to progress with career decisions with difficult profiles, for example, split profiles, where two high scores are tied that are not in adjacent regions.

8. The costs of the program, in terms of both hardware and licensing agreements, can be a barrier to some potential users. Due to the costs, DISCOVER is usually available only through institutional settings such as school, university, or organizational career centers. At the present time it is not available, for example, through web-based applications, to individual users.

DISCOVER is particularly useful as a career planning tool because it has been designed to move a user through the entire career planning process, from learning about self and career (Hall 1), to choosing occupations (Hall 2), to planning for education (Hall 3), and finally, to planning for work (Hall 4). It is a self-contained assessment, guidance, and information resource and is unique in its abilities to provide critical information-based resources through its extensive databases and links to other information-based sites on the Web, thereby not requiring any auxiliary information-based resources or tools. DISCOVER, Windows Version's multimedia capabilities make it particularly engaging for group programs and career classes, as well as for individual users.

OTHER COMPUTER-ASSISTED CAREER GUIDANCE SYSTEMS

SIGI PLUS, System of Interactive Guidance and Information

SIGI PLUS is one of the other most commonly used computerized career guidance systems. SIGI PLUS is offered by Educational Testing Services as a comprehensive, self-directed, interactive system of both career guidance and information. SIGI PLUS offers in-depth self-assessment that allows users to clarify their work-related values, identify their interests, and define their skills. The self-assessment results are then used to identify potential occupations which can be searched for information on 27 different dimensions, such as work activities; educational requirements; and beginning, average, and top earnings. SIGI PLUS can also be used to gather up-to-date information on colleges and graduate schools, including the education or training needed to match occupational requirements. SIGI PLUS can also help the user manage related issues in making career transitions, offering practical advice on such topics as financial aid, managing time, and finding day care facilities. The system also assists the user in evaluating the potential rewards and chances of succeeding in various career options and can help the user establish short-range goals and action steps needed to achieve them.

More information on SIGI, a demonstration disk, or a marketing video can be obtained by contacting:

Educational Testing Service
P.O. Box 6403
Princeton, NJ 08541-6403
1-800-257-7444
Fax: 609-734-1290
e-mail: *sigiplus@ets.org*
Internet: http://www.ets.org/sigi/

Other examples of Computer-Assisted Career Guidance Systems have recently been profiled in Kapes, Mastie, and Whitfield (1994). You may wish to review this resource for an overview of 15 computer-assisted career guidance systems. Examples of systems profiled by Sampson et al. (1994) include:

1. DISCOVER for Colleges and Adults (American College Testing Program)
2. SIGI PLUS (Educational Testing Service)
3. Career Information System (University of Oregon)
4. Guidance Information Service II (Riverside Publishing Company)
5. Choices (Careerware-ISM Systems Corporation)

You will also want to be aware of a very important and useful resource center for practitioners and researchers interested in identifying and locating information on the design and use of computer-assisted career guidance systems:

The Center for the Study of Technology in Counseling and Career
   Development
University Center, Suite A 4100
The Florida State University
Tallahassee, FL 32306
Phone: 850-644-6431
FAX: 850-644-3273
http://www.aus.fsu.edu/~Career/techcntr

CAREERHUB, Internet Site: (http://www.careerhub.org)

The Internet is fast becoming an enormously useful tool for career counselors and individuals in need of career planning and job search assistance. The proliferation of Internet sites intended to market and deliver career services, both those that are integrated as distance guidance components of existing career centers and those that stand alone as independent sites, has led to an unparalleled advancement in the ability of career counselors to serve their clients virtually anywhere, any time (Sampson, 1999; Harris-Bowlsbey et al., 1998).

You may wish to refer to the recent publication produced by the National Career Development Association (NCDA), *The Internet: A Tool for Career Planning* (Harris-Bowlsbey et al., 1998) for a very helpful overview of how web sites can be used in career counseling, a thoughtful evaluation of a variety of sites, and a review of key ethical issues that need to be considered in utilizing web-based career services. One of the concerns raised in NCDA's publication is the considerable unevenness in the quality of career-related web sites that are currently available. Counselors are encouraged, when referring clients to web-based career services, to be cognizant of the ethical issues associated with Internet use. Counselors can also be guided in their referrals by the recently developed *NCDA Guidelines for the Use of the Internet for the Provision of Career Information and Planning Services* (NCDA, 1997).

Careerhub, recently released by Consulting Psychologists Press, was selected as an example of an Internet-based career services web site because it was developed by psychologists and researchers specializing in career issues and its design is in alignment with the NCDA Guidelines mentioned above (e.g., information about the credentials and experience of the authors is provided, confidentiality is adhered to, and the site provides clear information about what the user can expect the site to do and what it cannot do). In addition, one of the co-authors of this publication was also one of the contributing authors and team members in the design of *Careerhub*, and was therefore able to provide additional insight into the development of this service. While this overview, as all others, is intended to be impartial, we do wish to caution readers to be alert to any unintended biases arising from this association. Details on *Careerhub's* development are available in the recent article, *Constructing a Quality Career Assessment Site* (Prince et al., 2000). According to the authors, *Careerhub* is designed to be a self-directed tool serving adults facing job and career choices and offering assistance with the critical task of career assessment within the context of the overall career planning process. Users are guided in navigating through the site by the *Careerhub* Map, designed like a subway map (see Figure 6.5), to show users where they are at any given time in the system.

Careerhub provides an overview of the career planning process in a four-step model that allows users to match their needs with the services and resources provided. Users are encouraged to work through the process in a step-wise fashion, but may also access the information in any order they choose.

Within the four-step model, users have the option to utilize resources that correspond to the typical steps in most career planning models. In Step (1), the *Career Change Package*, which is the only fee-based portion of the system, users can take assessment tools designed at CPP to gather self-knowledge. Step (2), *Research Links*, allows users to explore career options by reviewing annotated

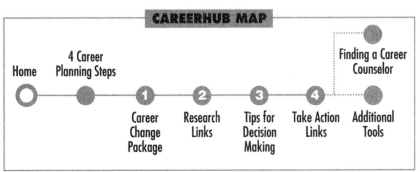

Figure 6.5 *Careerhub* **Logo and Map**

Note. Modified and reproduced by special permission of the publisher, Consulting Psychologists Press, Inc., Palo Alto, CA 94303, from Careerhub.org © 2000 by CPP, Inc.

descriptions of 5–10 of the best Internet sites for educational and occupational information, selected by *Careerhub's* authors, and then link directly to any sites of interest. Step (3), *Tips for Decision Making,* assists users in the process of evaluating and narrowing potential career options. In Step (4), *Taking Action,* users can take steps to move forward with the career options they have identified by reviewing annotated descriptions of key Internet sites for: (a) networking with others in the field, (b) volunteering for experience and professional development, (c) developing job search skills, and (d) identifying job listings. Users can also directly link to those sites. *Finding a Career Counselor* helps users determine when they might need a career counselor, reviews guidelines for selecting a career counselor, and accesses links to the National Board of Certified Counselors' web site for listings of certified counselors by city or state. *Additional Tools* describes other CPP assessments, such as the *Strong Interest Inventory* and *Myers-Briggs Type Indicator,* which must be administered and interpreted by a qualified career professional for those who wish to use more in-depth assessment tools.

The assessment package includes five assessment tools designed to assist users in assessing their interests, skills, and values; focusing their career planning; improving their problem-solving style; and developing resources for coping with stressful situations. The assessments include three established instruments: *The Career Factors Inventory, The Problem Solving Inventory,* and *The Coping Resources Inventory.* They also include two checklist tools, created for the site: *The Interests/Skills Checklist* and *Work/Life Values Checklist.* For more information on *Careerhub,* refer to Rapid Reference 6.8 The remainder of our discussion will focus on *Careerhub's* interest assessment, the *Interests/Skills Checklist.*

The Interests/Skills Checklist, Careehub's *Interest Assessment*

The *Interests/Skills Checklist* is a new instrument developed specifically for *Careerhub* (Prince, 1998). It is a checklist-style inventory designed to assist users in identifying general work interests and self-estimated skills for each of Holland's six personality types. The intended audience is adults making job or career changes. The inventory was designed to be completed, evaluated, and interpreted online, without the need for further interventions or interpretations by a professional counselor. Interpretative information is provided directly to the user to help with understanding and using the results. Users have the choice of

≡ Rapid Reference 6.8

CAREERHUB

Authors of site: Diane Silver, Judy Chartrand, and Jeffrey Prince

Publisher: Consulting Psychologists Press, Inc.
3803 East Bayshore Road
P.O. Box 10096
Palo Alto, CA 94303
Phone: 800-624-1765
http://www.careerhub.org
webmaster@cpp-db.com

Copyright Date: 1998

Description: *Careerhub* is a career planning web site that helps people with decisions relating to career development and job choices. *Careerhub* features five online assessments that help users identify what to look for in a career based on interests, skills, and work and life values; focus their career planning efforts; and improve their problem-solving and coping skills related to life and career transitions. *Careerhub* also offers free access to career planning information, including tips for making career decisions, annotated links to other useful career sites for researching educational and career options, and annotated links to sites that can assist the user with taking action on identified career goals.

The Interests/Skills Checklist is the interest assessment available through *Careerhub*.

Age Range: Adults, 17 to retirement

Administration Time: 5 minutes for the Career Factors Inventory
10 minutes for the Interests/Skills Checklist
15 minutes for the Work/Life Values Checklist
10 minutes for the Problem Solving Inventory
10 minutes for the Coping Resources Inventory

Qualifications: *Careerhub* is designed to be used independently and incorporates A-level instruments (i.e., those that can be self-interpreted and do not require a professional counselor or other career professional for interpretation).

Price: The Career Change Package can be purchased in a number of ways:
- Career Development Package (three tools for $19.00)
- Career Transition Package (all five tools for $24.95)
- Individual tools ($6.50 each)

Organizations: Quantity discounts are available for bulk purchases by organizations.

Note. Adapted from Careerhub, at www.careerhub.org.

completing the *Interests/Skills Checklist* alone or completing it along with as many of the other four tests in the assessment package as they wish.

The *Interests/Skills Checklist* consists of 60 items: 30 interest and 30 skill items. The scales are constructed so that there are five items for each of the six RIASEC Interest and six RIASEC Self-Estimated Skill scales. The response format provides four choices for respondents. In Part I, the Interests Checklist, respondents evaluate their level of interest by selecting one of four options in a free response format, including Very Strong Interest, Strong Interest, Some Interest, and Very Little Interest. In Part 2, the Skills Checklist, users rate their current level of skills in the activities using one of four response options: Very Strong Skill, Strong Skill, Some Skill, and Very Little Skill.

The *Checklist* takes approximately 10 minutes to complete. Users' responses are stored in a database, allowing individuals to revisit their results of the inventory at any time for up to 90 days following initial access to the package. The database also allows for the collection of data for determining reliability and validity statistics for the instrument and for ongoing refinement of the tool. Preliminary evidence suggests that the *Interests/Skills Checklist* works in an Internet environment. Ongoing research is being conducted on diverse samples to compile further data on the reliability, validity, and utility of this tool in an Internet environment (Prince, 1998).

How to administer and score

Individual users can access the Interest/Skills Checklist by going to the *Careerhub* site, http://www.careerhub.org, and purchasing it with a credit card either electronically on CPP's secure server or by calling CPP's customer service number. The user then receives a login and password that can be used at the "Members Login" location on *Careerhub's* home page to access the assessment package at any time for three months after initial login. Organizations who wish to offer their clients the package as a self-assessment tool can purchase the package in quantity and provide logins and passwords to their clients.

After users complete the *Checklist,* they click on the "Submit Responses" button and their responses are automatically scored online, and results along with interpretive material are presented in a matter of seconds.

How to interpret

Results of the *Interests/Skills Checklist* are summarized in a four-box matrix shown in Figure 6.6. Each box highlights a different possible pattern of inter-

Interests/Skills Checklist Results

We have summarized your interests and skills ratings into the four-box matrix below. Each box of the matrix highlights a different pattern of interests and skills revealing your unique profile and lets you compare your interests with your skills. The Career Types within each category reflect your patterns of interests and skills. The six types that show up here are based on psychologist John Holland's theory of career choice (1992), one of the most widely researched and recognized theories of career behavior.

The information that follows your summary will help you interpret your results and get some tips for directing your Career Change. You may want to print a copy of your summary and the more detailed results or take notes for future reference.

We recommend you investigate your results in the following order:

Category 1: Highest Priority, Both interested and skilled
Category 2: Worth Developing, Interested but little skill
Category 3: Worth Reconsidering, Skilled but little interest
Category 4: Lowest Priority, Little interest and little skill

Click on each Career Type within the boxes to read about your interests and skills. We recommend that you read these before checking out the tips in each category.

	Moderate to Strong Skill	Little Skill
Moderate to Strong Interest	**#1 Highest Priority** You report having interest and skill in: Investigative Artistic Conventional These Career Types are the ones for which you scored moderate-to-strong in both your interests and your reported skills. Since these are the areas in which your interests match your skills, these types of work activities are important ones to target first for further investigation. You are more likely to find satisfaction and success in these areas than in other areas at this time. Note: Not everyone has both interests and skills in particular Career Types. If you have no types listed here, go on to Category 2. Tips for Using Highest Priority Career Types	**#2 Worth Developing** You report having interest but little skill in: Realistic These are the Career Types for which you scored moderate-to-strong interest but in which you reported having little or no skill. These areas include options worth pursuing if you are able to develop the related skills. Note: If you have no Career Types in this Category, move on to Category 3. Tips for Using Career Types Worth Developing
Little Interest	**#3 Worth Reconsidering** You report having skill but little interest in: Social These are the Career Types for which you scored moderate-to-strong skill but for which you reported having little or no interest. These areas include options worth pursuing if you are able to develop or heighten your interest in these areas. Note: If you have no types in this Category, go on to Category 4. Tips for Using Career Types Worth Reconsidering	**#4 Lowest Priority** You report having little interest and little skill in: Enterprising These are the Career Types for which you scored both little interest and little skill. Consider holding off pursuing these areas at this time since you appear to have little attraction to these, and little confidence in your skill at succeeding at them. Nevertheless, take a few minutes to learn about your Lowest Priority Types. They can help you narrow your range of options by identifying career fields you may want to rule out at this time. Also, check out the tips. Tips for Using Lowest Priority Career Types If you have no types in this category and have gone over the other categories, go back to the Career Change Package Menu to select another inventory, or go to the Home Page to take some other steps toward your career goals.

Click on the   to select another tool.

Figure 6.6 Interests/Skills Checklist Results

Note. Modified and reproduced by special permission of the publisher, Consulting Psychologists Press, Inc., Palo Alto, CA 94303, from Careerhub.org © 2000 by CPP, Inc.

ests and skills in various combinations. *Career Types* (i.e., *Realistic, Investigative, Artistic, Social, Enterprising,* and *Conventional*), based on John Holland's theory of career choice (1997), are plotted into the appropriate box based on the user's scores on each of the six interest and six skill scales. When users score moderate to strong on both their interests and reported skills on a given Career Type, that type will be listed in the *#1 Highest Priority* box of the four-box matrix. When users score moderate to strong on their interests but report little skill on a given Career Type, that type will be listed in the *#2 Worth Developing* box. A combination of moderate to strong skills and little interest on a given type will result in that Career Type being listed in box *#3 Worth Reconsidering.* Finally, a combination of little reported skill and little interest on a given type will result in its inclusion in box *#4 Lowest Priority.*

The *Interests/Skills Checklist* results offer online, text-based advice and support for individuals along with recommendations on how to work with the results obtained. For example, it is recommended that users investigate their results by first exploring the career types listed in the #1 Highest Priority category, followed by #2 Worth Developing, then #3 Worth Reconsidering, and finally, #4 Lowest Priority. By clicking on the Career Types in each box, users are linked to descriptive pages highlighting relevant career information on that Career Type, including job activities, work environments, values and self-concepts, hobbies, competencies, programs for training and academic study, and occupations. The information included in these profiles is based upon the research of Holland (1973), Hansen and Campbell (1985), Hansen (1992), and others as reported by Harmon et al. (1994). The occupations listed for each Career Type are those whose members have endorsed that particular type as their highest code in research using the *Strong Interest Inventory* and its antecedents.

In addition to links to descriptions for each Career Type, each of the boxes in the matrix offers additional support and online suggestions. For example, for those types reported in the Highest Priority box, the supporting text recommends that these are highest priority areas because the user's interests match his or her skills, and it is in these areas that the user is most likely to find satisfaction and success. After reviewing each of the types, the user can link to additional tips for using the Career Types, relevant to the box in which they are located. For example, for those Career Types found in the Highest Priority box, the tips suggest the user evaluate his or her current work activities and roles in light of those preferred by the highest priority types to determine whether the current activities are a good fit, or whether the job responsibilities might be altered to produce a more satisfying match with the user's interests and strengths. The Tips sections also offer very useful recommendations on how the knowledge of Career Types can be used to research and evaluate new career options under consideration. Suggestions are also provided on how to apply this knowledge to the user's overall lifestyle for increased satisfaction, by expressing interests and skills in other life roles. The tips in these sections, as with each of the assessments offered by Careerhub, offer interpretive information similar to what might be provided by a professional career counselor. Refer to Rapid Reference 6.9 for a listing of the topics about which the user can receive substantive guidance for their *Interests/Skills Checklist* results.

The tips offer encouragement and a number of ways in which users can apply the information to their lives. The tips also discuss the impact that stereotypes, gender roles, or cultural expectations may be having in determining the user's results.

While the *Checklist* results are intended to be self-interpreted through the online analysis of results, counselor support can be useful in certain circumstances. For example, if a client receives four or more Career Types in the Highest Priority category, the counselor can assist the client in evaluating which of those might be in greatest alignment with the work values obtained in the *Work/Life Values Checklist* to help narrow the options. Also, for clients who are making a potential job or career change and are seeking information on additional career options based on their Career Types, counselors can assist them in linking their obtained Career Types to further occupational options, beyond those provided in the list of occupations for each type, by referring them to resources such as the *Dictionary of Holland Occupational Codes* (Gottfredson & Holland, 1996). Clients can then be supported in learning more about their options by reminding them to use the *Occupational Information* and *Take Action* links in Careerhub to explore their options through reading, networking, and participation in fields of interest.

Strengths and Limitations

Careerhub offers an important new development in Internet-based career guidance, with a career services site developed and delivered by an expert team in-

≡Rapid Reference 6.9

Topics Discussed in *Tips for Using Career Types*

Category	Topics Discussed
Category 1: **Tips for Using** **HIGHEST** **PRIORITY** **Career Types**	• Evaluate Your Current Situation • Research New Career Options • Evaluate Your Overall Lifestyle Activities • Select among Four or More Highest Priority Career Types
Category 2: **Tips for Using** **Career Types** **WORTH** **DEVELOPING**	• Evaluate Your Undeveloped Potential • Seek Ways to Increase Your Skills • Increase Your Confidence to Increase Your Options • Consider More Detailed Assessment
Category 3: **Tips for Using** **Career Types** **WORTH** **RECONSIDERING**	• "Been There, Done That" or Have You? • Investigate Your Hidden Interests • Is "Burnout" the Reason? • Consider Factors Other Than Your Interests
Category 4: **Tips for Using** **LOWEST** **PRIORITY** **Career Types**	• Confirm Your Results • Consider More Thorough Interests and Skills Assessment • Identify Factors to Avoid • Explore the Unknown

cluding psychologists who have specialized in career issues, are experienced researchers in career assessment, and have acquired exceptional expertise in providing career counseling support. One of the unique advantages of this Internet site is the commitment of the site's authors to ongoing research and development of the assessments and information provided at the site. The *Interests/Skills Checklist* assessment offers a useful application of Holland's typology in its explicit presentation of separate *interests* and *skills* assessments that allow users to gain an understanding of the relationship of their interests and skills on the important RIASEC dimensions. The utilization of the matrix format for presenting results yields a helpful and instructive way of thinking about interests and skills in combination. The tips that have been written for each box of the matrix offer self-contained, online, text-based counseling and coaching support that can be helpful with a variety of issues embedded in career decision-making. Another important strength of the *Interests/Skills Checklist* lies in the reliance on the established research of Holland, Hansen, and Campbell, among others, in describing the Career Types identified as a result of the assessment. The *Interests/Skills Checklist* demonstrates compliance with guidelines for Internet-based assessment, including, for example, recommending when the user may wish to consider working with a counselor. The *Interests/Skills Checklist,* the other assessments, the online counseling support, and the links to other useful Internet sites offer a free-standing, self-directed career intervention for the public. Similar expert guidance and support is unavailable at most Internet sites.

One of the limitations of *Careerhub* is that the number of specific occupations listed in the Career Types summaries for each Holland type is limited to 12–16 occupations. Instructions on how to derive three-letter Holland codes and to access additional career titles in resources such as the *Dictionary of Holland Occupational Codes* is lacking. Also, *Careerhub* users are encouraged to consider how their interests, skills, and values can be used together in evaluating career options, but the program does not provide an integrated summary of results across assessments.

As with many other computerized guidance systems, the results of the *Interests/Skills Checklist* are scored online and the user is then provided with an interpretation of the results. However, specific scores are not provided directly to the user. In cases of high flat profiles or low flat profiles, (e.g., four to six Career Types listed in the high priority or low priority box), the user is unable to assess intra-individual priorities among the Career Types within a box. It is not yet clear how often flat profiles occur among typical respondents, but it may be relatively common since scores are presented only according to four boxes. Additional research will show whether adjustments need to be made in scoring the items to reduce the number of Career Types appearing in these particular boxes. The strengths and limitations are summarized in Rapid References 6.10 and 6.11.

Applications

Careerhub's *Interests/Skills Checklist* is intended for use by adults seeking assistance either with making an initial career choice or with career development or

≡Rapid Reference 6.10

Strengths of *Interests/Skills Checklist* of *Careerhub*

- One of the few Internet-based career assessment sites developed by psychologists and researchers specializing in career issues.
- Site provides the public access to self-contained, quality, relatively low-cost career assessments, professional counseling support, and free online career planning information.
- Site complies with the guidelines for Internet-based assessment and provision of career information and planning services developed by NCDA.
- Site publisher is committed to ongoing research on the assessments in the site and ongoing development of the content and related links.
- New checklist instrument explicitly provides separate scores for the assessment of interests and skills in Holland's RIASEC dimensions.
- Matrix format for presenting results allows for a useful comparison of interests and skills for career planning purposes.
- Well-formulated, thorough, and ethically-based online counseling and coaching supports the assessment and other site content in a way that is easy to use and does not require the assistance of a counselor.
- The online counseling support offers psychologically sound observations and recommendations to individuals.
- Comprehensive and multifaceted descriptions of the Career Types are drawn from the research of Holland, Hansen, and Campbell, among others.
- Site offers several important, well-researched, and annotated links to other Internet sites relevant to the career planning process.

transition concerns. It can be successfully utilized by individuals as a self-contained application without the need for counselor support or intervention. Alternatively, it can be used as either a stand-alone component or as part of a self-assessment package in counselor-supported career interventions, such as individual counseling, group workshops, or career classes.

The Career Types generated in each of the matrix quadrants offer many kinds of applications. For example, "Highest Priority" Career Types suggest specific occupations that may be of interest to individuals searching for new career options. These Career Types also recommend programs of academic study or training for individuals who are contemplating continuing their education or

≡ Rapid Reference 6.11

Limitations of *Interests/Skills Checklist* of *Careerhub*

- Interest results are not integrated with results of other *Careerhub* assessments into a complete assessment summary report.
- The number of occupations listed in the Career Types summaries is limited; individuals may need further guidance to generate additional career options.
- Career Types are not presented in a three-letter Holland code format, which limits the user's ability to reference established resources for Holland-based occupational information.
- Users are not provided with either raw or standard scores, which makes it difficult to assess the degree to which Career Types, particularly those in the same box of the matrix, may be differentiated.
- Career Types are not linked directly to other Internet resources for easy access to expanded career and occupational titles or descriptions (e.g., O*NET).

returning for further training. For those who are seeking ways to enrich their jobs, specific job activities are described that could be incorporated into an individual's current job responsibilities. For those who are job seeking, the descriptions of environments can provide recommendations as to the type of departments or organizations that would be particularly rewarding to the individual. The listings of careers and hobbies in each Career Type can be used by individuals planning for retirement to identify second careers, leisure pursuits, or volunteer retirement activities that would likely be satisfying and productive options. The competencies listed in each Career Type can also guide individuals in designing their professional development plans. Individuals who wish to pursue careers or roles suggested by Career Types in Category #2, WORTH DEVELOPING, for example, could examine the competencies of that type and select one or more as a developmental goal, to be achieved through a variety of activities including courses, mentoring, modeling, reading, volunteering, etc.

For additional suggestions on how to apply the results of the inventory, see Rapid Reference 6.9, which suggests a variety of applications of the *Interests/Skills Checklist* based upon the category in which the Career Types are located.

OTHER INTERNET INTEREST ASSESSMENT EXAMPLES

Other examples of sites that assess interests have recently been profiled in NCDA's *The Internet: A Tool for Career Planning* (Harris-Bowlsbey et al., 1999). You may wish to review this publication for an annotated listing of several sites, including those that provide assessments, educational and training opportunities, occupational information, and information on job openings.

Examples of sites that assess interests suggested by Harris-Bowlsbey (1999) and others include:

1. *Career Interests Game*
   http://www.missouri.edu/~cppcwww/holland.shtml
2. *Find Your Career: US News*
   http://www.usnews.com/usnews/edu/beyond/bccguide.htm
3. *Student's Center.com About Work*
   http://www.aboutwork.com
4. *The Self-Directed Search*
   http://www.parinc.com
5. *Career Development Leadership Alliance, Inc.*
   http://www.careerguide.org

TALENT SORT 2000, A CARD SORT

Card sorts have been available over the last four decades as important qualitative methods of career assessment. While card sorts are less well-known and less frequently utilized than standardized tests, research has demonstrated that they are similar to more widely used assessments, such as the *Strong Interest Inventory* and *Self-Directed Search,* in effectively predicting career choice and reducing career undecidedness (Slaney et al., 1994). Slaney et al. provide an important summary of the historical origins and research on card sorts in *A Counselor's Guide to Career Assessment Instruments* (Kapes et al., 1994). The interested reader may also wish to refer to the brief overview Slaney et al. (1994) provide of 10 card sorts, seven of which use occupational titles for the sorts, and one each that uses values, interests, and skills as the basis for the sort.

Practitioners and researchers alike have discovered that card sorts offer an engaging and stimulating experiential method for clients to explore career options. As with other assessments that can be either self-administered or administered by a counselor, the client gains additional benefits with counselor support (Slaney et al., 1994). Williams (1978) suggested that the incremental value of a card sort, beyond generating occupational options, is in helping clients develop an understanding of their choices as they organize them into meaningful patterns and define the reasoning that underlies the groupings they have created.

Talent Sort 2000 (Farren, 1998), formerly known as *Deal Me In,* is a card sort distributed by Mastery Works that can be utilized by people making initial career choices and career changes to assess interests for determining a career focus and possible occupations. *Talent Sort 2000* card sort can also be used for a variety of other career-related applications, including job enrichment, skill building, and performance management, among others. The card sort was first published by Career Systems, Inc. as the *Deal Me In* card sort in 1985, and was later revised in 1992. Mastery Works, Inc. completed the second major revision of the card sort in 1998–99 and published this revision under the name *Talent Sort 2000*.

We are highlighting *Talent Sort 2000* because it is one of the few card sorts that uses interests as the basis for the sort, compared to occupational titles, values, or skills. Each card includes a gerund—for example, explaining, strategizing, or calculating—and a cartoon picture depicting that activity. The gerund form allows the cards to be used for both interests and skills sorts. See Figure 6.7 for an example of the cards.

The cards are engaging, colorful, lively, and contemporary in their look and feel. Users report enjoying working with the cards and in a short administration time of approximately 10 minutes, users have constructive information to work with in understanding their interest patterns and related career options.

Talent Sort 2000 includes 52 cards, with 13 cards representing each of the four categories: data, ideas, people, and things. These categories correspond to Prediger's (1976, 1996) bipolar dimensions of Data/Ideas and People/Things. *Talent Sort 2000* was designed by Farren and her associates to help individuals discover which of these dimensions represent their strongest preferences. They assumed that working in areas of natural interest and aptitude would lead people to their greatest happiness and highest performance in work (Farren, 2000).

Calculating

Developing

Negotiating

Building

Figure 6.7 Examples of Talent Sort 2000 Cards

Note. Talent2000 Sort Cards™ reprinted with permission of Mastery Works and Caela Farren.

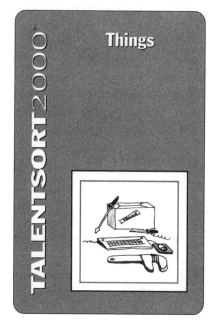

Figure 6.7 (*continued*)

This second revision of the card sort includes activities from a wide range of industries, professions, and jobs for salaried and nonsalaried workers. The developers sought activities that were easily understood by a variety of cultures, ages, and workers and that could be easily linked to the four interest areas or combinations of those areas. Initial activities were identified through interviews with a cross-section of people, and the list was further honed through several focus groups. The focus groups also assisted with the final categorization of the activities into the ideas, data, people, and things dimensions and helped develop the lists of occupations. A cartoonist created illustrations for the activities and these were subjected to focus group validation. In the 1998–99 revision, the interest/competency activities and the lists of occupations were updated to include more technology; a wider range of professions, trades, and crafts; and a broader range of industries (Farren, 2000).

To date, there have been no reliability or validity studies conducted for *Talent Sort 2000*. This is an area rich for exploration by authors, researchers, or practitioners involved in the area of interest measurement applications and research.

See Rapid Reference 6.12 for more information on *Talent Sort 2000*.

How to Administer and Score

The *Talent Sort 2000* card sort is often administered by a career professional as part of an individual intervention, group workshop, or career class. The card sort can also be self-administered. Each deck contains the basic instructions for "Solitaire," one of the card games used to assess career interests.

The instructions, included in the deck, ask the user to shuffle the 52 cards and then deal them, black and white side up (i.e., activity label and cartoon picture up), into four rows of 13 cards each. The user is then instructed to select 10 cards that best represent his or her interests.

By turning the cards over, the user then discovers their color coding (Blue-Data, Red-Ideas, Yellow-People, and Green-Things). By counting the number of cards he or she has in each "suit," the user determines the "scores" for each of the four dimensions: Data, Ideas, People, and Things. The user is then directed by the instruction cards to view the Occupations Card for that "suit" to select possible occupations the user may wish to further explore. There are six Occupations Cards to review, one each for Data, Ideas, People, and Things,

≡Rapid Reference 6.12

TALENT SORT 2000

Authors: Caela Farren, PhD and associates

Publisher: Mastery Works
7353 McWhorter Place
Suite 200
Annandale, VA 22003
703-256-5712 or 800-229-5712
703-256-9564 or 800-899-9564 (Fax)
http://www.masteryworks.com

Copyright Date: 1998

Description: *Talent Sort 2000* is a card sort that allows individuals to select cards representing different activities in which they are most interested. Cards can then be sorted, based on their color coding, into four categories or "suits": Ideas, Things, People, or Data. Users can then consult the appropriate Occupations card for a listing of possible occupations related to the "suit" that appeared most frequently. The accompanying guide, *It's in the Cards* provides 22 applications of the card sort to various career needs.

Age Range: High School to adult

Administration Time: 10 minutes

Qualifications: *Talent Sort 2000* is designed to be self-interpreted. As with most instruments, maximum benefit is generally obtained with counselor or practitioner support.

Price: $15 per deck of *Talent Sort 2000* cards.
$20 for the *It's In the Cards* guide

and two additional cards that suggest occupations based upon People and Ideas combined. Each Occupations Card suggests 21–25 occupations for consideration.

How to Interpret

The instruction card in the card deck directs the user to identify which of the occupations on the selected Occupations Cards are most appealing. The instructions also encourage the user to review the interests on the activities cards

≡*Rapid Reference 6.13*

Talent Sort 2000—Suggestions for Exploring Career Fields
From the Accompanying Guide

Activity	Suggestions
Card Activity	• Pick the appropriate occupation cards (People, Ideas, etc.) and scan the list of occupations. • Add occupations that come to mind after you review the list.
Discussion Tip	• Get your friends' input regarding your interests. Do they see you as a People, Data, Things, or Ideas person, or a combination of "types"? • Read through the occupations list for your interests and pick three to five you'd like to explore further. • Brainstorm a list of people you could talk with to learn more about the occupation.
Action/Next Steps	• Go to the library to learn more about the occupations. • Refer to the eight industry pages at the back of the guide for more ideas. • Track down companies in your geographic area. • Set up two or three informational interviews. You'll learn more about the field with minimal risk. • Network with your friends to learn about associations and trade journals in the field.

Source: It's in the Cards: Dealing with Work and Career Changes. (Cohan & Farran, 1992).

he or she had previously selected and consider several ways to add those activities to the user's current job. There are no further interpretive guidelines in the *Talent Sort 2000* card deck. There are, however, a number of important and helpful suggestions in the *It's in the Cards* guide, a useful and engaging guide that counselors can use as a reference or give to clients. A summary of several applications is provided in Rapid Reference 6.18. In addition, Rapid Reference 6.13 summarizes follow-up activities recommended in the guide for exploring occupations of interest.

In addition to the 21–25 occupations listed in each of the six occupations cards (data, ideas, people, things, data/ideas, people/ideas), the *It's in the Cards* guide includes sets of additional job titles for eight industries, including finance, health service, manufacturing, transportation, service, energy, government, and computer technology. Within each of the eight industries are an additional 15–25 occupations for each of the four data, ideas, people, and things preferences, resulting in about 150 additional occupational suggestions for each of the four areas, or about 600 additional occupations, beyond those provided in the occupations cards included in the card deck. See Figure 6.8 for an example of the additional occupations provided in the industry lists.

This card sort intervention assists individuals in gaining a clearer understanding of their interests and related occupational options in a self-administered format. As is the case with other card sorts, the user's understanding of their interests, insight into the underlying meaning behind the pattern of their choices, and knowledge of potential options can be enhanced through counselor-supported administrations of the card sort.

You can assist the client in understanding their motivations behind selecting key interests by supporting them in exploring these themes during the session. For example, in the Solitaire game or Exercise 1 in the *It's in the Cards* guide, users are instructed to pick either 10 cards or all of the cards, that best represent their interests or intrigue them most. After the client has selected the cards and before turning them over to discover the suits, you can ask exploratory questions to help your client probe the reasons behind their selections. You might ask open-ended questions such as, "How did you decide to select the cards you have chosen?" or "What patterns do you see in the cards you have selected?" to stimulate their reflection. Then summarize broad themes that you hear.

As with other assessments, counselors can be helpful in working with clients whose interests are undifferentiated or include preferences for opposite poles. Refer to Rapid Reference 6.14 for suggestions for working with clients who demonstrate these concerns.

Finally, you can help clients identify other career options by using the results from the card sort with other interpretive aids. For example, you might use the *Career Area Charts,* which can be ordered from the American College Testing Program, to identify 500 occupations within 23 job families that cover more than 95% of the labor force arranged within the Data, Ideas, People, and

INDUSTRY

FINANCE INDUSTRY - Exchange of money.

Organizations in this industry include: Banks, Insurance, Real Estate, Credit, Brokerage Houses, Investment Planning, and Financial Corporations.

PEOPLE (YELLOW)	DATA (BLUE)	THINGS (GREEN)	IDEAS (RED)
Chief Financial Officer	Comptroller	Systems Engineer	Systems Design Manager
Stockbroker	Real Estate Appraiser	ATM Machine Servicer	Economist
Mortgage Banker	International Tax Analyst	Microfilm Operator	Policy Analyst
Personal Banker	Portfolio Strategist	Engraver	Product Developer
Branch Manager	Insurance Underwriter	Brokerage Clerk	Bank Marketing Researcher
Financial Services Sales Rep.	Real Estate Title Examiner	Computer Service Technician	Venture Capitalist
Securities Underwriter	Contract Specialist	Locksmith	Investment Banker
Municipal Bond Trader	Securities Trader	Security Systems Specialist	International Currency Trader
Financial Planner	Securities Analyst	Financial Records Processor	Economic Forecaster
Bank President	Cost Estimator	Statement Clerk	Advertiser
Bank Teller	Accountant	Installer	Copyright Specialist
Credit Manager	Actuary	General Office Clerk	Product Developer
Real Estate Property Manager	Financial Analyst	Equipment Operator	Portfolio Manager
Real Estate Broker	Internal Auditor	Data Base Technician	Computer Systems Analyst
Project Manager	Loan Officer		Systems Integration Specialist
Receptionist	Credit Analyst		Operations Research Analyst
Clerical Supervisor	Budget Analyst		Forecaster
Insurance Salesperson	Insurance Claims Adjuster		
Mortgage Broker	Tax Specialist		
	Payroll Manager		
	Bank Examiner		
	Accounts Payable Clerk		
	Bookkeeper		
	Investment Portfolio Assistant		

Figure 6.8 Additional Occupational Examples Sorted by People, Data, Things, and Ideas in the Industry Lists for the Finance Industry.

Note. Reprinted with permission of Mastery Works.

Rapid Reference 6.14

Working with Clients with Problematic Card Sorts

Problem and Impact	Possible Solutions
Undifferentiated Interests In a forced choice card sort, for example, select 10 cards, the client has essentially equal numbers of cards in each suit.	• Try another sort using the full deck and allowing the client to select ALL the cards that interest him or her to see if larger differences can be obtained between the various suits (data, ideas, people, and things dimensions). • Help clients generate career options that would allow them to utilize the breadth of their interests in their work, such as jobs that combine interests and allow for a wide variety of tasks, roles, responsibilities, or projects. • Assist clients in considering the many contexts in their work lives in which their interests can be met; for example, the job itself, their department, the larger organization, or their profession. • Help clients consider that interests can be met in their lives as well as in work and assist them in identifying areas such as their family, friends, leisure activities, or volunteer or community service pursuits that could provide a context for the expression of interests that are not utilized at work. • Help clients understand the value of sequencing; that is, some interests may be met at one career stage, others in later stages, or in later jobs or career choices. • Complete another sort, this time sorting the interests "activities" into two skills categories, "do well" and "don't do well," or three skill categories, "high skills," "skills worth developing," and "low skills." Help your client explore occupations in the suits in the "high skills" or "skills worth developing" categories.

Dealing with Opposite Poles

Clients have strong interests that include categories at opposite poles, such as data and ideas, or people and things.

- Help client recognize there are fewer occupations in the world that incorporate interests that are opposite one another, such as people and things, or data and ideas. However, such occupations do exist. Examples include: teaching in technical fields (people and things), many of the medical specialties and technologies (people and things), and much of the work in the information technology area (ideas and data). Because people who have interests and skills in these opposite poles are also rare, they are highly valued. Help your client brainstorm possible options in the people/things categories, and both brainstorm with them and refer them to the data/ideas Occupations Card for ideas on this combination.

- Opposing interests can also be met by working with one set of interests in the environment of the other. For example, a job in finance management for an arts organization or scientific company combines interests in a data job and ideas environment.

- Interests in opposites poles can also be met by fulfilling one type of interest in work roles and the other through activities outside of work.

Things dimensions. You can also translate the Data, Ideas, People, and Things dimensions into Holland codes (see Rapid Reference 6.15). Based upon the priority order of the four dimensions and their Holland codes translations, create a three-letter Holland code for your client. For example, a client who selected cards in three suits in the order "People, Ideas, and Data," may want to explore occupations with Holland codes of SIE, SAE, SIC, or SAC or any of these in various combinations, depending on the strength of the scores. Assist your client in consulting Holland's *Occupations Finder* or *Dictionary of Holland Occupational Codes,* which can be ordered from Psychological Assessment Resources, Inc., to identify additional occupations of interest among 1,346 or 12,860 occupations, respectively, by the RIASEC codes.

Strengths and Limitations

The Strengths and Limitations of *Talent Sort 2000* are described in Rapid References 6.16 and 6.17.

≡ Rapid Reference 6.18

lications of *Talent Sort 2000* described in the *It's in the Cards* Guide

JOB SEARCH

- Determining a career focus and field
- Interviewing for information
- Writing a resume
- Preparing for an interview
- Dealing with relocation

JOB ORIENTATION

- Clarifying expectations with a supervisor
- Discussing "what counts" with colleagues
- Building a network of resources
- Setting priorities for improving service

PERFORMANCE AND REPUTATION

- Increasing interpersonal and managerial skills
- Responding to denied promotion
- Building public speaking skills
- Identifying and prioritizing critical skills for development

ENRICHMENT AND ENHANCEMENT

- Motivating a worker who is frustrated and stressed
- Preparing for the global market
- Tired of current work; need a change
- Getting a degree and still not getting ahead

REALIGNMENT AND RESTRUCTURE

- Maximizing talent during company downsizing
- Producing more results with less support
- Finding a position with better "fit"
- Suffering from "golden handcuffs"
- Securing freedom to redesign your position

Source: It's in the Cards. (Cohan & Farren, 1992).

≡ Rapid Reference 6.15

BiPolar Dimensions and Their Relationship to Holland Codes

BiPolar Dimensions	Holland's Themes
Things	Realistic
People	Social
Ideas or Ideas and Things	Investigative
Ideas or Ideas and People	Artistic
Data or Data and People	Enterprising
Data or Data and Things	Conventional

Applications

Farren and Cohen (1992) developed the companion guide, *It's in the Cards,* to give counselors, managers, and employees many more ways to use the cards beyond identifying potential career options. The guide provides a number of suggestions that allow the versatile interests/skills activity cards to be applied to a variety of career issues. The guide includes 22 different ways to use the cards, grouped into five different areas: **Job Search** or *Choosing a Career Niche;* **Job Orientation** or *Learning the Ropes in a New Job or Field;* **Performance and Reputation** or *Building Powerful Options;* **Enrichment/Enhancement** or *On-the-Job-Learning;* and **Realignment & Restructure** or *Managing Change.* See Rapid Reference 6.18 for an overview of the various applications of the card sort described in the *It's in the Cards* guide.

For example, in the application entitled *Getting a degree and still not getting ahead,* the employee is coached to sort the cards into current skills being used on the job and college-acquired skills. Next, the employee's manager is asked to sort the cards into skills needed in the current position and skills needed for the next advancement opportunity. The employee and manager can then discuss differences between what the employee's skills are and what is needed to advance, ways to apply newly-acquired skills to the current position, and other

≡ Rapid Reference 6.16

Strengths of *Talent Sort 2000* Card Sort

- One of the few card sorts that uses interests rather than occupational titles to help individuals identify potential career options, offering greater assistance to users who may be confused about career possibilities.
- Well-grounded in research on interest measurement, using the bipolar dimensions of interests as the underlying constructs.
- Cards are attractive and easy to use, with engaging drawings on the black-and-white face of the cards that describe activities and ingenious color-coding of the suits that reveals the interest or skill priorities after the cards have been sorted.
- Quick assessment method that offers useful information on interest patterns and related occupations in a short period of time.
- Can be self-administered or used with counselor support. With counselor support, interactive approaches allow counselors to assist clients in gaining greater insight into their interests patterns.
- Contemporary language for activities and up-to-date occupations create face validity.
- Useful supporting materials for identifying additional career options (occupations cards and *It's in the Cards* guide).
- Excellent supporting materials for additional applications of the card sort to a variety of career-related issues and needs (see Rapid Reference 6.19 for further information).
- Effective for use in a variety of settings, including schools, colleges, and organizational settings, and for a number of purposes, including career choice and change, employee development, career coaching, and outplacement and transition counseling, among others (see Rapid Reference 6.19 for further information).

≡ Rapid Reference 6.1...

Limitations of *Talent Sort ...*

- There is currently no technical documentation on t... card sort and no user's guide available to assist cou... ter grounded in the use of the tool.
- While the card sort categories are based upon wel... the bipolar dimensions of interests, the actual select... occupations into the four categories was based upo... terns and focus group input. There are a few instanc... rization of occupations is contrary to current resear...
- No research has been conducted to determine the ... the instrument.
- The instructions with the card sort are limited, altho... tions and supporting activities are provided in the *It'...* which can be purchased separately.
- Follow-up is somewhat limited for users seeking initi... reer changes, in that they are not referred to comm... ences or sources for occupational information availa...
- Users are not instructed in how to derive Holland c... Ideas, People, and Things priorities, which limits their ... tional career options through well-established resour... *nary of Holland Occupational Codes.*
- While the card sort can be self-administered, no sup... place for the individual user that explains the context ... ment or how the individual would fully utilize the info... the card sort. Consequently, the card sort is best utili... practitioner-supported intervention.

skills that may still be needed for development. In the application, *Tired of cur rent work; need a change,* a group of employees can work together and sort the cards into activities they like and would want to do on a daily basis. The employees are instructed to view one another's cards and, using company knowledge, identify an expanded list of job titles, departments, and projects for each person in the group. As part of an action plan, the employees can interview people who hold jobs of interest and volunteer to work on related projects with people from other work units.

The *Talent Sort 2000* cards may be used in a variety of ... ticularly helpful for use in organizations. Many activ... signed as important stimuli for conversations bet... managers. For example, the cards are in use in a variety ... including AT&T, Marriott, GTE, Ernst & Young, TRW... Lucent Technologies (Farren, 2000). In addition, the ca... variety of government agencies, universities, and schoo... ative and engaging activities developed for the card so... for individual, group, and organizational applications i...

≡*Rapid Reference 6.19*

Various Uses of *Talent Sort 2000*

Settings and Users	Applications
Career consultants	Assist clients in choosing professions, positions, industries, and organizations.
Managers	Work with employees in selection, development, and coaching to achieve greater career "fit."
Outplacement companies	Enliven career transition coaching, career seminars, individual coaching, and career resources centers.
Career counselors	Support vocational counseling, job search coaching, mid-career transition counseling, relocation assistance, executive coaching, career management seminars, workshops, and career resource centers.
High school teachers and counselors	Enrich Career Days, Career Fairs, and the curriculum, and as an aid in internship selection.
Organizations	Develop job posting systems and code volunteer positions.

Rapid Reference 6.19 summarizes the various ways in which *Talent Sort 2000* has been used (Farren, 2000).

OTHER EXAMPLES

As described in the introduction to this section, other examples of card sorts have been profiled in Kapes, Mastie, and Whitfield (1994). The interested reader may wish to review this reference to learn about additional card sorts, including:

1. Slaney Vocational Card Sort (1978)
2. Occ-U-Sort (Jones & Devault, 1979)
3. Vocational Exploration and Insight Kit (Holland, 1980)
4. Occupational Interest Card Sort (Knowdell, 1993)
5. Motivated Skills Card Sort (Knowdell, 1991)

🪶 TEST YOURSELF 🪶

1. **Items were selected for the UNIACT, DISCOVER's Interest Inventory, that would clearly distinguish gender-related differences in item responses.** True or False?

2. **DISCOVER's World-of-Work Map has two underlying dimensions which allow all occupations to be organized according to their involvement with data, ideas, things, and people.** True or False?

3. **When clients receive low, flat profiles on the Interest Inventory in DIS-COVER, they should be discouraged from viewing the job family videos.** True or False?

4. **When clients receive high, flat profiles on the Interest Inventory in DIS-COVER, they should be encouraged to evaluate which career options:**

    (a) Require their greatest talents

    (b) Fulfill their most important values

    (c) Are in greatest alignment with their resources

    (d) All of the above

    (e) Only A and B above

5. ***Careerhub* includes a checklist-style interest inventory and a skills confidence inventory comprised of items representing each of Holland's six personality types.** True or False?

6. **When *Careerhub* users score moderate to strong on both their interests and skills on a given Career Type, that type will be listed in the Highest Priority box of a four-box interpretive matrix.** True or False?

7. ***Talent Sort 2000* card sort includes cards representing each of Holland's six personality types.** True or False?

8. ***Talent Sort 2000* cards can be used in applications that include:**

    (a) Determining a career focus and field

    (b) Identifying skills for development

    (c) Both A and B

    (d) Neither A nor B

Answers: 1. False; 2. True; 3. False; 4. d; 5. True; 6. True; 7. False; 8. c

References

Chapter 1

American College Testing, Inc. (2000). *DISCOVER* [computer program]. Iowa City, IA: Author.

Campbell, D. P. (1992). *Campbell Interest and Skill Survey.* Minneapolis, MN: National Computer Systems, Inc.

Consulting Psychologists Press. (1999). *Careerhub* [computer program]. Palo Alto, CA: Author.

Farren, C. (1998). *Talent Sort 2000.* Annandale, VA: Mastery Works.

Harmon, L. W., Hansen, J. C., Borgen, F. H., & Hammer, A. L. (1994). *Strong Interest Inventory, Form T317 of the Strong Vocational Interest Blanks.* Stanford, CA: Stanford University Press.

Holland, J. L. (1994). *Self-Directed Search—Form R.* Odessa, FL: Psychological Assessment Resources.

Parsons, F. (1909). *Choosing a vocation.* New York: Houghton Mifflin.

Savickas, M. L. (1998). Interpreting interest inventories: A case example. *The Career Development Quarterly, 46* (4), 307–310.

Strong, E. K. (1927). Vocational Interest Test. *Educational Record, 8,* 107–121.

Walsh, W. B., & Betz, N. E. (1995). *Tests and assessment* (3rd ed.). Englewood Cliffs, NJ: Prentice-Hall.

Watkins, C. E., Jr., Campbell, V. L., & Nieberding, R. (1994). The practice of vocational assessment by counseling psychologists. *The Counseling Psychologist, 22* (1), 115–128.

Chapter 2

Borgen, F., & Grutter, G. (1995). *Where do I go next? Using your* Strong *results to manage your career.* Palo Alto, CA: Consulting Psychologists Press.

Campbell, D. P. (1996). The use of interest surveys with groups: A useful team-building technique. *Measurement and Evaluation in Counseling and Development, 29,* 153–162.

Dalton, G., & Thompson, P. (1993). *Innovations. Strategies for career management.* Provo, UT: Gene W. Dalton and Paul H. Thompson.

Grutter, J. (1998a). *Making it in today's organizations: Career advancement using the* Strong *and* MBTI. Palo Alto, CA: Consulting Psychologists Press.

Grutter, J. (1998b). *Making it in today's organizations: Career enrichment using the* Strong *and* MBTI. Palo Alto, CA: Consulting Psychologists Press.

Grutter, J. (1998c). *Making it in today's organizations: Career transition using the* Strong *and* MBTI. Palo Alto, CA: Consulting Psychologists Press.

Gutteridge, T. G., Leibowitz, A. B., & Shore, J. E. (1993). *Organizational career development. Benchmarks for building a world-class workforce.* San Francisco: Jossey-Bass.

Hansen, J. C. (1990). Leisure report. In A. L. Hammer (Ed.), *Strong Interest Inventory topical reports manual.* Palo Alto, CA: Consulting Psychologists Press.

Hansen, J. C., & Campbell, D. P. (1985). *Manual for the Strong Interest Inventory* (4th ed.). Stanford, CA: Stanford University Press.

Hansen, J. C. (1984). *User's guide for the SVIB-SCII.* Stanford, CA: Stanford University Press.

Harmon, L. W., Hansen, J. C., Borgen, F. H., & Hammer, A. L. (1994). *The Strong Interest Inventory: Applications and technical guide.* Palo Alto, CA: Consulting Psychologists Press.

Holland, J. L. (1997). *Making vocational choices: A theory of vocational personalities and work environments* (3rd ed.). Odessa, FL: Psychological Assessment Resources, Inc.

Prediger, D. J. (1982). Dimensions underlying Holland's hexagon: Missing link between interests and occupations? *Journey of Vocational Behavior, 21,* 259–287.

Prince, J. P. (1995). *The Strong Interest Inventory resource: Strategies for group and individual interpretations in college settings.* Palo Alto, CA: Consulting Psychologists Press.

Rumpel, S. K. & Lecertua, K. *Strong Interest Inventory Resource: Strategies for group and individual interpretations in high school settings.* Palo Alto, CA: Consulting Psychologists Press.

Super, D. E. (1984). *Career and life development.* In D. Brown, L. Brooks, and Associates (Eds.), *Career choice and development.* San Francisco: Jossey-Bass.

Swanson, J. L. & Hansen, J. C. (1988). Stability of vocational interests over 4-year, 8-year, and 12-year intervals. *Journal of Vocational Behavior, 33,* 185–202.

Chapter 3

Campbell, D. P., & Hyne, S. A. (1990; 1995). *Manual for the Campbell Organizational Survey.* Minneapolis: National Computer Systems.

Campbell, D. P. (1991). *Manual for the Campbell Leadership Index.* Minneapolis: National Computer Systems.

Campbell, D. P. (1996). The use of interest surveys with groups: A useful team-building technique. *Measurement and Evaluation in Counseling and Development, 29,* 153–162.

Hallam, G., & Campbell, D. P. (1994). *Manual for the Campbell-Hallam Team Development Survey.* Minneapolis: National Computer Systems.

Hallam, G., & Campbell, D. P. (1999). *User's guide for the Campbell-Hallam Team Leader Profile.* Minneapolis: National Computer Systems.

Holland, J. L. (1997). *Making vocational choices: A theory of vocational personalities and work* (3rd ed.). Odessa, FL: Psychological Assessment Resources.

Pugh, R. (1998). Review of the Campbell Interest and Skill Inventory. *Mental Measurements Yearbook.*

Chapter 4

Abe, C., & Holland, J. L. (1965). *A description of college freshmen: I. Students with different choices of major field* (ACT Research Report No. 3). Iowa City: The American College Testing Program.

Bardsley, C. A. (1984). Hooking management on career development: A workshop. *Training and Development Journal, 38,* 76–79.

Borgen, F. H., & Seling, M. J. (1978). Expressed and inventoried interests revisited: Perspicacity in the person. *Journal of Counseling Psychology, 25,* 536–543.

≡Rapid Reference 6.15

BiPolar Dimensions and
Their Relationship to Holland Codes

BiPolar Dimensions	Holland's Themes
Things	Realistic
People	Social
Ideas or Ideas and Things	Investigative
Ideas or Ideas and People	Artistic
Data or Data and People	Enterprising
Data or Data and Things	Conventional

Applications

Farren and Cohen (1992) developed the companion guide, *It's in the Cards,* to give counselors, managers, and employees many more ways to use the cards beyond identifying potential career options. The guide provides a number of suggestions that allow the versatile interests/skills activity cards to be applied to a variety of career issues. The guide includes 22 different ways to use the cards, grouped into five different areas: **Job Search** or *Choosing a Career Niche;* **Job Orientation** or *Learning the Ropes in a New Job or Field;* **Performance and Reputation** or *Building Powerful Options;* **Enrichment/Enhancement** or *On-the-Job-Learning;* and **Realignment & Restructure** or *Managing Change.* See Rapid Reference 6.18 for an overview of the various applications of the card sort described in the *It's in the Cards* guide.

For example, in the application entitled *Getting a degree and still not getting ahead,* the employee is coached to sort the cards into current skills being used on the job and college-acquired skills. Next, the employee's manager is asked to sort the cards into skills needed in the current position and skills needed for the next advancement opportunity. The employee and manager can then discuss differences between what the employee's skills are and what is needed to advance, ways to apply newly-acquired skills to the current position, and other

≡ Rapid Reference 6.16

Strengths of *Talent Sort 2000* Card Sort

- One of the few card sorts that uses interests rather than occupational titles to help individuals identify potential career options, offering greater assistance to users who may be confused about career possibilities.
- Well-grounded in research on interest measurement, using the bipolar dimensions of interests as the underlying constructs.
- Cards are attractive and easy to use, with engaging drawings on the black-and-white face of the cards that describe activities and ingenious color-coding of the suits that reveals the interest or skill priorities after the cards have been sorted.
- Quick assessment method that offers useful information on interest patterns and related occupations in a short period of time.
- Can be self-administered or used with counselor support. With counselor support, interactive approaches allow counselors to assist clients in gaining greater insight into their interests patterns.
- Contemporary language for activities and up-to-date occupations create face validity.
- Useful supporting materials for identifying additional career options (occupations cards and *It's in the Cards* guide).
- Excellent supporting materials for additional applications of the card sort to a variety of career-related issues and needs (see Rapid Reference 6.19 for further information).
- Effective for use in a variety of settings, including schools, colleges, and organizational settings, and for a number of purposes, including career choice and change, employee development, career coaching, and outplacement and transition counseling, among others (see Rapid Reference 6.19 for further information).

skills that may still be needed for development. In the application, *Tired of current work; need a change,* a group of employees can work together and sort the cards into activities they like and would want to do on a daily basis. The employees are instructed to view one another's cards and, using company knowledge, identify an expanded list of job titles, departments, and projects for each person in the group. As part of an action plan, the employees can interview people who hold jobs of interest and volunteer to work on related projects with people from other work units.

≡ Rapid Reference 6.17

Limitations of *Talent Sort 2000*

- There is currently no technical documentation on the development of the card sort and no user's guide available to assist counselors in becoming better grounded in the use of the tool.

- While the card sort categories are based upon well-established research on the bipolar dimensions of interests, the actual selection of items and related occupations into the four categories was based upon "common sense" patterns and focus group input. There are a few instances where the categorization of occupations is contrary to current research findings.

- No research has been conducted to determine the validity or reliability of the instrument.

- The instructions with the card sort are limited, although extensive instructions and supporting activities are provided in the *It's in the Cards* guide, which can be purchased separately.

- Follow-up is somewhat limited for users seeking initial career choices or career changes, in that they are not referred to commonly used print references or sources for occupational information available on the Internet.

- Users are not instructed in how to derive Holland codes from their Data, Ideas, People, and Things priorities, which limits their ability to identify additional career options through well-established resources such as the *Dictionary of Holland Occupational Codes*.

- While the card sort can be self-administered, no supporting structure is in place for the individual user that explains the context for interest assessment or how the individual would fully utilize the information obtained from the card sort. Consequently, the card sort is best utilized in a counselor- or practitioner-supported intervention.

The *Talent Sort 2000* cards may be used in a variety of settings and can be particularly helpful for use in organizations. Many activities are especially designed as important stimuli for conversations between employees and managers. For example, the cards are in use in a variety of private companies, including AT&T, Marriott, GTE, Ernst & Young, TRW, Lockheed Martin, and Lucent Technologies (Farren, 2000). In addition, the cards are being used in a variety of government agencies, universities, and schools. The number of creative and engaging activities developed for the card sort make it a useful tool for individual, group, and organizational applications in a variety of settings.

≡Rapid Reference 6.18

Applications of *Talent Sort 2000* described in the *It's in the Cards* Guide

JOB SEARCH

- Determining a career focus and field
- Interviewing for information
- Writing a resume
- Preparing for an interview
- Dealing with relocation

JOB ORIENTATION

- Clarifying expectations with a supervisor
- Discussing "what counts" with colleagues
- Building a network of resources
- Setting priorities for improving service

PERFORMANCE AND REPUTATION

- Increasing interpersonal and managerial skills
- Responding to denied promotion
- Building public speaking skills
- Identifying and prioritizing critical skills for development

ENRICHMENT AND ENHANCEMENT

- Motivating a worker who is frustrated and stressed
- Preparing for the global market
- Tired of current work; need a change
- Getting a degree and still not getting ahead

REALIGNMENT AND RESTRUCTURE

- Maximizing talent during company downsizing
- Producing more results with less support
- Finding a position with better "fit"
- Suffering from "golden handcuffs"
- Securing freedom to redesign your position

Source: It's in the Cards. (Cohan & Farren, 1992).

≡ *Rapid Reference 6.19*

Various Uses of *Talent Sort 2000*

Settings and Users	Applications
Career consultants	Assist clients in choosing professions, positions, industries, and organizations.
Managers	Work with employees in selection, development, and coaching to achieve greater career "fit."
Outplacement companies	Enliven career transition coaching, career seminars, individual coaching, and career resources centers.
Career counselors	Support vocational counseling, job search coaching, mid-career transition counseling, relocation assistance, executive coaching, career management seminars, workshops, and career resource centers.
High school teachers and counselors	Enrich Career Days, Career Fairs, and the curriculum, and as an aid in internship selection.
Organizations	Develop job posting systems and code volunteer positions.

Rapid Reference 6.19 summarizes the various ways in which *Talent Sort 2000* has been used (Farren, 2000).

OTHER EXAMPLES

As described in the introduction to this section, other examples of card sorts have been profiled in Kapes, Mastie, and Whitfield (1994). The interested reader may wish to review this reference to learn about additional card sorts, including:

1. Slaney Vocational Card Sort (1978)
2. Occ-U-Sort (Jones & Devault, 1979)
3. Vocational Exploration and Insight Kit (Holland, 1980)
4. Occupational Interest Card Sort (Knowdell, 1993)
5. Motivated Skills Card Sort (Knowdell, 1991)

🐟 TEST YOURSELF 🐟

1. Items were selected for the **UNIACT, DISCOVER's Interest Inventory, that would clearly distinguish gender-related differences in item responses.** True or False?

2. **DISCOVER's World-of-Work Map has two underlying dimensions which allow all occupations to be organized according to their involvement with data, ideas, things, and people.** True or False?

3. **When clients receive low, flat profiles on the Interest Inventory in DISCOVER, they should be discouraged from viewing the job family videos.** True or False?

4. **When clients receive high, flat profiles on the Interest Inventory in DISCOVER, they should be encouraged to evaluate which career options:**

    (a) Require their greatest talents

    (b) Fulfill their most important values

    (c) Are in greatest alignment with their resources

    (d) All of the above

    (e) Only A and B above

5. *Careerhub* **includes a checklist-style interest inventory and a skills confidence inventory comprised of items representing each of Holland's six personality types.** True or False?

6. **When** *Careerhub* **users score moderate to strong on both their interests and skills on a given Career Type, that type will be listed in the Highest Priority box of a four-box interpretive matrix.** True or False?

7. *Talent Sort 2000* **card sort includes cards representing each of Holland's six personality types.** True or False?

8. *Talent Sort 2000* **cards can be used in applications that include:**

    (a) Determining a career focus and field

    (b) Identifying skills for development

    (c) Both A and B

    (d) Neither A nor B

Answers: 1. False; 2. True; 3. False; 4. d; 5. True; 6. True; 7. False; 8. c

References

Chapter I

American College Testing, Inc. (2000). *DISCOVER* [computer program]. Iowa City, IA: Author.

Campbell, D. P. (1992). *Campbell Interest and Skill Survey*. Minneapolis, MN: National Computer Systems, Inc.

Consulting Psychologists Press. (1999). *Careerhub* [computer program]. Palo Alto, CA: Author.

Farren, C. (1998). *Talent Sort 2000*. Annandale, VA: Mastery Works.

Harmon, L. W., Hansen, J. C., Borgen, F. H., & Hammer, A. L. (1994). *Strong Interest Inventory, Form T317 of the Strong Vocational Interest Blanks*. Stanford, CA: Stanford University Press.

Holland, J. L. (1994). *Self-Directed Search—Form R*. Odessa, FL: Psychological Assessment Resources.

Parsons, F. (1909). *Choosing a vocation*. New York: Houghton Mifflin.

Savickas, M. L. (1998). Interpreting interest inventories: A case example. *The Career Development Quarterly, 46* (4), 307–310.

Strong, E. K. (1927). Vocational Interest Test. *Educational Record, 8,* 107–121.

Walsh, W. B., & Betz, N. E. (1995). *Tests and assessment* (3rd ed.). Englewood Cliffs, NJ: Prentice-Hall.

Watkins, C. E., Jr., Campbell, V. L., & Nieberding, R. (1994). The practice of vocational assessment by counseling psychologists. *The Counseling Psychologist, 22* (1), 115–128.

Chapter 2

Borgen, F., & Grutter, G. (1995). *Where do I go next? Using your Strong results to manage your career*. Palo Alto, CA: Consulting Psychologists Press.

Campbell, D. P. (1996). The use of interest surveys with groups: A useful team-building technique. *Measurement and Evaluation in Counseling and Development, 29,* 153–162.

Dalton, G., & Thompson, P. (1993). *Innovations. Strategies for career management*. Provo, UT: Gene W. Dalton and Paul H. Thompson.

Grutter, J. (1998a). *Making it in today's organizations: Career advancement using the Strong and MBTI*. Palo Alto, CA: Consulting Psychologists Press.

Grutter, J. (1998b). *Making it in today's organizations: Career enrichment using the Strong and MBTI*. Palo Alto, CA: Consulting Psychologists Press.

Grutter, J. (1998c). *Making it in today's organizations: Career transition using the Strong and MBTI*. Palo Alto, CA: Consulting Psychologists Press.

Gutteridge, T. G., Leibowitz, A. B., & Shore, J. E. (1993). *Organizational career development. Benchmarks for building a world-class workforce*. San Francisco: Jossey-Bass.

257

Hansen, J. C. (1990). Leisure report. In A. L. Hammer (Ed.), *Strong Interest Inventory topical reports manual*. Palo Alto, CA: Consulting Psychologists Press.

Hansen, J. C., & Campbell, D. P. (1985). *Manual for the Strong Interest Inventory* (4th ed.). Stanford, CA: Stanford University Press.

Hansen, J. C. (1984). *User's guide for the SVIB-SCII*. Stanford, CA: Stanford University Press.

Harmon, L. W., Hansen, J. C., Borgen, F. H., & Hammer, A. L. (1994). *The Strong Interest Inventory: Applications and technical guide*. Palo Alto, CA: Consulting Psychologists Press.

Holland, J. L. (1997). *Making vocational choices: A theory of vocational personalities and work environments* (3rd ed.). Odessa, FL: Psychological Assessment Resources, Inc.

Prediger, D. J. (1982). Dimensions underlying Holland's hexagon: Missing link between interests and occupations? *Journey of Vocational Behavior, 21,* 259–287.

Prince, J. P. (1995). *The Strong Interest Inventory resource: Strategies for group and individual interpretations in college settings*. Palo Alto, CA: Consulting Psychologists Press.

Rumpel, S. K. & Lecertua, K. *Strong Interest Inventory Resource: Strategies for group and individual interpretations in high school settings*. Palo Alto, CA: Consulting Psychologists Press.

Super, D. E. (1984). *Career and life development*. In D. Brown, L. Brooks, and Associates (Eds.), *Career choice and development*. San Francisco: Jossey-Bass.

Swanson, J. L. & Hansen, J. C. (1988). Stability of vocational interests over 4-year, 8-year, and 12-year intervals. *Journal of Vocational Behavior, 33,* 185–202.

Chapter 3

Campbell, D. P., & Hyne, S. A. (1990; 1995). *Manual for the Campbell Organizational Survey*. Minneapolis: National Computer Systems.

Campbell, D. P. (1991). *Manual for the Campbell Leadership Index*. Minneapolis: National Computer Systems.

Campbell, D. P. (1996). The use of interest surveys with groups: A useful team-building technique. *Measurement and Evaluation in Counseling and Development, 29,* 153–162.

Hallam, G., & Campbell, D. P. (1994). *Manual for the Campbell-Hallam Team Development Survey*. Minneapolis: National Computer Systems.

Hallam, G., & Campbell, D. P. (1999). *User's guide for the Campbell-Hallam Team Leader Profile*. Minneapolis: National Computer Systems.

Holland, J. L. (1997). *Making vocational choices: A theory of vocational personalities and work* (3rd ed.). Odessa, FL: Psychological Assessment Resources.

Pugh, R. (1998). Review of the Campbell Interest and Skill Inventory. *Mental Measurements Yearbook*.

Chapter 4

Abe, C., & Holland, J. L. (1965). *A description of college freshmen: I. Students with different choices of major field* (ACT Research Report No. 3). Iowa City: The American College Testing Program.

Bardsley, C. A. (1984). Hooking management on career development: A workshop. *Training and Development Journal, 38,* 76–79.

Borgen, F. H., & Seling, M. J. (1978). Expressed and inventoried interests revisited: Perspicacity in the person. *Journal of Counseling Psychology, 25,* 536–543.

Costa, P. T., Jr., McCrae, R. R., & Holland, J. L. (1984). Personality and vocational interests in an adult sample. *Journal of Applied Psychology, 69,* 390–400.

Crites, J. O. (1978). Review of the *Self-Directed Search.* In O. K. Buros (Ed.), *Mental measurement yearbook* (8th ed.). Highland Park, NJ: The Gryphon Press.

Daniels, M. H. (1989). Review of the *Self-Directed Search:* 1985 review. In J. Conoley & J. Kramer (Eds.), *Tenth mental measurements yearbook.* Lincoln, NE: Buros Institute of Mental Measurements of the University of Nebraska, Lincoln.

Farr, J. M. (1993). *The complete guide for occupational exploration.* Indianapolis, IN: JIST Works.

Farr, J. M. (1994). *America's top technical and trade jobs* (2nd ed.). Indianapolis: JIST Works.

Fouad, N. A., & Dancer, L. S. (1992). Comments on the universality of Holland's theory. *Journal of Vocational Behavior, 40,* 220–228.

Gottfredson, G. D., & Holland, J. L. (1975). Some normative self-report data on activities, competencies, occupational preferences, and ability ratings for high school and college students, and employed men and women. *JSAS Catalog of Selected Documents in Psychology, 5,* 192. (Ms. No. 859).

Gottfredson, G. D., & Holland, J. L. (1996). *Dictionary of Holland occupational codes* (3rd ed.). Odessa, FL: Psychological Assessment Resources, Inc.

Gottfredson, G. D., Jones, E. M., & Holland, J. L. (1993). Personality and vocational interests: The relation of Holland's six interest dimensions to five robust dimensions of personality. *Journal of Counseling Psychology, 40,* 518–524.

Holland, J. L. (1968). Explorations of theory of vocational choice: VI. A longitudinal study using a sample of typical college students. *Journal of Applied Psychology, 52,* 1–37.

Holland, J. L. (1985). *Manual for the Vocational Preference Inventory.* Palo Alto, CA: Consulting Psychologists Press.

Holland, J. L. (1990). *Form CP, Self-Directed Search.* Odessa, FL: Psychological Assessment Resources.

Holland, J. L. (1992). *Vocational exploration and insight kit.* Odessa, FL: Psychological Assessment Resources.

Holland, J. L. (1994). *You and your career.* Odessa, FL: Psychological Assessment Resources.

Holland, J. L. (1996a). Exploring careers with a typology: What we have learned and some new directions. *American Psychologist, 51,* 397–406.

Holland, J. L. (1996b). *The occupations finder.* Odessa, FL: Psychological Assessment Resources, Inc.

Holland, J. L. (1996c). *Form E, Self-Directed Search.* Odessa, FL: Psychological Assessment Resources, Inc.

Holland, J. L. (1997). *Making vocational choices: A theory of vocational personalities and work environment* (3rd ed.). Odessa, FL: Psychological Assessment Resources.

Holland, J. L., Daiger, D., & Power, P. (1980). *My vocational situation.* Palo Alto, CA: Consulting Psychologists Press.

Holland, J. L., Fritzsche, B. A., & Powell, A. B. (1994). *SDS Technical Manual.* Odessa, FL: Psychological Assessment Resources.

Holland, J. L., & Gottfredson, G. D. (1976). Using a typology of persons and environments to explain careers: Some extensions and clarifications. *The Counseling Psychologist, 6,* 20–29.

Holland, J. L., Johnston, J., & Asama, N. (1993). The Vocational Identity Scale: A diagnostic and treatment tool. *Journal of Career Assessment, 1,* 1–12.

Holland, J. L., Powell, A. B., & Fritzsche, B. A. (1997). *SDS professional user's guide*. Odessa, FL: Psychological Assessment Resources Inc.

Holland, J. L. & Rayman, J. R. (1986). The Self-Directed Search. In W. B. Walsh & S. H. Osipow (Eds.), *Advances in vocational psychology: The assessment of interests*. Hillsdale, NJ: Lawrence Erlbaum.

Holmberg, K., Rosen, D., & Holland, J. L. (1997). *The leisure activities finder*. Odessa, FL: Psychological Assessment Resources, Inc.

Jin, S. R. (1991). A study of the relation between vocational interests and personality. *Bulletin of Educational Psychology, 24,* 91–115.

Kelso, G. I., Holland, J. L., & Gottfredson, G. D. (1977). The relation of self-reported competencies to aptitude test scores. *Journal of Vocational Behavior, 10,* 99–103.

Krieshok, T. S. (1987). Review of the *Self-Directed Search. Journal of Counseling and Development, 65,* 512–514.

Lacey, D. (1971). Holland's vocational models: A study of work groups and need satisfaction. *Journal of Vocational Behavior, 1,* 105–122.

Lee, D. L., & Hedahl, B. (1973). Holland's personality types applied to the *SVIB* basic interest scales. *Journal of Vocational Behavior, 3,* 61–68.

Manuele-Adkins, C. (1989). Review of the Self-Directed Search: 1985 review. In J. Conoley & J. Kramer (Eds.), *Tenth mental measurements yearbook*. Lincoln, NE: Buros Institute of Mental Measurements of the University of Nebraska, Lincoln.

Morgan, R. L. (1990). *Classification of instructional programs*. Washington, DC: National Center for Educational Statistics.

National Crosswalk Service Center. (1994). *NOICC Master Crosswalk, Version 4.0* [computer program]. Des Moines, IA: Author.

Overs, R. P. (1971). *Avocational Activities Inventory (Revised)*. Milwaukee, WI: Curative Workshop of Milwaukee.

Prediger, D. J. (1981). A note on the *SDS* validity for females. *Vocational Guidance Quarterly, 30,* 117–129.

Reardon, R. C., & Lenz, J. G. (1998). *The Self-Directed Search and related Holland career materials: Practitioners guide*. Odessa, FL: Psychological Assessment Resources, Inc.

Rezler, A. G. (1967). The joint use of the *Kuder Preference Record* and the *Holland Vocational Preference Inventory. Psychology in the Schools, 4,* 82–84.

Richards, J. M., Jr., Holland, J. L., & Lutz, S. W. (1967). The prediction of student accomplishment in college. *Journal of Educational Psychology, 58,* 343–355.

Rosen, D., Holmberg, K., & Holland, J. L. (1997). *The educational opportunities finder*. Odessa, FL: Psychological Assessment Resources, Inc.

Rounds, J., & Day, S. X. (1998). Describing, evaluating, and creating vocational interest structures. In M. L. Savickas & A. R. Spokane (Eds.). *Vocational Interests: Their meaning, measurement and use in counseling* (pp. 103–133). Palo Alto, CA: Davies-Black.

Shahnasarian, M. (Ed.). (1996). *The Self-Directed Search in business and industry:* A resource guide. Odessa, FL: Psychological Assessment Resources, Inc.

Spokane, A. R. (1985). A review of research on person-environment congruence in Holland's theory of careers. [Monograph]. *Journal of Vocational Behavior, 26,* 306–343.

Tracey, T. J., & Rounds, J. B. (1993). Evaluating Holland's and Gati's vocational-interest models: A structural meta-analysis. *Psychological Bulletin, 113,* 229–246.

U.S. Department of Labor. (1991). *Dictionary of Occupational Titles*. Washington, DC: Government Printing Office.
U.S. Department of Labor Statistics. (1998–1999). *Occupational outlook handbook*. Washington, DC: Bureau of Labor Statistics.

Chapter 6

ACT, Inc. (1999). *DISCOVER Professional Manual*. Iowa City, IA: Author.
American College Testing. (1988). *Interim psychometric handbook for the 3rd edition ACT Career Planning Program*. Iowa City, IA.
Cohen, J., & Farren, C. (1992). *It's in the cards: Dealing with work and career changes*. Washington, DC: Career Systems, Inc.
Farren, C. (1998). *Talent Sort 2000*. Annandale, VA: Mastery Works.
Farren, C. (2000). Personal communication on the development of *Talent Sort 2000*. Mastery Works.
Gottfredson, G., & Holland, J. (1996). *Dictionary of Holland Occupational Codes* (3rd ed.). Odessa, FL: Psychological Assessment Resources.
Hansen, J. (1992). *User's guide for the Strong Interest Inventory*. Stanford, CA: Stanford University Press.
Hansen, J., & Campbell, D. (1985). *Manual for the Strong Interest Inventory* (4th ed.). Stanford, CA: Stanford University Press.
Harmon, I., Hansen, J., Borgen, F., & Hammer, A. (1994). *Strong Interest Inventory applications and technical guide*. Stanford, CA: Stanford University Press.
Harris-Bowlsbey, J., Dikel, M., & Sampson, J. (1998). *The Internet: A tool for career planning* (1st ed.). Columbus, OH: National Career Development Association.
Holland, J. (1973). *Making vocational choices* (1st ed.). Englewood Cliffs, NJ: Prentice-Hall.
Holland, J. (1985). *Making vocational choices: A theory of vocational personalities and work environments* (2nd ed.). Englewood Cliffs, NJ: Prentice-Hall.
Holland, J. (1997). *Making vocational choices* (3rd ed.). Odessa, FL: Psychological Assessment Resources.
Holland, J. L., & Associates. (1980). *Counselor's guide to the vocational exploration and insight kit* (VEIR). Palo Alto, CA: Consulting Psychologists Press.
Jones, L. K., & DeVault, R. M. (1979). Evaluation of a self-guided career exploration system: The Occu-Sort. *The School Counselor,* 334–341.
Kapes, J., Mastie, M., & Whitfield, E. (1994). *A counselor's guide to career assessment instruments* (3rd ed.). Columbus, OH: National Career Development Association.
Knowdell, R. L. (1991). *Manual for Motivated Skills Card Sort*. San Jose, CA: Career Research and Testing.
Knowdell, R. L. (1993). *Manual for Occupational Interests Card Sort Kit*. San Jose, CA: Career Research and Testing.
Kuder, F. (1977). *Activity interests and occupational choice*. Chicago: Science Research Associates.
National Career Development Association. (1997). *NCDA guidelines for the use of the Internet for the provision of career information and planning services*. Columbus, OH: Author.
Prediger, D. J. (1976). A world-of-work map for career exploration. *Vocational Guidance Quarterly, 24,* 198–208.

Prediger, D. J. (1981). A note on *Self-Directed Search* validity for females. *Vocational Guidance Quarterly, 30,* 117–129.

Prediger, D. J. (1982). Dimensions underlying Holland's hexagon: Missing link between interests and occupations? *Journal of Vocational Behavior, 21,* 259–287.

Prediger, D. J. (1996). Alternative dimensions for the Tracey-Rounds interest sphere. *Journal of Vocational Behavior, 48,* 59–67.

Prediger, D. J. (1998). Is interest profile level relevant to career counseling? *Journal of Counseling Psychology, 45,* 204–212.

Prediger, D. J. & Johnson, R. W. (1979). *Alternatives to sex-restrictive vocational interest assessment* (ACT Research Report No. 79). Iowa City, IA: American College Testing.

Prince, J. (1995). *Strong resource guide, strategies for group and individual interpretations in college settings.* Palo Alto, CA: Consulting Psychologists Press.

Prince, J. (1998). *Interests/Skills Checklist.* Palo Alto, CA: Consulting Psychologists Press.

Prince, J., Chartrand, J., & Silver, D. (2000). Constructing a quality career assessment site. *Journal of Career Assessment, 8,* 55–67.

Silver, D., Chartrand, J., & Prince, J. (1999). *Careerhub.* Palo Alto, CA: Consulting Psychologists Press.

Sampson, J. (1999). Integrating Internet-based distance guidance with services provided in career centers. *The Career Development Quarterly, 47* (3), 243–254.

Sampson, J. P., Reardon, R. C., Wilde, C. K., Norris, D. S., Peterson, G. W., Strausberger, S. J., Garis, J. W., Lenz, J. G., & Saunders, D. E. (1994). A Comparison of the Assessment Components of Fifteen Computer-Assisted Career Guidance Systems. In J. Kapes, M. Mastie, & E. Whitfield, *A counselor's guide to career assessment instruments* (3rd ed.). Columbus, OH: National Career Development Association.

Slaney, R., Moran, W., & Wade, J. (1994). Vocational card sorts. In J. Kapes, M. Mastie, & E. Whitfield, *A counselor's guide to career assessment instruments* (3rd ed.). Columbus, OH: National Career Development Association.

Swaney, K. B. (1995). *Technical Manual: Revised Unisex Edition of the ACT Interest Inventory (UNIACT).* Iowa City, IA: ACT, Inc.

Williams, S. (1978). The vocational card sort: A tool for vocational exploration. *The Vocational Guidance Quarterly, 26,* 237–243.

Annotated Bibliography

Chapter 1

Mapes, J. T., Mastie, M. M., & Whitfield, E. A. (1994). *A counselor's guide to career assessment instruments* (3rd ed.). Alexandria, VA: National Career Development Association.

This outstanding resource is widely used by counselors, educators, and researchers in the field of career development. It includes brief reviews of 52 career assessment instruments by 63 authors and co-authors. Instruments include aptitude, achievement, interest, values, personality, and career development measures. Reviews address the following areas: Description, Use in Counseling, Technical Considerations, Computer-Based Version (if available), Overall Critique, and References. Additional chapters and appendixes list over 200 additional assessments, provide addresses of publishers, address issues surrounding the selection and use of career assessment instruments, and highlight standards for ethical and multiculturally fair usage.

American Educational Research Association, American Psychological Association, & National Council for Measurement in Education. (1999). *Standards for educational and psychological tests.* Washington, DC: American Psychological Association.

Three professional associations through a joint committee of the American Psychological Association have published this primary reference source that provides detailed guidance for professionals in the use of tests for a wide range of domains, including career counseling. The new Standards *reflects changes in federal law and measurement trends affecting validity for individuals with disabilities or from different linguistic backgrounds. The* Standards *also address technical issues of test development and use in education, psychology, and employment.*

Lowman, R. L. (1991). *The clinical practice of career assessment.* Washington, DC: American Psychological Association.

This text reviews and integrates the three divergent domains of interests, abilities, and personality assessment to provide a practical model for conducting career assessment. Material is presented in a clear manner with illustrated vignettes and sample test data. Specific guidance is provided for giving feedback to clients and for writing assessment reports.

Walsh, W. B., & Betz, N. E. (1995). *Tests and assessment* (3rd ed.). Englewood Cliffs, NJ: Prentice-Hall.

This well-written undergraduate and graduate textbook aims to help students develop assessment skills and to improve their knowledge about assessment techniques and tests. It provides an excellent review of the fundamental statistical and measurement foundations of testing, and offers brief reviews of a range of instruments, including assessments of career interests and development, personality, cognitive ability, and human development.

Chapter 2

Harmon, L. W., Hansen, J. C., Borgen, F. H., & Hammer, A. L. (1994). *Strong applications and technical guide.* Palo Alto, CA: Consulting Psychologists Press.

A comprehensive guide for both administration and interpretation of the Strong. *Contents include detailed descriptions of scale development, reliability, and validity. Also included are detailed strategies for using the* Strong *with clients of diverse ethnic backgrounds and ages.*

Hirsh, S. K. (1995). *Strong Interest Inventory resource: Strategies for group and individual interpretations in business and organizational settings.* Palo Alto, CA: Consulting Psychologists Press.

This guide provides human resource and organizational development professionals with a complete set of materials for using the Strong *in organizational settings. Instructions, scripts, and workshop exercises focus on issues such as job dissatisfaction, job fit, and balancing work and leisure. 128 pp, plus 90 reproducible masters in a three-ring binder.*

Prince, J. P. (1995). *Strong Interest Inventory resource: Strategies for group and individual interpretations in college settings.* Palo Alto, CA: Consulting Psychologists Press.

This guide provides college counselors with customized materials for delivering both individual and group interpretations of the Strong. *It supplies detailed scripts, instructions, and overheads for easy workshop delivery. Sections cover topics such as choosing a college major, career, or graduate program. In addition, specific guidelines are provided for using the* Strong *with diverse college populations such as reentry students and multicultural students. 144 pages, plus 94 reproducible masters in a three-ring binder.*

Rumpel, S. K., & Lecertua, K. (1996). *Strong Interest Inventory resource: Strategies for group interpretations in high school settings.* Palo Alto, CA: Consulting Psychologists Press.

This guide provides instruction and support materials for counselors administering and interpreting the Strong *in high school settings. It offers detailed lesson plans for incorporating the instrument in the classroom for career explorations, and for involving parents and guardians in the career planning process. 92 pages, plus 51 reproducible masters in a three-ring binder.*

Grutter, J. (1998). *Making it in today's organizations: Using the* Strong *and the* MBTI. Palo Alto, CA: Consulting Psychologists Press.

This professional workshop and presentation binder of three books offers individuals and organizations help in dealing with career enrichment, career advancement, and career transition. Strategies and resource materials focus on expanding beyond basic interpretations of either instrument alone. Presentation materials address the Strong *and the* MBTI *jointly in a range of workshop options. Particular focus is placed on combinations of* MBTI *functions and attitudes with* Strong *themes and scales.*

Borgen, F., & Grutter, J. (1995). *Where do I go next? Using your* Strong *results to manage your career.* Palo Alto, CA: Consulting Psychologists Press.

This highly useful interpretive workbook helps clients understand and use their Strong *results for career decision-making. It offers expanded interpretive information on the General Occupational Themes, Basic Interest scales, and Personal Style scales, along with expanded lists of occupations, work tasks, and skills.*

Gottfredson, G. D., & Holland, J. L. (1996). *Dictionary of Holland occupational codes* (DHOC) (3rd ed.). Odessa, FL: Psychological Assessment Resources, Inc.

This 768-page book links Holland occupational codes to seven of the most widely used occupational classifications and information sources in the United States. In addition to providing Holland occupational codes for each occupation listed in the Dictionary of Occupational Titles *and its supplements, the* DHOC *provides empirically derived cross-references between Holland occupational codes and the Occupational Employment Statistics system, the* Standard Occupational Classification Manual, *the* Census Occupational Classification, *the* Classification of Instructional Programs, *the* Guide to Occupational Exploration, *and the* Occupational Outlook Handbook. *The* DHOC *includes both alphabetical and code-classified indices for quick and easy referencing.*

O*NET—Occupational Information Network *(at* http://www.doleta.gov/programs/onet_hp.htm).

*This Internet-based database contains comprehensive information on job requirements and worker competencies. Each occupation has a Holland Theme code descriptor. (O*NET replaces the older, print-based reference, the* Dictionary of Occupational Titles.)

Chapter 3

Campbell, D. P., Hyne, S. A., & Nilsen, D. L. (1992). *Manual for the* Campbell Interest and Skill Survey. Minneapolis, MN: National Computer Systems, Inc.

A comprehensive technical guide that describes the development and applications of the Campbell Interest and Skill Survey. *Contents include detailed descriptions of scale construction and reliability and validity statistics. Also included are in-depth strategies for reviewing self-reported interests and skills in combination and guidelines for delivering individual and group interpretations of the* CISS.

Boggs, K. R. (June, 1998). Career decisions: The Campbell and Ms. Flood. *Career Development Quarterly, 46,* 311–319.

This article provides an approach for interpreting the Campbell Interest and Skill Survey. *The article is one of a series of interpretations of various assessment instruments for the same client. Suggestions for orienting the client to the* CISS, *using the Interest/Skill Pattern Quadrant Worksheet, integrating the various scales of the survey, and applying the results to the client's previous and current career choices are provided.*

Pugh, R. C. (1998). Review of the Campbell Interest and Skill Survey. *Mental Measurements Yearbook, 13,* 167–170.

This review of the CISS, *one of two in the 1998* Mental Measurements Yearbook, *provides an overview of the survey, a description of the scales, and a summary of the rationale for including skill items in the instrument. The reviewer describes the* Profile *report and discusses its utility while also cautioning users about the use of two of the Interest/Skill pattern labels.*

Gottfredson, G. D., & Holland, J. L. (1996). *Dictionary of Holland Occupational Codes (DHOC)* (3rd ed.). Odessa, FL: Psychological Assessment Resources, Inc.

This 768-page book links Holland occupational codes to seven of the most widely used occupational classifications and information sources in the United States. In addition to providing Holland occupational codes for each occupation listed in the Dictionary of Occupational Titles *and its supplements, the* DHOC *provides empirically-derived cross references between Holland occupational codes and the* Occupational Employment Statistics *system, the* Standard Occupational Classification Manual, *the* Census Occupational Classification, *the* Classification of Instructional Programs, *the* Guide to Occupational Exploration, *and the* Occupational Outlook Handbook. *The* DHOC *includes both alphabetical and code-classified indices for quick and easy referencing.*

O*NET—Occupational Information Network (at http://www.doleta.gov/programs/onet_hp.htm).

This internet-based database contains comprehensive information on job requirements and worker competencies. Each occupation has a Holland Theme code descriptor. (O*NET replaces the older, print-based reference, Dictionary of Occupational Titles.*)*

Holland, J. L. (1994). *Occupations finder.* Odessa, FL: Psychological Assessment Resources.

This 15-page booklet lists the three-letter summary Holland codes for 1,335 of the most common occupations in the United States. Listings include the nine-digit number from the Dictionary of Occupational Titles, *along with an estimate of the educational level required for the occupation.*

Chapter 4

Holland, J. L., Fritzsche, B. A., & Powell, A. B. (1994). *SDS technical manual.* Odessa, FL: Psychological Assessment Resources, Inc.

This revised and expanded technical manual describes the history of the SDS, *development of the fourth edition, and research and technical information about all forms of the* SDS.

Holland, J. L., Powell, A. B., & Fritzsche, B. A. (1997). *SDS professional user's guide.* Odessa, FL: Psychological Assessment Resources, Inc.

This guide provides counselors comprehensive information about the four forms of the SDS, *including a description of Holland's theory. It presents practical guidelines for administration, scoring, and interpreting the* SDS.

Holland, J. L. (1997). *Making vocational choices: A theory of vocational personalities and work environments* (3rd ed.). Odessa, FL: Psychological Assessment Resources, Inc.

This 312-page source book is the most comprehensive resource for information on Holland's theory. It details the components of the interactive model, including thorough descriptions of the six personality types. In addition, it provides practical ideas for helping clients attain vocational satisfaction.

Reardon, R. C., & Lenz, J. G. (1998). *The Self-Directed Search and related Holland career materials: Practitioner's guide.* Odessa, FL: Psychological Assessment Resources, Inc.

This 332-page book is an excellent resource for using the SDS. *It provides a thorough review of the history and use of the* SDS. *It describes Holland's theory and how it fits with other career theories. Chapters focus on how the* SDS *works as a simulated guidance activity. Detailed descriptions are provided for the four* SDS *forms. Other Holland-based career guidance materials also are discussed.*

Shahnasarian, M. (Ed.). (1996). *The Self-Directed Search in business and industry: A resource guide.* Odessa, FL: Psychological Assessment Resources, Inc.

The authors of the chapters in this 170-page book address applications of Holland's theory and the SDS *to organizational settings. Topics include employee selection, training, and development, and using the* SDS *in combination with other career instruments.*

Reardon, R. C., & Lenz, J. G. (1999). Holland's theory and career assessment. *Journal of Vocational Behavior, 55,* 102–113.

This excellent review article describes how the Self-Directed Search *can be used to increase understanding of an individual's Personal Career Theory (PCT). It describes practical applications of Holland's constructs, and details uses of Holland's theory for career assessment, service delivery, and counselor training.*

Rayman, J. R. (1998). Interpreting Eleanor Flood's Self-Directed Search. *The Career Development Quarterly, 46,* 330–338.

This journal article provides an expert demonstration interpretation of the Self-Directed Search *using a true client's profile. The author poses 10 critical questions to shape the interpretation session.*

Gottfredson, G. D., & Holland, J. L. (1996). *Dictionary of Holland Occupational Codes (DHOC)* (3rd ed.). Odessa, FL: Psychological Assessment Resources, Inc.

This book links Holland occupational codes to seven of the most widely used occupational classifications and information sources in the United States. In addition to providing Holland occupational codes for each occupation listed in the Dictionary of Occupational Titles *and its Supplements, the* DHOC *provides empirically derived cross references between Holland occupational codes and the* Occupational Employment Statistics *system, the* Standard Occupational Classification Manual, *the* Census Occupational Classification, *the* Classification of Instructional Programs, *the* Guide to Occupational Exploration, *and the* Occupational Outlook Handbook. *The* DHOC *includes both alphabetical and code-classified indexes for quick and easy referencing.*

Gottfredson, G. D., & Holland, J. L. (1991). *The Position Classification Inventory (PCI).* Odessa, FL: Psychological Assessment Resources, Inc.

The PCI, *an 84-item inventory that can be completed in 10 minutes or less, allows a job incumbent, supervisor, or job analyst to describe and classify positions according to the RIASEC typology. This instrument can help clarify the demands of a specific position and evaluate the degree of fit with a person's Holland type.*

U.S. Department of Labor Statistics. (1998–1999). *Occupational outlook handbook.* Washington, DC: Bureau of Labor Statistics.

This handbook is completely revised every two years and is the best single source for information about occupations. The Occupational Outlook Handbook *is a comprehensive, up-to-date, and reliable source of career information. The* Handbook *profiles 250 occupations that in 1996 accounted for over 114 million jobs: six out of every seven jobs in the United States. For each career, it describes work activities and environment, earnings, as well as the types of education, training, and personal qualifications needed to have the best prospects. This standard reference typically is available in public libraries and career library collections. In addition, it is available in paper, hardcover, and CD-ROM.*

U.S. Department of Labor. (1991). *Dictionary of Occupational Titles (DOT).* Washington, DC: Government Printing Office.

This 1,300-page, two-volume reference assists job seekers, employers, educational and training institutions, researchers, and others by detailing tasks performed, educational requirements, and skills needed for more than 12,000 types of jobs. Also available online with a retrieval program that enables you to search using words or numbers on any of the 28,800 job titles.

O*NET (Occupational Information Network). (1998). (http://www.doleta.gov/programs/onset_hp.htm). Washington, DC: Government Printing Office.

This Internet database replaces the 1991 print version of the DOT. It contains comprehensive information on job requirements and worker competencies. Each occupation has a Holland Theme code descriptor. O*NET *provides access to information for over 1,100 occupations listed in the DOT. It is organized in a relational database, available on CD-ROM, diskettes, and Internet download. It offers the capability of locating occupations through skill requirements or key words, and offers electronic linkages that crosswalk* O*NET *occupational titles to eight other classification systems. Information includes employment levels, occupational outlook, and wages, along with short "Occupational Profiles" that provide data descriptions on each occupation.*

Chapter 6

Gottfredson, G. D., & Holland, J. L. (1996). *Dictionary of Holland Occupational Codes (DHOC)* (3rd ed.). Odessa, FL: Psychological Assessment Resources.

This book links Holland occupational codes to seven of the most widely used occupational classifications and information sources in the United States. In addition to providing Holland occupational codes for each occupation listed in the Dictionary of Occupational Titles *and its Supplements, the* DHOC *provides empirically-derived cross-references between Holland occupational codes and the* Occupational Employment Statistics *system, the* Standard Occupational Classification Manual, *the* Census Occupational Classification, *the* Classification of Instructional Programs, *the* Guide to Occupational Exploration, *and the* Occupational Outlook Handbook. *The* DHOC *includes both alphabetical and code-classified indexes for quick and easy referencing.*

ACT Inc., *DISCOVER: Career Guidance and Information System, Overview.* (1999). Iowa City, IA: Author.

This publication provides a detailed overview of the features of the Windows Version, Macintosh Version, and DOS Version of DISCOVER and details about the World-of-Work Map and ACT.

ACT, Inc., *Research Support for DISCOVER Assessment Components.* (1999). Iowa City, IA: Author.

This publication summarizes key findings in the research that has supported the development of the assessments used in DISCOVER, including the research underpinnings of the World-of-Work Map, the ACT Interest Inventory (UNIACT), the Inventory of Work-Relevant Abilities (IWRA), and the Inventory of Work Preferences (IWP). Research on the use of multimedia assessment of interests and abilities as compared to paper-and-pencil administrations is also provided.

ACT, Inc., *DISCOVER Professional Manual.* (1999). Iowa City, IA: Author.

The Professional Manual *can be downloaded from DISCOVER, Windows version, and other versions. The Windows Version of the* Manual *provides details about the various modules of the DISCOVER system (referred to as Halls). Details include information on each of the inventories and how to use inventory results; choosing occupations by the inventories or WWM features; finding majors, schools, and financial aid; and planning for work through various activities. It also describes technical features and options of the system and offers suggestions on how to use DISCOVER with counselor support.*

Swaney, K. (1995). *Technical Manual: Revised Unisex Edition of the ACT Interest Inventory (UNIACT)*. Iowa City, IA: ACT, Inc.

This manual details the 1989 revision of the Unisex edition of the ACT Interest Inventory (UNI-ACT). It provides documentation of the redevelopment process, an overview of the inventory and related interpretive aids such as the World-of-Work map, and information on the psychometric properties of the instrument, including its norms, reliability, and validity statistics.

Index

Acknowledgments

Authors never write a book alone. We would like to acknowledge the many people who supported us in this venture.

We would first like to express our heartfelt appreciation to our partners, Richard Keller and Michael Sommer, who demonstrated enormous patience and willingly sacrificed many nights and weekends to support us through the many months of our work. Through it all, they provided uplifting encouragement, almost total "life maintenance" support, and late night computer consulting. We are grateful for their belief in us and for their unfailing love, encouragement, and support that saw us through it all.

We would also like to thank our parents, Raymond and Lillian Prince and Gene and Vera Heiser, for their support. They provided us the means to pursue our educations and expressed the confidence in our interests and abilities that enabled us to comfortably pursue the work we truly love. Lisa would also like to say a special thanks to Gene and Vera Heiser, who coped in remarkable ways with cancer during this past year. Their invaluable demonstrations of grace, humor, generosity, perseverance, acceptance, humility, courage, heart, understanding, hope, laughter, and uncommon wisdom have strengthened and supported her throughout this past year as in all previous years.

We would like to express our appreciation to Jo-Ida Hansen, PhD, who taught a seminar class on the *Strong-Campbell Interest Inventory* the first year we were students together in graduate school at the University of Minnesota. Jo-Ida expressed the best of the scientist/practitioner model in her capacity to explain in captivating detail her research on scale construction and at the same time demonstrate the enormous interpretive powers of this assessment with such consummate skill. It is our hope that this book can convey some of the same enthusiasm for the underpinnings of these instruments, and appreciation for the potential these tools have to be life-changing and -enhancing, that Jo-Ida first revealed to us in that seminar room so many years ago.

We would like to thank David Campbell, PhD, another exceptional leader and mentor in our field, for the opportunities we have had to learn from him about his innovative work on the *Campbell Interest and Skill Survey*. His unique blend of knowledge, expertise, and humor, in both his teaching and writing, makes learning from him both enlightening and fun. Special thanks are due to David for the time he took to ensure the technical accuracy of our review of his work on the *CISS*. We would also like to thank him for his affirming support of our work, and for his encouragement to "loosen up" in our writing style. While we may not have achieved that goal entirely, it would be a good developmental pursuit for our future and we have him to look to as a master teacher in that regard.

We would also like to add our thanks to John Holland, PhD, whose contributions in this field have been acknowledged many times over. John took the time to sit with us and go through edits page by page. He ensured, with his characteristic intelligence, humility, and colorful wit, that we did not overly complicate our review of the *SDS* so that counselors can comfortably utilize his most extraordinary and accessible work.

We wish to thank Judith Grutter and Diane Silver, who reviewed the chapter on the *SII*, for being exceptional professionals from whom we have learned so much about the *Strong*, even when we thought we knew it well. Their generosity in sharing their expertise and providing essential edits to this chapter have benefited us all.

Thanks are due as well to Diane Ducat, PhD, for the obvious care she took in providing the extremely useful edits to the chapter on the *CISS*. Her suggestions and examples enabled us to clarify several important points in the chapter.

We wish to thank Robert Reardon, PhD, and his colleague, Janet Lenz, PhD, who reviewed the chapter on the *SDS*, for sharing their expertise and useful editorial suggestions. Their research, writing, and teaching on this tool continue to enlighten us all.

Our thanks also go to Marilyn Maze and Dale Prediger, PhD, at ACT for their important clarifications and suggestions on the chapter section on DISCOVER. Their generosity of time and expertise, particularly given the pressure of our deadlines, were most appreciated.

We also thank Caela Farren, PhD, for her uplifting encouragement and helpful information on Talent Sort 2000, delivered by fax and e-mail as she was consulting around the country.

Our sincere thanks are extended to Gabrielle Blanc for sharing her life story with us and permitting us to use her assessments to demonstrate the power of these instruments in affirming and clarifying major career and life decisions. We wish her well in all the future holds.

We wish to thank Tracey Belmont, our editor, for her important editorial suggestions, her patience with our "moving" deadlines, and her encouragement regarding the content we were developing.

We would like to thank our colleagues who supported us in the day-to-day activities of researching, writing, editing, complaining, wondering, and hoping as we made our way through this process. Jeff wishes to thank his colleagues at the University Health Services at the University of California, Berkeley for their support, with special thanks to Dinorah Meyer, who compiled many useful research articles for our background work. Lisa wishes to thank her supervisor, Richard Kilburg, PhD, who encouraged her to undertake professional writing and believed she could do it more than she did. Lisa would also like to thank her colleagues in the Career Management Program at The Johns Hopkins University, Evan Anderson, Jennifer Patton, Diane Tracey, and Gail White-Moore, who, more than any others, both understood the content of the book and demonstrated caring support regarding its completion. Thanks are due as well to the Wintergreen Board of Directors: Rick Benner, Maureen Doherty, Nedra Hartzell, Audrey Hudson, Art LaSalle, Bruce Ritter, and Mac Saddoris, for their emotional support during this past year.

Finally, and perhaps most importantly, we would like to thank our clients over the years, who have allowed us into their lives and who have taught us about interest assessment from a personal perspective. As we have shared the results of their inventories with them, we have learned from them how to weave the value of information offered by assessment with their dreams, hopes, and experiences into compelling visions of the future and clarifying pictures of the present and past.

We most sincerely appreciate everyone mentioned above and others, including family, friends, and colleagues, whom we regrettably do not have space to mention here, for supporting us in so many ways. With their help, this vision of creating a career counselor's resource for understanding and confidently using the most common instruments in career interest assessment has become a reality. We hope that career counselors now and in the future will find it to be a useful companion guide!

About the Authors

Lisa J. Heiser, MA, is the Director of the Career Management Program for Faculty and Staff at The Johns Hopkins University in Baltimore, MD, where she designed and developed an internal career development program that serves over 8,500 employees. Lisa is a National Certified Counselor with over 20 years of experience providing career counseling and assessment services to students and adults. Lisa earned her MA in Counseling Psychology from the University of Minnesota and is a graduate of the Fellows in Change Management Program at Johns Hopkins University. Before Johns Hopkins, she delivered career counseling services to students as a Program Director at the University of Maryland's Career Center and as the Director of the College of Liberal Arts Career Development Office at the University of Minnesota. Lisa has served as an officer of the Maryland and Minnesota Career Development Associations. She consults with organizations on the development of internal career programs and services and presents nationally, regionally, and locally on topics related to career counseling and coaching and adult development.

Jeffrey P. Prince is the Associate Director of Counseling and Psychological Services at the University of California at Berkeley. Dr. Prince is a licensed psychologist with a specialization in career assessment and career development. He has over 20 years of experience as a counselor, trainer, and teacher. He is a part-time faculty member at San Francisco State University, and has taught in the graduate programs of the California State University at Hayward and the University of Maryland. He also has served as a staff psychologist and counselor on a number of college campuses, including the Catholic University of America, the University of Maryland, and the University of Minnesota. Dr. Prince also provides career development consulting and training to organizations, and offers certification as well as advanced training in the *Strong Interest Inventory* through G/S Consultants. Dr. Prince received his PhD in counseling psychology from the University of Minnesota, and his bachelor's degree in psychology from Cornell University. He has contributed a number of professional journal articles and book chapters on the topics of interest assessment and career development. He is the author of the book, *Strong Interest Inventory Resource: Strategies for Group and Individual Interpretations in College Settings,* and of the *Strong Interest Inventory College Profile.* He is also co-author of the Internet-based career assessment site, *Careerhub.org.* He is a frequent presenter at the American Psychological Association and other professional conferences on topics related to career assessment and career development.